Reel Talk

Irreverent Insights
on
Cinema and Television

Chelsey Cosh

ALSO AVAILABLE

FICTION

Shannon Hollow

To my parents who showed me movies,
To my sister who quotes them,
and to my fiancé who laughs at the bad ones
with me.

This book is a collection of thoughts and theories
regarding pop culture.
It in no way intends to make allegations
upon those mentioned herein.
These personal essays are merely
musings on media.
(There are many spoilers. You have been warned.)

Table of Contents

A Message from the Author

I am a rock; I am an island. I am a PC. I am Inigo Montoya. I am Heisenberg. I am a pop culture aficionado.

Often devalued as unmemorable junk that rots your brain, pop culture gets a bad rap. In fact, pop culture is a major source of communication. It's an ice breaker with new friends. It's a memory with old friends. It marks important steps in your life: the first R-rated film you watched; your favourite holiday film; the magazine you renewed each year on your birthday; the first time you beat that boss level in a tough video game; the TV show you rushed home to watch; the CD you played in your first car; the song that played at your wedding; and the website you check into every morning before work. We relate to each other and form identities through pop culture. Our preferences tell us so much. The guy who likes *Beavis and Butthead* and *Dumb and Dumber* is different from the fellow who quotes *Citizen Kane* and listens to Bach. Like it or not, pop culture is important.

As a connoisseur of television, film, music, and technology, entertainment always comes first. It's not the nuances of this or that; it's whether or not you enjoyed it, whether you connected with it, whether you quote it fifteen years later, which matters most. When we gather details, it's not a competition. It's a labour of love. Trekkies aren't trying to outdo each other; they see a bit of themselves in the Enterprise's crew. And it doesn't have to be hardcore sci-fi for fanaticism to take hold. It can be anyone. Anyone who ever said, "That's what she said," is a fan. Those who chose between McSteamy and McDreamy are fans. Team Jacob. Team Edward. Swifties. Beliebers. The black-clad listeners of Stevie Nicks. The black-clad listeners of Marilyn Manson. The glitter-clad listeners of the Spice Girls. The twelve-year-old wearing a Batman shirt or a Bart Simpson shirt. Women who call themselves a Carrie or a Samantha. Even those who argue of the merits of Bach over Beethoven. No one is exempt. I am still convinced that my fiancé and I are Lily Aldrin and Marshall Erikson from *How I Met Your Mother*. Like I said, it can be anyone. It can be you. In fact, I dare say it is you.

In *Reel Talk*, what I aimed to do was go in-depth, investigating a little further than the entertainment level that we, the world at large, sit at. I looked at pop culture I did like. I looked at pop culture I didn't. I did something daring: I took a stance. For the truly well versed pop culture aficionados, this collection of essays may not break new ground. But considering the range of topics, from love triangles to TV moms, from Julia Roberts to Will Ferrell, I feel there is something here for everyone. I do hope it encourages you to look deeper at that which has provided fascinating conversations over the years, the kind of premium water-cooler material that stands the test of time, even after it goes off-air and off Netflix.

And if it gently nudges you towards something you've never seen before, I've done my job.

Move Over, Meryl:

The Search for A Better Film Actress

Rotten Tomatoes is "the most trusted measurement of quality for filmed entertainment," a review aggregation website for film and television. Beloved by film buffs and movie-goers alike, Rotten Tomatoes aims to please by dispensing a percentage score for each film, including one based on the opinions of critics and another from the audiences. For the sake of this experiment, I relied on critical scores. Why? While far from infallible, film critics must stand by their statement, whereas the average filmgoer can and may be fickle, changing their mind as the wind blows.

Every film actor will have their fifteen minutes; every film actor will have their flop; and virtually every film reviewed is in the Rotten Tomatoes database. The roller coaster careers of Tinseltown can be observed mathematically. It isn't a single film but the body of work in its entirety that determines the quality of an actor. If all the films in one's repertoire are totalled and averaged, a B-movie actor will probably warrant a percentage score akin to a B. The trashy actress who only appears in throwaway projects may not break into double digits. Surely, Meryl Streep, considered the greatest film actress alive, nominated for eighteen Academy Awards and winner of three (the greatest number of wins by a living actor-actress), has the greatest score imaginable on Rotten Tomatoes.

That is surprisingly not the case. All the hoopla given to superstar Streep, darling of award shows and frequent topper of 'best of' lists, may be bestowed upon the wrong one. Don't get me wrong. With a Rotten Tomatoes average score of 67.12% (rounded to the nearest hundredth and as of late 2014), Meryl is a delightful actress worthy of praise, but someone else has been dodging the spotlight.

This actress had a unique upbringing. At five, her mother, a Jew with ancestry from all over Europe, succumbed to a nervous breakdown. Eventually she overcame it and became a psychotherapist, citing her experiences as a form of career training. A half-Jewish Spanish diplomat, her maternal grandfather heroically forged travel documents in 1940 to save French Jews from the growing anti-Semitic forces. Her paternal family is just as intriguing. She is the great-granddaughter of a First-World-War-era British prime minister on her father's side, hailing from a respected and aristocratic English lineage. Alas, at thirteen, this actress's banker father suffered paralysis after a routine operation. When the procedure also left him partially blind and in a wheelchair, she became self-reliant and found an agent, dealing with her father's ailments by burying herself in as much work as she could, escaping drama with drama.

Thrust into the spotlight with no training, she was a celebrated film actress at nineteen. Initially typecast as the Merchant-Ivory corset-donning virgin, she wanted to break free of that rut. As early as the nineties, she was compared to Meryl for her eagerness to accept challenging roles, ones that forced her to stretch herself as an actress. A slightly eccentric young lady, she stayed with her parents in their beautiful London home until past her thirtieth birthday. She struggled to grow up and adopted a style all her own, both personal and physical. Never one to wear skimpy or overly feminine dress, her fashion sense is as notorious as her acting. She now lives with her long-term partner, a director who shares in her quirkiness. Together, they are parents and colleagues, the marvellous actress frequently appearing in his cinematic works. Her body of work is more critically acclaimed than Meryl Streep's. She has an average Rotten Tomatoes score of 70.33% (again, rounded to the nearest hundredth). This actress is Helena Bonham Carter.

I understand your resistance. Bellatrix Lestrange? Are you sure? For the Streep admirers, the argument may turn to the sheer size of Meryl's body of work. When you work as long and as hard as Streep, you're bound to encounter a stinker. Let me stop you right there. Meryl Streep isn't even the hardest working woman in Hollywood. Helena has eighty-one acting credits. Meryl has an embarrassing seventy-four. In comparison, Meryl just doesn't stack up.

And you haven't heard the worst of it. Shockingly, Helena Bonham Carter isn't the only one to trump Streep. After scouring through today's many living actresses of acclaim, from Jodie Foster (with a threateningly close score of 66.72%) to Angelina Jolie (with a comparatively abysmal 44.74%), Sigourney Weaver (a formidable 61.83%) to Uma Thurman (50.18%), Natalie Portman (60.69%) to Amy Adams (58.10%), it seems at least another five actresses stand alongside Helena. Please don't shoot the messenger.

We'll start first with a woman who shares more than a few things with Helena: Oscar-winner Emma Thompson. Both have been described as intelligent feminists, unconventional and distinctive. Both are liberal Londoners. And both fell for the same man. Helena's first serious relationship was with actor Kenneth Branagh, a romance that started up during Thompson's public divorce from him; some even argue his attraction to Helena triggered the split, something Bonham Carter vehemently denies. And now, with Emma warranting a score of 69.35%, the two women have something else in common.

Standing tall with a score of 70.24%, Cate Blanchett does it all. She's an awards show mainstay. She directs plays at Australia's largest theatre company, the Sydney Theatre Company, which she happens to run with her playwright husband. She was appointed as the sole woman on a ten-member steering committee for Kevin Rudd, the then-prime minister of Australia. But let's focus on her glory as an actress. She is considered one of the most versatile actresses of all time, able to play anything from the virgin queen Elizabeth I to folk singer-songwriter Bob Dylan. Public consensus seems to be that she's an energetic multi-tasker, a global busy-body who has earned respect as a hybridized "artist, administrator and intellectual." Streep should be proud to bow down to Blanchett.

Then, following close behind are two Dames: Maggie Smith at 69.76% and, at her heels, Judi Dench at 69.28%. These great women have much in common. Judi's father was a doctor and Maggie's a pathologist, each working for a lofty institution, the Theatre Royal and Oxford University, respectively. Both were drawn into the world of acting through their fathers, Judi joining her dad at work to observe the performances and Maggie involving herself in the university's Dramatics Society and its productions. An Oscar winner in 1969 and again in 1978, Maggie Smith started her career in the fifties in the British theatre circuit, actively pursuing the plays of Shakespeare, Ibsen, and Chekhov. Judi Dench debuted in 1957 as Ophelia in *Hamlet* at the Old Vic. She then spent three decades as part of the Royal Shakespeare Company, playing all the Bard's female leads. It seemed to prepare her for her late-in-life Academy Award moment; Dench nailed her mere eight-minute performance as Queen Elizabeth I, finally nabbing that Oscar gold in 1999.

They didn't limit themselves to mere film and stage. They each took time out to do television. Judi worked for the BBC on *Hilda Lessways* and continued on other series, like *A Fine Romance*. Meanwhile, Maggie is a frequent Emmy nominee for her role as Dowager Countess Violet Crawley in *Downton Abbey*. They're not just British roses. Judi Dench found international fame through the *James Bond* film franchise, taking on the role of Bond's boss M from the nineties onward. Maggie Smith gained international recognition as Professor McGonagall in the *Harry Potter* film franchise.

Even their personal lives are oddly identical. They married in the mid-seventies and their husbands both died of cancer three years apart. In recent years, both dealt with health scares. Dench is losing her eyesight through macular degeneration, while Smith underwent treatment for breast cancer. They're even good friends, co-workers who build each other up instead of tearing down the competition. They've appeared together in a number of films, including *A Room with a View*, *Tea with Mussolini*, and *The Best Exotic Marigold Hotel*. In 1988, Judi Dench became a Dame, and two years later, Maggie received the same royal title. Both ladies will eerily become octogenarians this December and show no sign of slowing down. Together they oust Streep from the spotlight.

Finally, twenty-four-year-old Jennifer Lawrence merits a 67.79% score. The Academy of Motion Picture Arts and Sciences, the body that hands out Oscars, has a reputation for consisting of old, white men. With a median age of sixty-two amongst its electors, few voters are youthful newcomers. However, winners and nominees and other substantial artists are brought into the fold year after year, offered membership by the Academy itself. The pint-sized winner Anna Paquin joined at age eleven. Saoirse Ronan and Dakota Fanning were in their mid- to late-teens. There's only a handful of twenty-somethings, too, but Jennifer Lawrence can count herself among them. No wonder, considering her precocious prestige. The Kentucky-native broke box office records with 2012's *The Hunger Games* and is much lauded for her acting chops and work ethic. At seventy-six, veteran actor Donald Sutherland extolled a twenty-one-year-old Lawrence as "a wonder" and called her "Jennifer Lawrence Olivier" in a comparison to the late British acting great Sir Laurence Olivier. Her talent doesn't translate into confidence, though. She was uncomfortable acting until her surprising success with the indie film *Winter's Bone* introduced her at twenty to the awards circuit. Granted, Lawrence's body of work is vastly smaller in total number of pictures than the company she's joined, but as the youngest three-time Oscar nominee and one-time winner, Jennifer Lawrence does, mathematically speaking, trump Meryl.

When these actresses come head to head, the truth about Ms. Streep is all the more evident. Meryl has never won the Academy Award in a category where any of these women have also been nominated. In fact, in 1979, Maggie Smith won the Academy Award for her supporting role in *California Suite*, beating Meryl who was nominated for *The Deer Hunter*. The same thing happened again in 2014 with *Blue Jasmine*'s Cate Blanchett snatching the Best Actress Oscar from under Streep for *August: Osage County*.

This *Moneyball*-style analysis reveals that those who are applauded, the fan favourites and critical darlings, aren't necessarily the most consistent in their wondrousness. We trust our instincts to interpret the value of art, but the numbers don't lie. So, when the historical drama *Suffragette* hits theatres in January 2015 and co-stars Streep and Bonham Carter find themselves sitting side by side both on the ticket and in the Dolby Theatre, you know who I'm betting on to get that gold.

To Do or Not To Do:

John Hughes and the Virginity Question

Teens and sex. Teens and sex. Teens and sex. Since time immemorial, parents have been worrying about their precious babies falling in with that rebellious gang or that trollop June. Even teens themselves are fascinated by the boudoir behaviours of others.

The Adolescent Family Life Act passed in 1981. The first grants were authorized, and, by 1982, funding started for the precursor of abstinence-only sex education from the federal government. A lesson on contraceptives was no longer taught. Everything was built around keeping that information from teens. Instead, gym teachers spouted "chastity and self-discipline", whatever that meant to an uninformed and confused hormonal adolescent.

Enter John Hughes. He wasn't an educator, not in the formal sense. He was a filmmaker who specialized in the teen perspective, an often neglected demographic that is oh-so-relied upon for their disposable income. Everything available is for them to buy but not necessarily for them to consume. In the eighties, no one was writing a story for teenagers about teenagers, so Hughes did what he did best. He used his films to talk frankly to teenagers at a time when abstinence-only education prevailed, when teens were thought too stupid to manage their lives, including but not limited to their sex lives.

Sixteen Candles, Hughes's directorial debut, starts to reveal his feelings towards teen sexuality. Samantha Baker's best friend Randy mocks Samantha's idealistic birthday wish, embellishing it with the notion of sex "on a cloud without getting pregnant or herpes." This twist is a blunt wake-up call. Teens, always considered the dumbest generation no matter what the time period, are far from misinformed. They're aware of the risks involved with sex, the incurable sexually transmitted diseases and the all-too-common unplanned pregnancy. Besides, Randy and Sam aren't playing with fire; they're just talking.

And the conversation continues in a yawn-inducing class as they pass notes back and forth, asking if Sam's ever done the deed and, if not, with whom would she bump uglies. As a sixteen-year-old sophomore, Sam responds innocently and honestly to these questions. She knows that, given the chance to have sex, she would, she guesses. That's the best she can muster, those three little words: "I guess so."

Despite the overindulgence that teens are sex-crazed animals, the reality is that fewer and fewer teens are having sex. In America, the adolescent birth rate has experienced a decline over the past half-century. It reached its height in 1957 with 96 births per thousand women aged fifteen to nineteen; since then, it has steadily dropped and, as of the year 2000, the rate was as low as 49 per thousand, the lowest it has ever been. Abortion rates didn't skyrocket to counteract the trend; teens were just choosing safe sex or no sex. Between 1988 and 1995, the number of teens abstaining increased two percent and the number of sexually active teens using contraceptives also increased two percent. Due to improved contraceptive use, pregnancy rates simply dropped. Teens were making smart decisions about their bodies. They were waiting and abstaining or making their choices in a state other than a drunken stupor.

And *Sixteen Candles* captures that. The first time we see Samantha Baker, she's examining herself and determining she doesn't feel or look like a sixteen-year-old sex goddess; it's just not who she is. She tells anyone who will listen that she's waiting to give her V-card to someone special. She's not throwing it around. Her family don't seem particularly concerned, either. In fact, Sam's grandparents diminish her sexuality. As they look at her developing body, they refer to her breasts as "perky" specimens that one needs a magnifying glass to inspect. Hardy har-har.

To contrast, there's the beautiful buxom blonde prom queen Caroline Mulford, the teen with a womanly body that Sam glimpses in the shower and concludes must be the sex goddess she'll never be. Caroline's a party girl, for sure, but even she holds herself accountable when it comes to sex. She's on birth control, and even though she considers the pill some form of magic that allows her to be "really super careless", the audience can see that she's already taken the precautions to protect herself. Caroline's not winging it. She's smarter than even she gives herself credit for. If she's having sex, it's going to be safe sex.

Which brings us to the big male-female question. There's this double standard presented in pop culture, an idea that has existed for seemingly ever, that idea that teen girls are responsible and knowledgeable about how sex works and its consequences while teen boys are…what? Part-ape? Most depictions in media of teen boys boil down to sex-crazed animals rubbing up against anything they can, when the reality is that there is little to no statistical difference between sexually active male and female teenagers. (Actually, the few years it wasn't perfectly equal, the girls were doing it more than the boys.)

Sixteen Candles deals with this ridiculousness with a touch more dignity. After all, John Hughes was once a teenage boy himself. He shows two perspectives, one exaggerated and stereotypical with the geeky Ted and one that's simultaneously realistic and romantic with the popular jock Jake Ryan. Ted, more often labelled the Geek, spends his time bothering Sam, hovering around her and sniffing her hair. He can barely contain his burgeoning erection. Ted points out that, as a virile male, he would hand over his lunch money to any woman because he's "too torqued up to say no." His hormonal body is rattling his brain, so much that he automatically assumes the only reason Sam won't have sex with him is because she has venereal disease. (She corrects him.) Ted's ultimately unfamiliar with women, so sure that there's a conspiracy amongst them to keep men waiting to do that ever-revered "it." Meanwhile, Jake can get any woman he wants, but he wants something more than that. Jake wants reciprocated love. "I think a ton of guys feel the same way you do," Ted tells Jake. "It's just that they don't have the balls to admit it." More than three-quarters of males admitted they felt sexually pressured by the culture around them in a survey of over a thousand men between ages fifteen and twenty-two. That

explains why thirty percent lie about their level of
sexual experience. The geeky Ted validates that
theory, proving that even he's too scared to say that
he wants love, more than just sex. In an intimate
moment of self-disclosure, Ted reveals his darkest
secret to Samantha: He's "never bagged a babe", a
confirmed virgin. For him, it's all talk, all about
appearances and reputation. He'd rather show off
Sam's undies like a mounted deer-head than
actually embrace her. In Ted's world, panties are
currency, no matter how they're obtained.

Jump to *Weird Science*, which revolves
around two awkward prepubescent boys, Wyatt, 15,
and Gary, 16. The premise is nothing more than a
Frankenstein story. Bored and horny, the computer-
savvy Wyatt programs their dream woman one
weekend, a twenty-something bombshell they name
Lisa. Lisa meets Gary's parents halfway through the
film. They're depicted as the stereotypical old-fogey
parents, curmudgeons with antiquated notions of
what it means to be a teenager. In a satirical bit of
wit, Lisa paints the party she's throwing as "your
basic high school orgy", which Hughes is trying to
point out is scarcely the reality. Parents may fret but
the gross majority of teenage parties aren't the
sexual Valhalla they've imagined. Lisa then reveals
quite openly that the only sexual act Gary's ever
performed is masturbation, which is still enough to
shatter their ideas of purity. The essential point of
Weird Science boils down to this: Teenage boys
may build up in their imaginations (or in this film,
in a computer) their dream girl as a scantily clad
woman in her early twenties, the kind of woman
they refer to as a "sexpot", but nobody wants an
empty shell. It speaks volumes that Lisa repeatedly
throws herself at Wyatt and Gary and there is never

any reciprocation. They worry about Lisa's feelings as they fall in love with girls their age, but neither feels genuine all-encompassing love for her. Neither sleeps with her. All talk, no action.

The Breakfast Club offers the gamut of high school types, a derivative of every clique, and though this diversity, it is the most helpful to digest John Hughes's views on teenage sexuality. The "criminal" bad boy John Bender uses Claire's sexual inexperience to mock her, calling her "cherry" and whatnot. To a point, her virtue is worth defending, dodging his questions and scoffing at his remarks. The school's wrestling superstar Andrew Clark even rushes to her aid. Meanwhile, Brian Johnson, the timid academic, is embarrassed of his virginity and lies about it, inventing women that he's "laid lots of times." These adolescents view sexuality as "a double-edged sword"; use it and you're branded as a hussy or player, but don't use it and you're a frigid prude. Neither option is acceptable when you want to belong. And as it turns out, Allison, the guidance counsellor's pet project, admits that, while a virgin, if she met the right person, someone she loved and who loved her back, she would sleep with him. You have to realize the level of bravery it takes to make a bold statement like that amongst high schoolers. Claire reluctantly admits that she feels the same, wanting to feel loved and respected before jumping in the sack. The guys remain mostly quiet during this discussion, but their lack of objection speaks louder than any words they could say. The polarity of promiscuity and abstinence, it seems, is too much for any of them; admitting to either end of the spectrum is social suicide, so all students find somewhere safe in the middle, regardless of the truth. They find comfort in ambiguity.

And treating preteens with this preciousness, covering their eyes and ears to block out the naughty bits, is an act in futility. They know what's going on. Take *National Lampoon's Vacation*, an account of a cross-country family trip with periodic breaks along the way. One particular pit-stop is at the wife's cousin's farmhouse in Kansas. They introduce their kids to each other, Chicagoans Audrey and Rusty to Kansan Vicky and Dale.

The four kids, in their early to mid-teens, scamper off into the yard. Audrey and her second cousin Vicky exchange idle chit-chat as they ride a seesaw. From the outside, it looks like a scene of children playing in the yard. However, the conversation is slightly more adult. Farm-girl Vicky tells city-slicker Audrey that she French kisses now and Audrey's response is telling: "So? Everybody does that."

Meanwhile, Rusty spends time with another second cousin Dale. Bored with playing with worms, again a childish activity, Dale leads Rusty to his bedroom to show him his collection of pornographic magazines. Rusty examines the centerfold with great excitement, asking if he can have the magazines. Dale objects to the idea, referring to them as necessities considering his masturbatory frequency. And you get further glimpses into the mind of family-man Clark Griswold's preteen son in the sequel *National Lampoon's Christmas Vacation*; here we're shown a signed cheesecake poster of a scantily clad lingerie model hanging above the top bunk in his bedroom.

Awareness does not equate to interest, though. In *Home Alone*, eight-year-old Kevin's entire family is going to France for Christmas. The house is filled with Kevin's cousins and siblings stuffing their knapsacks and suitcases. Bouncing from room to room, young Kevin enters his teenage brother Buzz's room. Substantially older than Kevin, Buzz is having a conversation with his teenage cousin that's a bit mature for Kevin's ears. Solemn about travelling with his family, Buzz brightens at the idea of nude beaches in France, only to become disappointed when his cousin points out that it's winter.

Buzz seems to be the only vocal teenager in *Home Alone*, but his unfiltered drivel doesn't last long. After being left, as the title promises, home alone, Kevin steals from Buzz's secret stash of goodies in his room. While fishing through his belongings, Kevin uncovers a bounty of loot: BB gun ammo, cash, and a stack of Playboys. Only eight years old, Kevin discards the magazines, uninterested. "No clothes on anyone," he remarks. "Sickening."

In the sequel, *Home Alone 2: Lost in New York*, Kevin is older but still just nine, not a teenager and thus not really a prime candidate for talking about John Hughes's views on adolescent sexuality. However, Kevin does have a slight curiosity about the human anatomy. For example, he lingers a little too long in the bathroom when his uncle takes a shower. Later, he comments to a New York hotel concierge about how his father wouldn't travel to the Big Apple "to get his naked rear end spied on." He wants to know more, simple as that, but it's no fixation. Parents needn't be worried about their kids learning too much too soon; they should actually help out, rather than contributing to the spread of misinformation.

In *Uncle Buck*, Bill and Cindy Russell have three children, a fifteen-year-old daughter and two under ten. Their only son, Miles (played by the actor who played *Home Alone*'s Kevin, the legendary child actor Macaulay Culkin) is learning the vernacular for his anatomy. "What's the other word for balls?" he asks his parents. They ignore him, shooing him off to bed. On his own, he discovers a synonym: "Nuts!" His six-year-old sister Maizy isn't more proper because she's a girl; she refers to kissing as "slipping the tongue." They're children but they're not stupid. They're not oblivious to the world around them, but they don't fully comprehend it. Too precious about their precocious son, Bill and Cindy Russell are too embarrassed and distracted to teach Miles the medical names for his own body parts. Whether or not they sit down to discuss it, he'll still know bits and pieces. No need to fret, as long as they start a conversation soon.

Their concern is instead with their eldest, belligerent teenager Tia. When her uncle arrives to pick her up from school, he can see Tia kissing her boyfriend Bug on the steps. She rushes over to the car and gets in, but her uncle decides to chat with Bug. He warns him that "if you gnaw on her face in public like that again," there will be consequences. Tia doesn't bat an eye; their behaviour is, in her opinion, harmless. But not to Uncle Buck; no, he sees a predator-prey relationship, "zooming the girls [with] a pretty face." Tia divulges that her love life is her own, not his to meddle in, but Uncle Buck is unsatisfied. His concern lies in how much her parents know about their daughter, which Tia reveals is effectively zero. There's no communication. She presumes they have neither time nor interest in her boyfriends, never bothering to meet Bug, never showing interest in her emotional state.

Uncle Buck fears for Tia's safety, though, as she tends to draw the wrong kind of acquaintances. For example, a sleazy guy nicknamed "Pal" at the bowling alley hits on Tia, attracted to her appearance as a college-age cheerleader type. Pal has no idea she's a minor until Buck storms over and chases Pal away. Buck routinely hunts down Tia, even venturing into the woods to collect her from a bonfire. But despite his distrust, Tia ultimately decides for herself and doesn't respond to Bug's pressure to have sex. She secretly appreciates but doesn't need a watchful eye. Tia takes charge and decides if and when she's ready to jump in the sack. No amount of nagging from Bug is going to change her mind, even when he breaks up with her on a whim to bed a different girl. You see, the Russells don't need to worry about their children; they just need to care.

Tia's situation is an ideal one. There's another not-so-ideal situation that must be addressed, and John Hughes addresses it in *Ferris Bueller's Day Off*. Most of the film is light-hearted and deals with a "righteous dude" playing hooky with his hypochondriac best friend and loyal girlfriend. But we must remember Ferris Bueller's sister, Jeanie. She offers a different facet of teen sexuality, specifically the topic of rape. Twenty-five percent of teenage girls under eighteen suffer sexual assault. About a third of victims are attacked between twelve and seventeen years of age. In fact, adolescents between sixteen and nineteen are more vulnerable to rape attempts than the general population, 3.5 times more likely to be targeted. So, when Jeanie goes home from school to verify that her brother is a big faker, she becomes alarmed when she encounters a strange man in her house. Her immediate reaction is to call the police. She tells the emergency operation, "I am very cute. I am very alone. And I'm very protective of my body. I do not want it violated, or killed, all right? I need help!" Jeanie's reaction is to immediately report it to the police, and nothing has even happened yet. Scary as it is, when things do happen, when it's not just a scare anymore but a crime committed, people are more hesitant than ever to report it. There's a million different reasons why people don't, and fear often reigns supreme. But Jeanie shows that, when you're scared, that's when you need to call for help. If parents want to worry about something, the topic of rape is where they should focus their anxieties. Knowing what to do in a situation where they are more exposed to a sexual assault is vital; if they teach their children one thing, this should be it.

Pretty in Pink returns to the original messages conveyed through *Sixteen Candles*, *The Breakfast Club*, and *Weird Science*. In *Pretty in Pink*, Duckie Dale makes flirtatious remarks to his best friend Andie throughout much of the film, but at prom, when a young lady makes eyes at Duckie, he is floored. He can't believe that this girl is interested in him. For him, sex is a punch line, not an activity. Only one character gets between the sheets in *Pretty in Pink*, a rich snob called Steff, but he's a twerp, a character the audience is supposed to hate, not relate to. The same goes for *Some Kind of Wonderful* with arrogant lothario Hardy Jenns. *Some Kind of Wonderful* centers not on Hardy, but

on Keith Nelson. Keith has a gigantic crush on
beautiful Amanda Jones. Although they're from the
same community, she's friends with the rich snobby
kids and Keith hangs out with his loyal tomboyish
friend Watts. In Watts's mind, his fascination with
her is purely sexual, but Keith rebuts. He claims his
interest in Amanda is more than that, but he doesn't
know anything else about her. As an artist, he paints
her face but not her soul. Watts struggles to believe
that Keith's love for Amanda runs deep. She warns
him, "Don't go mistaking paradise for a pair of long
legs." Amanda has a similar problem, a fascination
with the surface of things. She's attracted to "the
boy with the car." This is the aforementioned Hardy
Jenns, the rich boy with no respect for Amanda.
Amanda knows Hardy is unfaithful to her. She
brushes it off several times, but one day, she can't
take it anymore. Fed up with Hardy's cheating
ways, Amanda only stoops to talk to Keith to make
Hardy jealous. She agrees to a date with Keith in
retaliation, throwing it back in Hardy's face. For
Amanda, sex is a weapon. Audiences are meant to
see themselves in Keith and Watts, your average
teenage boy and girl. They're the microphones for
John Hughes. And while Amanda and by proxy
Hardy convey purely physical facets of desirability,
superficial sexed-up stereotypes that parents worry
about, the truth is that everyone is Watts and Keith.
They are realistic representations of companionship
and emotional intimacy. The spark of their love
grows out of something other than their thighs.

John Hughes's message remained the same,
that most teen sexuality is discussion of the deed
and rarely execution of it. Parents were and still are
freaking out over nothing but talk. The media think
they're sex addicts, but they're more like

sexologists, studying it from afar in their spare time, constantly educating themselves about every type of peccadillo.

In the end, John Hughes was open and honest and told it like it is, but he knew that sex wasn't the point. None of Hughes's films were built around teen sex fantasies, not at the core. They were about the average teenager, almost to a boring point. You saw yourself, the person you were, not the person you aspired to be. Few girls were buxom and the guys outwardly seemed sex-crazed but secretly wanted more for themselves than fulfilment of carnal lust. No, Hughes was emphatic about how teens need love far more than sex. In his words, he saw the adolescent experience as incredibly "romantic – as wanting a relationship, an understanding with a member of the opposite sex more than just physical sex." Class dismissed.

Jack of All Trades, Master of None:

The Many Faces of Will Ferrell

A butcher, a baker, a candle-stick maker… Whatever your profession, we expect a degree of accountability, a sort of pride in your work. You want that quality control as consumers, as citizens of society at large, and for that, we have bosses. Larger companies include performance evaluations as part of their management policy. Unfortunately, work assessments are often poorly designed and executed. There are major issues of "appraisal reliability and validity", according to *Administrative Science Quarterly*. These performance evaluations are ineffective and subjective, garnering massive differences in scores from one evaluator to the next. And that's the companies that do use these measures. According to the 2014 Performance Management survey, less than a third of workplaces evaluate its employees yearly. (If that's not enough, over half of workplaces don't evaluate new employees after their first three months.)

The Peter Principle worsens matters. For those who are unfamiliar with the term, the Peter Principle tells us that an employee in a hierarchical workplace will be promoted continuously until the employee reaches a position in which they're incapable of effectively working. As a result, most of the higher-ranking positions in a company are filled by people that can't do their jobs.

Enter Will Ferrell. Over the span of eighteen movies and five television series, Ferrell has played a *Washington Post* investigative reporter, a NASCAR racing driver, an Olympic figure skater, a rancher, the "five-time Emmy-award winning anchor" of San Diego's News Center 4, a Democratic congressman, a forensic accountant turned "desk jockey" police officer, a nefarious henchman, a time-travelling palaeontologist, a Nazi playwright, a federal wildlife marshal, a poison factory worker, an essay-writer running an academically dishonest operation, a television actor (twice), a vitamin salesman turned kids' soccer coach, the "incredibly handsome criminal genius and master of all villainy", a Renaissance Fair jouster, a singer-turned-GM of the Flint Tropics, and a toy-making elf. He's only fired three times onscreen.

That's pretty amazing, considering what he does. He is deplorable, professionally speaking. Let's look at his résumé.

In *Elf*, Will Ferrell plays Buddy. As a baby waiting for adoption, Buddy slips out of his crib and crawls into Santa's sleigh. From thereon forth, Buddy lives at the North Pole and is raised as an elf. Elves have three vocational choices: baking cookies in a tree, cobbling shoes, or building toys in Santa's workshop. Of course, Buddy opts for building toys, but he's too large for the job, his oversized fingers not nimble and dextrous enough. He makes a paltry eighty-five Etch-a-Sketches compared to the quota of a thousand. After his abysmal work performance, Buddy's demoted to testing jack-in-the-boxes. Due to the overwhelmingly pleasant work environment in Santa's workshop, Buddy doesn't lose his job. Instead, upon learning of his status as a human, not an elf, he decides to travel – on foot, no less – from the North Pole to New York in search of his father. Thank goodness because he was holding those poor elves back.

In *Bewitched*, Will Ferrell plays Jack Wyatt, a down-on-his-luck actor switching from film to TV to play Darrin in a reboot of the classic series *Bewitched*. He's switching mediums because of his personal failures as an actor. He chooses the wrong projects and is no longer bankable after a big-screen flop. He even tests poorly with TV audiences earning only 32% favourability. Furthermore, Jack's not exactly the easiest person to work with; he's a demanding diva, insisting on a coffee machine that only he can use and claiming a greater and greater number of lines in the script. Here he's not just a lousy worker, but a lousy guy.

In *Austin Powers: International Man of Mystery* and *Austin Powers: The Spy Who Shagged Me*, Will Ferrell plays Mustafa, the henchman to Dr. Evil. Mustafa jumps between roles as an assassin and a device engineer, dabbling in fiery trap-holes and cryogenics alike. He fails to design gadgets to his boss's expectations and equally fall shorts in the assassination department. Ordered to kill Austin Powers in the sequel, Mustafa chases him in a car, eventually flying off a cliff. Miraculously, Mustafa lives and climbs back up the cliff where he is subjected to Austin Powers's questioning. Due to his compulsion to answer questions once they're repeated thrice, he doesn't stand up to interrogation. Twice, Mustafa is murdered, once by his own trap-hole and again by a poison dart to the throat. Both incidents are hits ordered by Mustafa's boss, Dr. Evil. That's right; Mustafa dies twice. In the business of evil, they terminate lives, not jobs.

In *Semi-Pro*, it's 1976 and the two basketball leagues, the ABA and NBA, are undergoing a merger. The NBA will only take four teams from the ABA and the remainder will dissolve, leaving each GM with a generous payout. Will Ferrell's character, Jackie Moon, however, the disco-era singer-turned-Flint Tropics owner/coach/power forward, will not take this merger sitting down. The problem is that – no surprise – Jackie's terrible at his job. In order to qualify for the NBA, he needs an average two thousand fans in attendance per game. Unfortunately, Jackie is an inferior promoter, struggling with low game attendance and jumping to increasingly desperate gambits to raise that tent-pole. He even falsifies sponsorships to appear more legitimate. As a player, he's not much better. His unsportsmanlike behaviour regarding the calls made by referee Father Pat is persistent, permeating the majority of games. While in the locker-room, it becomes abundantly clear that he cannot plan out plays for the team. He doesn't know how. Even Jackie himself realizes his limitations. "I'm not a tactician," he declares. "I'm a motivator." Ultimately, Jackie confuses his roles as businessman and athlete.

The Producers thrusts Will Ferrell's Franz Liebkind into the limelight as a member of the Nazi party who writes an atrocious script, a play so politically incorrect that the titular producers are convinced it will close in one night. Franz believes in Adolf Hitler like a religious zealot to a saint, leading him to pen a musical called *Springtime for Hitler*. The producers are certain his play will be a massive flop, but they decide to stack the cards anyway. They cast Franz, a man with no acting experience whatsoever, as the lead. On opening night and with no understudy to assist him, he fails to perform, breaking his leg. He fails as a writer, a performer, and a Nazi.

Will Ferrell is Dr. Rick Marshall in *Land of the Lost*, a disgraced palaeontologist who believes that time travel is possible. He's bad at taking criticism, frequently lashing out at everyone from a middle-school student to reporter Matt Lauer. In fact, the film opens on an interview with Matt that turns to fisticuffs. Whether it's requesting grants and other funding or comparing his intellect to those of his peers, Rick doesn't have the most tact. He is also prone to lows from his theories being constantly discredited by the academic community. To put it bluntly, Rick has become a punch line, a laughingstock amongst bone-dusters.

As the animated Megamind in DreamWorks's *Megamind*, Will Ferrell shows how poor he is at villainy. He is predictable in the means he uses to provoke his rival, Metro Man. His lack of creativity is somewhat intentional, though. He secretly likes the back-and-forth with Metro Man and having a superhero to fight gives Megamind's life meaning. However, he accidentally puts an end to Metro Man and takes over Metro City in the aftermath, giving himself the title of Evil Overlord. At first, Megamind is giddy with his surprise victory, but this achievement only gives him pleasure for a short time. Megamind becomes bored and sorrowful with no opposition. There's no challenge without a hero to retaliate and defend Metro City. Megamind even considers giving up being evil. When your only job requirement is to not defeat the city's hero, you'd think Megamind would be able to do so.

As "a stupid cowboy" with low intelligence, high ignorance, and poor self-preservation instincts, Will Ferrell plays redneck Ricky Bobby to a tee. In *Talladega Nights: The Ballad of Ricky Bobby*, Ricky becomes a race-car driver who consistently wins. That spells out a decent work performance under normal conditions, but things start to go awry in no time. First, he is disrespectful to his boss, Larry Dennit, Jr.; frankly, Ricky's arrogance is astounding, convinced that he's invincible, some kind of racing god. His boss seeks out some fresh meat to replace Ricky and finds French Formula One driver Jean Girard. Ricky Bobby can't handle the competition and suffers a mental collapse. He hallucinates his car going up in flames, and is admitted to the hospital for exhaustion. There, Ricky believes he is paralyzed from the hips down, but the doctor explains that it's all psychological. Ricky Bobby can't overcome his fears. It seems he'll never get back behind the wheel, obviously stunting his performance in such a way that he's dropped by his boss and many sponsors.

Will Ferrell is known for his now-iconic *Anchorman* role as Ron Burgundy, San Diego's number-one news anchor. Set in the seventies, Ron Burgundy is a hard-partying male chauvinist pig who struggles to accept the growing trend in gender diversity in the workplace, especially when beautiful Veronica Corningstone joins the news team and is promoted to co-anchor. Ron doesn't handle this competition well, consistently butting heads with Veronica and even brawling with other news teams in the streets. He's also not the best news anchor, regardless of what the ratings say. Why? He can't think on his feet, reading any typos that crawl across the teleprompter. Ron Burgundy is sloppy and sexist but he's celebrated at any rate.

His greatest work performance may be in the Spanish-language film *Casa de mi Padre*. There, Will Ferrell fills the role of rancher Armando Alvarez. He's naïve and innocent but honest. Armando is a decent rancher but not a good businessman, constantly criticized by his father and brother for being stupid.

But this role is an anomaly. He swiftly returns to his old ways in full force for *The Campaign*, in which incumbent Democratic congressman Cam Brady, played by Will Ferrell, campaigns for his fourth term in U.S Congress as Representative of the 14th District of North Carolina. At first, he is running unopposed, but eventually a Republican candidate steps forward, throwing a wrench in Cam's plans. After a much publicized lewd phone call to the wrong number, his approval rating drops from 62 percent to 42 percent. Cam can't handle his rage against his opponent. He accidentally punches a baby when he swings and misses his opponent Marty Huggins. Finally, Cam admits to the public that he is "a horrible congressman." He slowly but surely details his own incompetence, explaining how he "never reads the bills" and holds an abysmal voting record. He even admits to accepting bribes from those financing his campaign.

And this isn't Will Ferrell's first shady role. He also appears in *Zoolander*. A quick synopsis: When the new Malaysian prime minister agrees to improve workers' rights and increases wages, high-ranking members of the fashion industry are enraged. The sweatshops they rely upon for cheap labour are becoming more expensive, so together

they decide to put an end to Prime Minister Hassan.
And who do they put in charge of the operation?
Why, fashion designer Jacobim Mugatu, of course!
Played by Will Ferrell, Mugatu selects vain male
model Derek Zoolander to pull off the assassination;
because of Zoolander's severe lack of intelligence,
Mugatu can easily manipulate him. Even the
modelling agent who represents Derek, Maury
Ballstein, calls him "a sweet simpleton." Anyway,
Mugatu tells Derek to visit "a very exclusive day
spa" to prepare for the runway, but, in reality,
Mugatu's subjecting the receptive model to
brainwashing techniques. A quick recap: Mugatu
exploits sweatshop workers; he conspires to kill a
world leader; and he indoctrinates a gullible rube.
That should be enough, but alas there's more.
Besides being reprehensible from a moral
standpoint, Jacobim Mugatu is also an awful boss.
He calls his models fat and throws hot latte at his
loyal assistant. He throws his weight around and
flaunts his status. Mugatu feels invincible and, when
he's satisfied that either his models have run their
course or served their particular purpose, he orders
them to be killed. He's not just a horrific
professional; he's an all-round horrific person.

Will Ferrell appears as a wildlife marshal in
Jay and Silent Bob Strike Back named Willenholly.
Willenholly reports to an animal testing lab, the site
of an animal abduction by activists. The first thing
he does is crash his motorbike into a stationary
object. The next thing he does is misinterpret the
actions of two fools as a serious threat, taking to the
airwaves to report upon their idle chatter. The two
idiots he confuses for kidnappers then smuggle an
ape out of a diner that the Federal Wildlife Marshal
has surrounded. How do they smuggle the ape out?

By dressing it up like a child. Everyone else is aware of what they're doing and tries to warn the marshal, but Willenholly insists he knows better. I'd gamble that the Federal Wildlife Marshal should be able to distinguish an ape from a child. After realizing his error, Willenholly willingly jumps off a dam to chase after the two ape-loving dopes, endangering his life. (Without the help of movie magic, he would surely be dead.) Then he chases these fools to Hollywood and promptly rushes onto the set of a children's TV show where he shoots and presumably kills an unarmed man with a shotgun wound to the stomach. A few minutes later, Willenholly fires wantonly into a crowd of people. Somehow convinced that he's done his job well, he is shot finally by the ape that he was pursuing. But don't worry; it's only a tranquilizer dart, nothing like the bullets he sprayed across the room a few seconds earlier. Fearing that he's paralyzed as the tranquilizer numbs his lower extremities, Willenholly slips into a moment of deep confession. He reveals to a criminal that he failed the examination required to work for the FBI, so, in a moment of pity, the criminal who has outsmarted Willenholly at every turn bargains with him for a reduced sentence; for his own personal gain, Willenholly gladly makes a deal with this international criminal. I don't think I need to explain why Willenholly is an awful Federal Wildlife Marshal.

This preposterous slipshod amateur act is nonstop. As Detective Allen Gamble in *The Other Guys*, he opens fire in the office. As Olympic figure skater Chazz Michael Michaels in *Blades of Glory*, he shows up late to the games and makes it clear that he has a drug problem, a big no-no in the sports world. As Coach Phil Weston in *Kicking & Screaming*, he becomes an over-caffeinated winning-obsessed tyrant that threatens and intimidates ten-year-old children in order to win the kids' soccer league finals. As Phil's son articulates, "He taught us exactly how not to play soccer." And as *Washington Post* reporter Bob Woodward in *Dick*, a fictionalized account of the Watergate scandal, he is adamant against revealing the identity of Deep Throat. Normally, that wouldn't be something I could fault him for. The problem is, though, that Woodward isn't protecting the informants so much as himself. He's embarrassed to admit that everything he knows stems from two fifteen-year-old girls who divulged all their secrets over a prank phone call. His anonymous sources can't provide documentation because "the dog ate it." Bob Woodward and his partner Carl Bernstein risk their credibility on a pair of dizboes who spend their time discussing Mick Jagger's lips. I wouldn't call him top-notch in the journalistic ethics department.

This sloppy unprofessionalism transfers from film to television. In "Addicts", a 2001 episode of *Undeclared*, Will Ferrell plays Dave, a "townie" who sells undergrads college papers. He's an inconsistent writer, though, with his essays getting A's one second and D's the next. He also can't meet deadlines, especially when he's suffering hallucinations due to his amphetamine addiction. Then, in typical show-within-a-show fashion on *30 Rock*, Will Ferrell plays Shane Hunter, star of the sexist action drama *Bitch Hunter*. Every time an episode of *Bitch Hunter* aired, the public outrage it incited often led to an influx of women-friendly television programming on the network. Although this show elicits a negative reaction, it still seems to air, as it is mentioned in a negative light in the fourth season and appears again in an ad in a seventh season episode. In spite of how cancellation-happy networks can be, Shane Hunter is bizarrely not fired.

In "Mr. Saturday Knight", the ninth episode of the third season of *Family Guy*, the titular family guy, Peter Griffin, decides to become a jouster at the Quahog Renaissance Fair. He chooses to do this because he remembers back to a time when he was eighteen, high on hallucinogens, and leaped off the Ren Fair entrance sign. He was saved from injury by the Black Knight, the star jouster who raced towards him and caught him on the back of his horse. However, when Peter decides to work with him, the Black Knight, voiced by Will Ferrell, proves to be a dreadful colleague. Not only is he a lousy mentor to the new jousting recruits, but he's also prone to using bullying tactics, his arrogance getting the best of him.

Next, Will Ferrell appeared in the seventh season of *The Office*. His character, Deangelo Vickers, is the new Scranton branch manager of Dunder Mifflin Paper. On his first day, he tries to bulldoze over the effective routines that the previous manager, Michael Scott, put in place. One paper salesman, Andy Bernard, describes Deangelo as "a terrible salesman." And he's an equally terrible manager. He struggles to adapt to his new work environment and often says something inappropriate. He suffers a number of internal struggles. For one, he has a contentious relationship with food that leads him to grab handfuls of cake, taste them, and then throw them away. These angry outbursts are over food, though; his relationship with his employees is far more important. He's obsessed with being liked and seeming cool. As office administrator Pam Halpert puts it, "What could he possibly stand to gain from a real juggling routine?" Deangelo shows favouritism to a select few male employees, referred to as his "inner circle", which irritates another employee, Angela Martin. Deangelo displays sexism, ignoring the female heads of both the accounting and customer service departments. Other female employees feel they are denied opportunities and aren't privy to the same information as the men. Deangelo even switches two employees' positions in the customer service department so that the female head must report to a male supervisor. Trying to show off his masculinity, Deangelo attempts an epic slam dunk in front of the whole office that downs the basket in the warehouse. As he tumbles hanging from the rim, Deangelo smashes his head on the concrete and is rushed to the hospital, ostensibly ending his career at Dunder Mifflin.

Finally, as one of the main characters on the adult animated series, *The Oblongs*, Will Ferrell plays Bob Oblong, a family man who works at the poison factory, Globocide. With no limbs due to residing in a irradiated valley, Bob uses his mouth to put the lids on jars for a living, but after an incident at a Globocide-sponsored fairground causes Bob to suffer a jaw injury, Bob finds himself on worker's comp. Eager to avoid a lawsuit, Globocide provides Bob with a mechanical body, the Arms and Legs 2000. Up until that point, Bob was ill-equipped and thus inefficient at his job. How well would you fare trying to screw caps on jars with no arms or legs? Using just his mouth, Bob rarely hits his quota. But instead of using his new robotic body

to improve his work performance, Bob grows
enamoured with his higher quality of life. He
swiftly becomes arrogant and distracted, dancing
instead of working on the factory assembly line.

Ostensibly, Will Ferrell consistently plays a
guy bad at his job, no matter what the film. At this
level of ineptitude, he should be dismissed. Yet he
isn't. Frankly, it's not his output that matters; it's
his input. Even at his worst, he brings something to
the table. In *Semi-Pro*, he's an enthusiastic multi-
tasker, spinning all the plates. He exhibits a sense of
loyalty towards his team uncommon in the ever-
changing world of sports. In *Undeclared*, he's well
read, polishing off, as he estimates, "eight or nine
books a week." In *Jay and Silent Bob Strike Back*,
he doggedly chases after who he believes to be a
criminal mastermind. (He's wrong, but at least he's
dutiful.) In *The Oblongs*, he is dedicated, hardworking, and optimistic, overcoming his physical
disability. In *Elf*, he brings enthusiasm, an agreeable
colleague with a can-do attitude that keeps morale
high. Similarly, in *The Other Guys*, he is irritatingly
optimistic and supportive of his colleagues at the
NYPD. In both *Austin Powers* films, he is inventive.
In *Casa de mi Padre*, he is devoted and
hardworking; this is true, too, in *The Producers*
with his boundless devotion to the realization of his
play. In *The Office*, despite his obnoxious power
moves and pissing contests, he wishes to improve
the workplace by replacing an old chair in HR with
an ergonomic one, paying for education and training
programs for minority employees, and
implementing "ice-cream Thursdays" for everyone.
In *Land of the Lost*, he ardently believes in his
research on tachyons, the research that his peers
laughed at, and through perseverance and some

serious fieldwork, he is able to prove that he was
right all along. In *Anchorman: The Legend of Ron
Burgundy*, he earns the nickname "Mr. Dependable"
for his punctuality, never missing a broadcast. In
The Campaign, he gives speeches with ease,
tailoring them to his audience; he adeptly humiliates
the competition and is always ready for a patriotic
photo op. He knows that he "will do anything it
takes to win." In *Bewitched*, he is equally
ambitious; he genuinely wants to succeed. Sure, he
sucks, but he wants to do better. And he's
downright desperate for success in *Zoolander*; as
Mugatu, he "sold his soul" to a syndicate of the
world's fashion designers. His devotion to his
business translates to his devotion to them as "a
punk-ass errand boy"; he'll do anything to stay rich
and famous. But with all he brings to the table, it's
still unfathomable how he maintains employment.
Most could dismiss this phenomenon as a product
of the imaginary world where his work performance
is not only acceptable but at times commendable.

Not so fast. Remember the Peter Principle.
Given enough promotions, Will Ferrell would be as
incompetent as the next guy. It's not far off from
our reality. This silly world that we laugh at in
Ferrell's long list of slapstick comedies, the one his
characters inhabit with outwardly no regard to his
professional behaviour, is our world. (Will Ferrell
just disguises it well by making his vocational
calling seem like the most epic thing in existence.)

Perhaps he has pursued so many career paths
because of these promotions. Despite continuously
failing to fill the Tropics stadium in *Semi-Pro*,
Jackie Moon advances to a PR job at the NBA. In
fact, Will Ferrell's characters were at the summit of
their professions in *Anchorman, Talladega Nights*,

Megamind, *Blades of Glory*, *The Campaign*,
Zoolander, *Dick*, his episodes on *Family Guy* and
The Office, and oddly enough, *The Producers*. It's
not unheard of for him to change lanes when he hits
his own personal glass ceiling. In *Zoolander*, prior
to inventing the piano key necktie and taking the
fashion world by storm, Will Ferrell's character was
the keytarist for the band Frankie Goes To
Hollywood. Unfortunately, he'd been promoted past
competence. Stagnating as a musician, he switches
career paths, opting for fashion design instead. As
Congressman Cam Brady in *The Campaign*, Will
Ferrell chooses to withdraw from the race, so his
opponent Marty Huggins wins by default. Don't
worry; Will is rewarded by becoming Marty's chief
of staff, another job he proves terrible at, mixing up
folders and interrupting during an illegal campaign
financing trial. As ice skater Chazz Michael
Michaels, he switches to partners' figure skating
with his sworn enemy Jimmy MacElroy after being
stripped of his medals and banned from men's
singles figure skating. As Bob Oblong, he quits his
job at Globocide to become a lifeguard. He takes to
his new trade, getting into the beach culture and
learning CPR. Too bad his robotic suit isn't
waterproof. Even Megamind swaps out being a
villain for being the hero. So, what do you do when
you can't go up? You leave of your volition. You do
something new.

So, don't blame Will. Nobody can do
everything and he's one of the few brave enough to
venture out into a new, possibly green, but probably
brown, pasture. And if it's too brown to handle, he
can always drown his regrets with scotchy scotch-
scotch.

What Doesn't Kill You Makes You Depressed:

How America's Sweetheart Survived,

Won An Oscar, and Still Cannot Be Happy

Julia Roberts is known as a dramatic actress and romantic comedienne. Risky endeavours are typically allotted to adventurous casts of the action and epic persuasion, neither of which Roberts has ever been a part of. Fewer explosions, weapons, and death-defying leaps – simply put, she should be a "safer" actress by virtue of the genres she's selected.

Yet Julia Roberts can scarcely make it through the roles of her early career. Her characters' stories brush close to fatality, some of which meet tragic ends. It's an inevitability that ties together all of her early work. After her *Erin Brockovich* win, her roles consist of ones in less dire situations, but all of the characters are unhappy, suffering from clinical depression. If her entire career was one person, a psychologist would see her more recent roles as evidence of PTSD. The Oscar may have saved her life, but it didn't improve it.

Let's handle her least dangerous roles first. In *Something to Talk About*, Julia plays Grace King Bichon, a genteel Southern lady from Savannah, Georgia, who has caught her husband cheating. Now, Grace's husband, Eddie Bichon, isn't just the once-in-a-lifetime affair man, but rather a serious philanderer who sleeps with seemingly all the women in his wife's social circle. Considering his anti-monogamous attitude towards sex, Julia's character's chances of dying are probably in proportion to Eddie's, a direct correlation through her increased chances of catching a serious STI from him.

In the yesteryear era in which *Something to Talk About* is set, there weren't hepatitis B or HPV vaccines (not until 1981 and 2006, respectively), so that method of prevention is out. The majority who have contracted an STI don't show symptoms. They don't realize they're infected. The virus can wreak havoc in silence, damaging a woman's reproductive health, in addition to various effects on the rest of her body. Let's say Grace goes to the doctor and gets checked. Identifying the problem may not suffice. Her diagnosis may be grim since only half of the eight "biggies" in the world of STDs are curable; since herpes, hepatitis B, HPV, and HIV aren't treatable, they should be prevented at all cost. The advice of the World Health Organization and the Guttmacher Institute is to abstain or have "mutually monogamous" sex. Eddie's put his ship in every port, though, and I have doubts he'll stop. As of 2012, the Centers of Disease Control reported that the state of Georgia had a greater than national average rate of reported cases of common sexually transmitted diseases. In fact, of the fifty states, Georgia was in the top eight for reported incidence of both chlamydia and gonorrhea, and for primary and secondary syphilis, they were number one. And that's just the detected cases! If any of his numerous partners contract something, it's unlikely they'll notify him, considering the stigma adultery carries.

And then Eddie still has to tell his wife. There are many variables in this grapevine, a number of unreliable links in a chain to even get to Julia Roberts's character. Considering Eddie puts the onus of his infidelity on his wife, Grace, informing her that he cheated because she didn't follow through on her career dreams (a lousy excuse from a philanderer if I've ever heard one), I suspect there will always be another cockamamie defence waiting in the wings for why Eddie's suddenly got a rash on his nether-regions.

  Another of Julia's sounder roles comes from "The One After the Super Bowl", an episode in the second season of *Friends*. A make-up artist, Susie Moss (played by our Julia), recognizes Chandler (played by Matthew Perry). She knew him from grade school, but he doesn't recognize her. She describes herself as the bespectacled little girl who "carried a box of animal crackers like a purse" and they reminisce about when he jokingly pulled her skirt up to reveal her underwear during the fourth grade play. Susie flirts with Chandler until he invites her to dinner; she continues to suggest sex, innuendo after innuendo. At dinner, she asks him to meet her in the men's room where she has him undress down to her skivvies. She takes off with his clothing in an act of revenge almost two decades in the making. It may seem small beans in comparison to the more grandiose roles in Julia's oeuvre, but the effect of revenge on health can't be dismissed. It does challenge one's chances of living. The psychological effects on the body are self-evident. Our mind affects our health. Although revenge is sought out to revel in that feeling of catharsis, that's rarely what comes of any vengeful act. Psychologists call it the revenge paradox: getting revenge actually leaves you unhappier. Perhaps Susie Underpants should just let it go.

Looking for a more physical threat? Roberts has a cigarette in her mouth in both *My Best Friend's Wedding* and *Mystic Pizza*. She even gets in trouble for smoking in a hotel in the former. Twenty percent of all American deaths annually are caused by cigarette smoke. Smoking cuts one's life expectancy by at least a decade. It leads to respiratory and cardiovascular disease, cancers, bone disease, cataracts, diabetes... The Center of Disease Control couldn't be clearer when they call smoking "the leading preventable cause of death in the United States."

Not only does Julia smoke like a chimney, but she also drinks like a fish. In *Mystic Pizza*, Julia's character Daisy Araujo destroys her boyfriend's car while inebriated. At one point, Daisy throws her arms up in the air, guzzling back her own six-pack. "How the hell do I know where I'll be ten years from now?" she replies. "I could be dead for all I know." Then, in *My Best Friend's Wedding*, as Julianne Potter, Julia Roberts becomes stressed and binge drinks to quell the pain when her plan falls apart before her eyes. "Death by a mini-bar," her token gay friend George describes it. Between ages sixteen and fifty-four, the more alcohol a woman consumes, the greater chance she will die. It is, as medical statisticians put it, "a direct dose-response relation."

Things get more serious for Julia Roberts from hereon forth. Starting at the very beginning, Roberts first appeared in a small role on the fourth season finale of *Miami Vice*. After sustaining a concussion, Detective Crockett suffers amnesia, believing that he is Sonny Burnett, his undercover identity. He gets swept into the life of a drug dealer, unbeknownst to Crockett that he is in fact a police officer. It is through drug boss Miguel Manolo that Crockett meets our positively infantile Julia Roberts. She plays Polly Wheeler, his assistant.

"I like hoods," she confides, admitting her fascination with drug dealers. "They're so much more upfront with their treachery." Her proximity to the illegal narcotics industry puts her in grave danger. She deals directly with investors, deciding who makes it through to see her big, bad boss. The criminal element that surrounds Polly often get, as Crockett describes it, "trigger spasms." In the late eighties and early nineties, narcotics-related homicide rates soared to what was then a record high, and refugee populations grew in Miami, bolstering the drug trade in the city. Fifteen percent of deaths in 1980 alone were tied to the drug trade. Fast forward eight years. The homicide rate for Miami in 1988 skyrocketed to nearly fifty deaths per hundred thousand people. Approximately thirty percent of male homicide perpetrators tested positive for cocaine. Half of the homicides in Dade County, Florida, occurred at night with obvious links to the Miami drug scene. To claim that drug trafficking was a safe vocation would be misguided.

This isn't the first role Julia has taken involving an illegal trade. In *Pretty Woman*, Julia Roberts plays Vivian Ward, a prostitute who can't pay her rent. She dodges her landlord to keep from homelessness while her roommate Kit De Luca spends their money wantonly on drugs. Walking through town, Vivian sees a prostitute dead in the Dumpster. The murder rate for American female prostitutes as of 2004 is approximately 204 for every hundred thousand people. Working girls, as

they're called, are nearly eighteen times more likely
to be killed than women of equivalent age and race.
It is the most dangerous American occupation. The
next worse job for women in the eighties would be
employment in a liquor store at a meagre four
homicides for every hundred thousand people.
Don't think that because it's women's work it's any
less dangerous. In fact, in the early nineties when
Pretty Woman was released, fishermen – a
predominantly male occupation and "the most
deadly occupation since 1992", according to the
U.S. Bureau of Labor Statistics – had a mortality
rate of a mere 140 per hundred thousand people
over five years. If she follows the occupational
average, Vivian will be dead before thirty-five.

And that's homicide alone. There are other
crimes that don't kill you but leave a lasting
impression nonetheless. For example, from a San
Francisco sample of two hundred sex workers, 164
were assault victims and 136 were on-the-job rape
victims. Prostitutes get attacked regularly, but they
have nowhere to turn when things go awry. They
struggle to report an incident without facing arrest
themselves. The annual average of Americans
arrested for prostitution-related crimes ranges
between seventy and eighty thousand people, and of
that number, the gross majority are female
prostitutes at seventy percent of arrests. (Pimps and
male prostitutes constitute twenty percent and
customers amount to only ten.) So you either die or
you get arrested. This is the fate of a Hollywood
hooker.

The story of *Pretty Woman* itself doesn't
offer anything better for Vivian. A businessman
named Edward Lewis pays Vivian three thousand
dollars to be his escort for six days and nights. She

tries to live up to his exacting standards, something that doesn't come easily. Considering that Edward couldn't reconcile with his father after the loss of his mother and dismantled his father's company in an act of revenge, what chance does Vivian stand if she gets on Edward's bad side? And Mr. Lewis doesn't keep the best company, either. Edward's trusted attorney, Philip Stuckey, physically assaults Vivian, an act that is only halted by happenstance. If she isn't killed on the street, she could just as easily be killed in the Penthouse.

From one title to the next, Julia broaches death. As the titular character in *Mary Reilly*, Julia is housemaid to Dr. Jekyll and his infamous dark side Mr. Hyde. Mary becomes romantically entangles with the two, but Hyde is the embodiment of evil, a man chased by the police who has murdered and could easily murder again. She lies to protect him, but when Hyde's nature is revealed to her, she decides she must leave. As Mary tries to flee, she is attacked by Hyde, a knife at her throat.

Don't forget *Flatliners*, in which Julia plays Rachel Manus, a medical student who flatlines to catch visions from the afterlife. Her and her fellow med student friends are literally playing with life and death. When it's Rachel's turn to actively die, a power outage threatens her chances of resuscitation. Need I say more?

A weird turn of events catapults Julia Roberts into danger in *Runaway Bride*. When columnist Ike Graham writes an article on Julia's character, Maggie Carpenter, about how she consistently leaves her fiancés at the altar, Maggie writes a furious letter to the editor. Ike loses his job, but he perseveres, travelling to Hale, Maryland, to follow Maggie as she prepares to get married for the fourth time. His research shows that she's fled on motorcycle and horseback, both of which carry their fair share of danger (seventy-two deaths per hundred thousand for motorcycles, according to the U.S. National Highway Traffic Safety Administration, while equestrian activity leads to an accident at least once every 350 hours). After her upcoming fourth wedding, she plans to spend her honeymoon mountain-climbing at Annapurna. You don't need statistics to know how dodgy mountain-climbing is. Even if I exclude her iffy family medical history (a mother who died prematurely and a father with an alcohol dependency problem), Maggie still finds a way to endanger herself through her actions alone. In order to prevent the gossipy columnist from writing a second slanderous story about her, Maggie breaks into his room at the inn and steals his research notes. When he catches her in the act, Maggie leaps through the window and shimmies around the building. If she falls at that height, I'm sure she'd make a horrible splat sound.

In *Sleeping With the Enemy*, Julia's Laura Burney lives in the lap of luxury in her husband Martin's beach house in Cape Cod. However, there are rules to living there, as Martin reminds Laura. The labels of canned food must face the front of the cupboard. The edges of the towels must be aligned when they hang down over the bar. We learn that Martin won't allow his wife to work longer hours at the library on account of a late supper. Worse still, Martin forbade Laura from attending her own mother's funeral, convinced she was trying to run away from him. He's an abusive man, venting his frustrations in the form of clenched fists at his wife.

Asked by their new neighbour to go aboard their boat, Martin insists that Laura come with him, even though she can't swim. The weather grows rough. The sail tears away. Martin rushes to help with the jib. When he turns back, Laura is gone. Martin searches for her and alerts the authorities. When her life-jacket is found floating in the water, Laura is declared dead. Unbeknownst to Martin, Laura has secretly learned how to swim at the YWCA. She clings to a buoy and swims back to shore in the middle of the night, chopping off her hair, grabbing a small bag of clothes and cash, and tossing her wedding ring down the toilet. Then, Laura takes the Greyhound to Iowa and rents out a home of her own. She starts a new life under the alias Sara Waters. Her life begins to improve, finding a sweet romance with her neighbour Ben.

Unfortunately, a friend of Laura's from the YWCA calls Martin to offer her condolences when she hears the news. She talks about how she knew Laura, revealing to Martin that his wife did know how to swim after all. Enraged, Martin begins to search through her belongings for some indication of where she may have gone. He visits the nursing home in Minneapolis where Laura's mother died six months previous… or so he thought. The chief of staff informs Martin that Laura picked her mother up and told them that she was coming to live at home with the two of them. Convinced Laura couldn't take her disabled mother far, Martin hires a private investigator to track down the old lady. In no time, he has an address. Martin follows the trail of breadcrumbs from a nursing home to a carnival where he watches his wife kiss her new boyfriend on the Ferris wheel. He pursues his wife, sneaking into her home armed with a gun. Laura knocks the gun from his hands and grabs it. She dials the police, aiming the gun at him, and alerts them to an intruder she just shot. As she hangs up, she shoots her husband thrice.

I don't know where to begin with the dangerousness of this role. First of all, she's a battered wife. According to the United Nations, 275 women in every hundred thousand in the States have been physically assaulted by their partner. Injuries swiftly turn to something graver in America. The romantic partners of American women are responsible in thirty percent of reported female homicide cases. That's not including the estimated eleven percent of female homicide cases perpetrated by exes, data that the U.S. Bureau of Justice Statistics ignores. Her status as an abused wife aside, Julia's character puts herself further in peril when she tries to escape from her malicious husband. She leaps into the Atlantic Ocean on a cold stormy night, and, at its warmest, the water temperature at Cape Cod rarely exceeds eighteen degrees Celsius. When the body is first immersed in chilly water, human beings experience "a cold shock response." Hyperventilation begins for up to three minutes, enough to potentially drive the swimmer under the water and cause death by asphyxiation. If one survives that shock, one may last up to twenty minutes before suffering muscle exhaustion and diminished circulation to the limbs. At this point, the swimmer needs a flotation device to survive. In *Sleeping With the Enemy*, the only reason Laura survives is because she clings to the buoy. Without it, she'd be dead for certain. Not to mention that it was only six months prior that Laura learned how to swim. Her chances are slim.

Thankfully, there's a lighter quality to *Notting Hill*, in which Julia takes on the role of Anna Scott, a megastar actress. What a stretch.

Donning shades and a beret, she travels without a bodyguard through London. Then, after colliding with a local man who spills food down her clothes, she agrees to go to his home to clean up. Considering her fame, one must ask how foolish must she be to enter a stranger's home alone. Anna has known him for no more than fifteen minutes. This man obviously recognizes her, but she doesn't know him from Adam. He could be, at worst, a serial killer seizing the opportunity to lure her to his oh-so-conveniently adjacent home under the pretence of altruism. Nevertheless, a little further into the film, Anna goes to Thanksgiving dinner hosted by a bunch of strangers. What else can we expect from her at this point? In a moment of deep self-disclosure to these strangers, Anna admits that she's had "a series of not-nice boyfriends", including a physically abusive man who attacked her. She also admits to a great deal of body image issues, admitting that she underwent two plastic surgeries – a rhinoplasty and either a genioplasty or a mentoplasty, she implies – to obtain and maintain a movie-star calibre of beauty. This self-loathing is indicative of a greater problem. Media studies professor Jib Fowles once calculated that the celebrity suicide rate is higher than the average Joe's, approaching four times more likely.

Let's tally up the risk Anna Scott incurred so far. She travels without a bodyguard. The supremely rich and famous generally never go anywhere alone, and if she's as famous as the story implies, then she should have at the bare minimum someone to protect her life. Secondly, she was the victim of domestic abuse. As aforementioned regarding *Sleeping With the Enemy*, up to two-fifths of all female homicide cases are caused by their romantic partners, including ex-boyfriends. Thirdly, she has the medical procedures stacked against her. With all the risks that they entail, including potential fatality from infection, hemorrhage, or anaesthetic reactions, Anna has a one in twenty chance of death from the chin augmentation alone, never mind the nose job. And that's not to mention the diverse range of occupational hazards associated with acting. Let us dunk you in this pool of water, Anna. Stand on your mark on the edge of that cliff, Anna. Each gig has its unique set of hazards. It's virtually impossible to determine what danger she faces based on what *Notting Hill* tells us, but there's a guarantee that she's faced at least some. As for overall risk, this role is perhaps on the safer end of the spectrum since no one is shooting her except with a photo lens, although Anna Scott is definitely not what a reasonable person would call secure.

Death continues to follow Roberts in *The Pelican Brief*. Julia Roberts is Darby Shaw, a twenty-four-year-old "eager-beaver" law student from New Orleans who believes in justice. When two Supreme Court justices are assassinated, Darby is confused why these two men with seemingly nothing in common would be killed on the same day. She begins researching them feverishly. Insatiable, Darby looks up case files and spends every waking hour hunting for answers. She writes an essay that implicates the White House and lets her boyfriend, Thomas, read it. He hands it over to his best friend, Gavin Verheek, who just happens to work for the FBI. In no time, it has worked its way up to the president's hands. Then, one night, as Thomas turns the key in the ignition, his car explodes in a fiery blaze. Darby witnesses everything. After a night spent distraught at the police station, she realizes that the car bomb was intended for her.

Throughout *The Pelican Brief*, Darby is targeted multiple times for assassination. After the car bombing, a man waits for her at Thomas's funeral and then chases her through her hotel and the streets of New Orleans. Later, a contracted killer disguises himself as Thomas's best friend Verheek to meet and murder Darby. More follow her through a parking garage, some on foot shooting at her and a lead-footed one motoring towards her in a car. Being targeted by the government for assassination must hurt your chances of survival.

Conspiracy Theory is a poor man's *Pelican Brief*. In much the same fashion, Julia Roberts plays Alice Sutton, a government lawyer this time, who flees with Mel Gibson's character, Jerry, a paranoid New York City taxicab driver. Bullets fly, an apartment explodes, and car chases ensue, not to mention the risk of taking off with Jerry, a presumed mentally unstable man.

There are a few roles in Julia's lengthy filmography that are a bit unique. For one, it's hard to quantify the risk of death of Julia's Tinkerbell in *Hook*. It's a fantasy world with fantasy rules. Mortality works differently there. Let's mark this film as an otherworldly neutral.

Then, there is *The Player*. Julia's role here boils down to a minor cameo appearance. *The Player* is a satirical film that mocks the Hollywood film industry and the plot revolves around the deals made by studio film exec Griffin Mill (played by Tim Robbins). Handed "an American tragedy in which an innocent woman dies", Griffin Mill intends to cast a Julia Robert-type for the part of Marsha Kent, the woman on death row. This move is made instead by Griffin Mill's ostensible competitor, Larry Levy, the new kid on the block. Levy modifies the artsy picture to have a Hollywood happy ending, filling it with celebrities. Julia Roberts is one of them. As a movie-within-a-movie, we only see the film's final scene, which means Julia delivers one lone line. However, we know more about the part she plays as it's fleshed out long before principal photography begins. The film initially dictates that her character's to die in a gas chamber for a crime she didn't commit, but after rewrites reshape it, Marsha Kent is suddenly the damsel in distress who is swept off her feet, saved by the district attorney who put her away. Yes, Julia Roberts is playing a version of herself in the movie, but as the Russian dolls open and another one pops out, there's room to state that she's playing Marsha Kent, too. And as Marsha Kent, she's literally scheduled to die, only for the Bruce Willis leading man to shoot through the glass and plunge into the foggy room to save her. She almost dies and yet she doesn't. She survives.

Perhaps the most telling of Julia's early performances is her role in *Steel Magnolias* as Shelby Eatenton Latcherie. The film opens at Easter time. Truvy's Beauty Spot is the go-to salon and Shelby Eatenton is preparing for her wedding. Jackson Latcherie and Shelby, the soon-to-be newlyweds, are suffering a touch of turbulence. Shelby has made it known to her fiancé that she's not particularly inclined to having children, so Jackson sneaks in her window and begs his betrothed to promise she'll marry him. With a smirk, she agrees. "I'll be the one in the veil down front," she says.

It's a hectic affair, especially for Shelby's run-ragged mother, M'Lynn. Sitting in the salon chair at Truvy's Beauty Spot, Shelby admits that her reason for marrying is that she "just likes the idea of growing old with somebody." All the while, M'Lynn contorts her face into fretful grimaces. When asked if she'll quit her position as a nurse in a maternity ward, Shelby insists she won't. Her mother M'Lynn complains that her daughter "should not be on her feet all day long", for the sake of her circulatory system. M'Lynn is truly concerned for Shelby.

But why? Without warning, sitting in the chair with Truvy fluffing her hair, Shelby refuses to raise her head. She begins to tremble and sweat. Everyone in the salon jumps into action. M'Lynn tries to force candy into her daughter's mouth past her clenched teeth while the former mayor's wife Clairee Belcher rushes to the fridge to retrieve some juice. Uncooperative, Shelby begins to cry, resisting her mother. The blushing bride is a diabetic with low chances of pregnancy in her future. Jackson insists that they'll go the adoption route instead. Fast forward eight months to Christmastime. Eager for her mother's approval, Shelby tells M'Lynn that she's pregnant. M'Lynn is far from overjoyed, but Shelby is delighted. M'Lynn's concerns rest on her daughter's well-being.

"Your poor body has been through so much. Why would you deliberately do this to yourself?" M'Lynn protests.

"Diabetics have healthy babies all the time," Shelby rebuts.

"You are special, Shelby," M'Lynn argues. "There are limits to what you can do."

Nonetheless Shelby's son Jack Jr. is born healthy and Shelby lives albeit a bit worse for wear. She's on dialysis now because pregnancy and childbirth strained her kidneys to the point of failure. Shelby plans to have a kidney transplant and talks nonchalantly about her health while her mother's friends grow concerned about whether she'll find a suitable organ donor. M'Lynn informs them not to fret as she's giving Shelby one of hers.

A handful of months later, the transplant is done and dusted. Shelby rushes home to take her son trick-or-treating, unsteady as she pulls him into his clown costume and lifts him up. Her body can't handle the weight; she finds herself on the ground, unable to stand. She scrambles for the phone to call for help, but passes out before dialling. When Jackson comes home to find his wife unconscious, Shelby's rushed into a hospital bed attached to breathing tubes and an array of machines. M'Lynn stands by her side, humming to her, talking to her, encouraging her daughter to wake up. Locked in a comatose state, M'Lynn moves her daughter's legs to a Jane Fonda workout and reads to her from beauty magazines to stay abreast the latest trends. Everyone watches M'Lynn suffer through the torment of her daughter's state. It's not long before they call it a day and unplug Shelby. *Steel Magnolias* is one of the few films where the Grim Reaper wins the race against Roberts.

Finally, we come to *Erin Brockovich*. As if at the end of her rope, it is in this film that Julia Roberts asks, "Are you going to be something else that I have to survive?" Addressing head-on the ever-growing shit-pile, her character, Erin – and, in a way, Julia herself – realizes that something must give. She won't merely survive anymore; gone are the days of aggressive threats pinning her down and intimidating her, all the while her life hanging in the balance. And so we hit our turning point. On March 25, 2001, Julia Roberts beat out her four fellow nominees to win her first ever Oscar for playing Erin. Judging by her roles thereafter, this moment is the last time she'd ever be happy again.

According to the National Institute of Mental Health, major depressive disorder is "a combination of symptoms that interfere with a person's ability to work, sleep, study, eat, and enjoy once-pleasurable activities." Women are twice as likely as men to suffer from depression. It can present itself in a great number of ways. Feelings of guilt; problems sleeping or excessive sleeping; a bleak outlook; poor concentration; loss of appetite or significant weight gain; a short temper; aggressive or violent tendencies; hallucinations; increased dependency on alcohol and drugs; a propensity towards reckless behaviour, dangerous sports, and gambling; withdrawal from social situations or sex; and self-criticalness are all symptoms. Worst of all, it is tragically under-diagnosed with fewer than half of all mental illness symptoms recognized by doctors. You have to really be looking for those warning signs.

Cue Julia's role in *Confessions of a Dangerous Mind*. It is a bit of a mystery. Roberts plays an agent firmly enmeshed in the assassination biz. She gives the protagonist, Chuck Barris, his directives in Helsinki, Finland, and West Berlin, Germany. She hesitates to give Chuck her name, offering him her alias, "Olivia," but she relents. "It's Patricia, actually," she clarifies. Patricia Watson has a bit of a thing for Chuck, a confusing manifestation of passion that looks like it could easily turn to murder. She's aggressive and impulsive, sleeping with Chuck on a whim. Her love-making is aggressive, animalistic, and verging on violent. She fits the assassin profile to a T.

Unfortunately, Chuck doesn't realize that Patricia likes to be in control. When Chuck doesn't meet Patricia, she hunts him down in the States. She is pissed. She spits insults at him in front of his girlfriend and storms out. After a period of isolation, Chuck re-emerges, visiting Patricia in Boston. She's still ensconced in the assassination business, telling Chuck how the other agents fingered him as the mole in their secret agency. As she waxes on about the goings-on since Chuck left, her depression-soaked personality dimly shines through. She looks at life through grey-coloured glasses with anarchistic leanings derived from a life as a cold contracted killer. She quotes Nietzsche, one of the more pessimistic philosophers. Her personality traits read like the list of symptoms for major depressive disorder.

However, Julia's character feels no remorse when she kills, a bit like a spider driven by instinct. She talks to her prey as they fall to the ground. She engages in premeditated murder like it's a sport, her eyes only ever gleaming as she participates in a dangerous cat-and-mouse game. Guilt is a symptom of depression, but Patricia Watson hasn't got an ounce of it. However, for an adept killer, her actions are a touch reckless, turning away from her target and missing his actions. She overestimates her skill, leaving her prey dangling and never expecting him to find a way out. She fails to focus when she should. Patricia's guilt-free conscience is cancelled out by her wildness and poor concentration. This is her undoing.

Overall, Patricia Watson is a curious case in the story of Julia Robert's career. *Confessions of a Dangerous Mind* shows her at her most melancholy, but only two years off her Oscar win, it harkens back to a previous life. Patricia bridges the gap between pre-*Brockovich* Julia – for a woman chasing death for a living is equally chased by it – and a sad and lonely post-*Brockovich* Julia experiencing the symptoms of depression for the first time. I see this movie as the post-traumatic transitional film.

Julia Roberts shows a much softer side acting as Kiki Harrison in *America's Sweethearts*. As a personal assistant to her movie star sister, Kiki Harrison spends her days dealing with the unrealistic demands of a spoiled overreacting actress, Gwen, made even crankier by a much publicized divorce from her former leading man, Eddie. Kiki brings Gwen tea. She carries Gwen's things. She ensures people don't smoke within Gwen's space. She knows everybody's name so Gwen doesn't have to. Other people would love to live Kiki's life. Not Julia. She plays Kiki as a mildly depressed woman who begrudgingly mixes family and business. She looks at her brother-in-law with longing. Her glance conveys yearning for Eddie to return to her life in some shape or form. It becomes all too clear that Kiki sacrifices her happiness to benefit her sister Gwen.

Again, the typical signs and symptoms are there. For one, Kiki has no discernible life of her own. She gave that up many moons ago, along with sex and even a modicum of selfishness. She's merged her life with her sister's. She has no friends of her own, unless you count Lee the publicist. Despite constantly being in the public eye, albeit two steps behind her scene-stealing sibling, Kiki has in fact withdrawn herself from social situations. Her life is unique but the song remains the same.

Yet she is reckless. She is willing to chuck it all away if given a shot at Eddie. She risks the wrath of her family; she risks her cushy job; and, more importantly, she risks it on a whim for a married guy who repeatedly tells her he's still in love with his wife and intends to get her back.

Next, we have evidence of an appetite for self-destruction, or, rather, lack of appetite. As Lee admires Kiki, commenting on her hair and tan, a visibly annoyed Gwen blurts out, "She lost sixty pounds." Later, Kiki admits to dreaming about bread, but deprives herself of it nonetheless. Substantial weight loss is indicative of major depressive disorder, as is guilt. There is evidence of Gwen using her sister's troubled conscience to her advantage, manipulating Kiki to do her dirty work for her. Gwen exacerbates Kiki's guilt, an element of her psyche already prevalent because of her depressed mental condition.

Eventually, with only thirty minutes left in the film, Kiki breaks. Her temper flares. She throws eggs into a person's lap. She yells and storms out. She binge eats carbohydrates until they doggy bag everything. Lee points out that they may need a forklift to take it all. Aggression and overeating are two more steps down the road towards clinical depression.

Julia's role as Tess is rather small in *Ocean's Eleven*, so we'll work with what we do know. Casino owner Terry Benedict is dating Tess, the ex-wife of grifter Danny Ocean and art curator at the museum above one of Benedict's casinos. Initially, Tess Ocean is racked with guilt, not for anything she did but for what her convicted con artist husband did. They had insurance, but her reputation was destroyed. She fled town and started anew in Las Vegas. Tormented by the raucousness of her first marriage, Tess has sought refuge in the arms of a wealthy control freak, Benedict. We watch her trot across the casino floor in a glittering golden gown and a trench-coat, heading to dinner. When her ex-husband Danny follows her to her reserved table, she's short-tempered with him. Unaware of his release, she greets him with hostility, declaring him "a thief and a liar." When Danny asks if Terry makes her laugh, she hesitates, a pained expression crossing her face. She replies, "He doesn't make me cry." A rather bleak view on love, Tess has opted for numbness. Despite sharing words over dinner, we never see Tess eat a meal or drink wine. We never see her do much of anything. There are a few signs here and there, but with little to draw from, it would be inappropriate to draw any conclusions in either direction.

Regrettably, *Ocean's Twelve* gives us little more to go on. In the sequel, Tess and Danny Ocean are re-entering society. Danny has adopted the moniker Miguel Diaz and Tess is mixing paints for their new home. Unfortunately, Terry Benedict shows up on their doorstep, demanding repayment and generally disturbing the peace. Julia's character doesn't return until over an hour later, pulled into the con game once Danny and several other con men are arrested. Julia Roberts then plays Tess Ocean imitating – who else? – Julia Roberts. She recklessly agrees to help in the theft of a Faberge egg, one of France's national treasures. However, she can't seem to concentrate on what she's doing, flitting around the hotel room as Bruce Willis shows up to say hello; she's struggling to remember the details of her fake identity. Tess is worried about her husband Danny and gets mired in pessimism. Then, when she finally catches up with the old ball and chain, her violent temper flares. Tess slaps and pounds Danny. "That is for making me a master thief," she says with a thump to his chest followed by an elbow to the groin. Again, there's evidence here and there, but nothing substantial enough to draw any conclusions. Overall, this role has been a limited one with minimal screen time to show Tess's persona.

Tess Ocean isn't the first role Roberts has played with a quieter personality. *Charlie Wilson's War* opens on April 6, 1980, with Texas Congressman Charlie Wilson in a hot tub with strippers and a Playboy cover model at a drug-fuelled party in Vegas bordering on orgiastic. Julia Roberts is nowhere near that kind of thing, playing well-to-do Joanne Herring. After sleeping with Charlie at a screening party, Herring, the sixth wealthiest woman in Texas, tells Charlie she wants him to save Afghanistan and end communism. She's "ultra-right-wing" and always gets what she wants, so she doesn't bat an eyelash at Charlie as he states his qualms about "taking up with Muslims" when most of his campaign contributors are Jewish Americans. Joanne doesn't care. She's aggressive and short-tempered. Don't ask her to tell you twice.

In terms of signs of depression, this role is perhaps the weakest. We don't know what motivates her. We never see or hear about her previous husbands. We never see her sleep but that doesn't mean that she's an insomniac. We never see her eat but that doesn't mean she's anorexic. It would require a great number of assumptions to diagnose her, one way or the other. Simply put, socialite Joanne Herring shows one thing: stubbornness. With little else to draw from, we'll call this role an anomaly on Julia's upwards trend (or is it downwards?) towards clinical depression.

Then there's *Larry Crowne*. Here's another Tom Hanks-centred film in which Julia plays second fiddle. This time, Ms. Roberts plays Mercedes Tainot, a community college professor teaching speech and communication. Her attitude needs work; she's convinced that she's "a fraud" that never gets through to her undergraduates. Her outlook is break, her fuse is short, and her self-criticism is subtle but abundant, all of which are signs of clinical depression. That's not to mention her perpetually tired expression, indicative of insomnia or some other sleep disorder. Her concentration is poor, a condition that insufficient rest could only worsen. This focus problem interferes with her work performance. For one, she can't listen to what her students are saying, an issue in any class but astronomically worse in a public speaking class. Mercedes withdraws from her professional life, abandoning any classes that have fewer than ten students and never investing the time to learn the names of the students in her slightly larger classes. When she gets home, she self-medicates with alcohol, guzzling down booze while her husband buries his face in Internet porn. Their relationship has lost its spark, resulting in a full-fledged fight while under the influence of "demon rum", as she describes it. Her depression affects her life, whether at the college or in her home.

She's not just a sad sack, though, a pitiful lost soul. No, she also has anger inside of her, fire that only comes through in counterproductive bursts. When one student naps in her class, Mercedes throws objects at him to rouse him from his slumber. Considering the multitudes of methods she could've used to wake him, throwing things veers into the more aggressive territory. Depression and aggression go hand-in-hand, a clear symptom of major depressive disorder.

Let's tally it up, shall we? Mercedes is a self-critical, sleep-deprived, miserable, unfocused, short-fused, aggressive alcoholic who has withdrawn from work and sex and social interaction altogether. A diagnosis of clinical depression is well within the realm of possibility for Professor Tainot. Hey, it could be worse. She could be a guilt-stricken gambler, too. All I'm saying is I'm glad she doesn't live in Las Vegas.

This isn't the first time Julia Roberts played a professor. Years earlier but still after *Erin Brockovich*, Julia played Katherine Watson in *Mona Lisa Smile*, an art professor who transferred from Oakland State to Wellesley College, where the all-women classes actually read the textbook. At first she is intimidated by the rapid-fire responses of her whip-smart undergrads. She feels out of her depths and loses focus. She cries and frets and trembles at the thought of going back into that lecture hall. But she does, from a different angle, one that goes against the grain, disturbing how they've learned to learn. She asks them to be critical thinkers, to examine things outside of the syllabus, and to notice things others haven't. This is an interesting case because of her area of study. Art has long had links to depression. There have been generations upon generations of artists whose genius waded through the murky waters of depression. The creative are statistically twice as likely to suffer a mental illness, with depression being the most common among them. Compare your artists to your scientists and the numbers will speak for themselves; in one study, less than thirty percent of the scientists polled suffered some form of psychopathology while over eighty percent of the poets did. And there are arguments, too, that it is through depression that true art is created and appreciated. Sufferers visualize their world in a unique way. Their mental illness allows them the creative insight, literally seeing what others cannot. And what does Katherine do in *Mona Lisa Smile*? She asks that her students delve into the deepest recesses of their minds and see things differently. They are forced to examine art in the way that only a depression sufferer could, a way that the rest of the world doesn't. I'm more than a little suspicious that Katherine may have major depressive disorder, but, to be fair, not every art professor is depressed. So I must push on and examine her character further.

This is the point that I should bring up the recurring mention of marriage in *Mona Lisa Smile*. A common symptom of depression is a tendency to be asocial, withdrawing from sex and romance and even friendship. Despite being engaged once before and then again for a split-second, Katherine has never married. And it's the fifties. She doesn't want a companion, though. Once she arrives at Wellesley, she moves in with some other teachers where she remains celibate for close to a year. Again, it is 1953, but even for the times, she is especially wary of men, systematically removing them from her life. She doesn't mind that the house rules dictate that no men are allowed in the rented boudoir. Canoodling is forbidden in Katherine's heart as much as in her room. Although she says she assumes she'll marry one day, I think otherwise. It's obvious she prefers to be alone. She lacks the constitution to compromise even a little bit, including the kind of compromises that are mandatory to maintain a successful relationship. In fact, she proves that she is unwilling to make concessions when she decides to leave Wellesley because, after receiving complaints, the administration question her teaching methods and place conditions of censorship upon her. The film gives her a dramatic exit, but Katherine Watson could have continued to do well in her position as an art history professor, teaching the students without overstepping her bounds. If she truly was a wonderful teacher, you'd think she'd want to continue teaching the best and brightest. No, there's something fishy about Katherine Watson. Maybe there's a reason she doesn't spend any time around the psychology department.

Valentine's Day, an overall jolly film, suffers a bit of a downer every time Julia appears onscreen. She's first seen on a plane, dressed in fatigues. The audience swiftly learns through the Q-and-A dialogue that Julia Roberts is playing a captain in the U.S. Army, Captain Kate Hazeltine. It's been fourteen months since she's been home; she's returning only for one day. She's on a fourteen-hour flight home and tomorrow she'll be on another fourteen-hour flight back. At one point during the flight, Kate goes to the washroom, but the plane starts to experience turbulence. She acts uncomfortable as if she's about to cry. She seems worn down. As we all can imagine, the rate of depression is higher in the military, but surprisingly, research has found that this mental illness is present when they enlist before they're deployed. In fact, major depressive disorder has a prevalence rate amongst soldiers five times that of your average civilian. Captain Kate Hazeltine wears her tell-tale frown and furrowed brow like a badge of courage, but it's not brave or strong enough to hide that hurt inside.

Our introduction to Julia's character in *August: Osage County*, Barbara, is a stellar example of depression eating away at a person's will. Barbara's teenage daughter Jean answers the telephone; it's "Aunt Ivy, from Oklahoma", calling to speak to her sister Barbara. Jean beckons for her mother, but she doesn't answer. She climbs the stairs and opens the bedroom door to find her mother lying in bed, head buried below the comforter. Barbara's intentionally ignoring the phone, thinking it's her husband. Her relationship with him is strained, their marriage destroyed by his penchant for younger women. When Barbara arrives at her mother's house, her aunt Mattie Fae grabs her by the shoulders, struck by how slender she's become. Barb's lost a great deal of weight since the family's last seen her. She's holding onto some weight, though, not physical but mental. It's the weight of guilt that pulls her down, guilt that she moved away from Oklahoma, guilt that she didn't become a writer like her late father wanted her to be, and guilt that she didn't return when her mother Violet received her cancer diagnosis. But she keeps it well hidden. When Barbara isn't cold and hard, she's crying… and she holds back those tears for awhile. On her own, Barbara can tally up the warning signs to realize that major depressive disorder is written all over her face.

And then there's the family. Neither of Barbara's parents were happy; they both suffered depression, characterized by her father's alcoholism and her mother's prescription pill addiction. Her father commits suicide and her mother did nothing to prevent it. There are genetic connections to mental illnesses, including but not limited to major depressive disorder. Having a parent with clinical depression can triple your likelihood to develop the disease yourself. Furthermore, those whose parents have recurrent depression have an even greater chance, closer to five times as much as someone with no relatives who have suffered. Now, if one parent has the combination of genes that increases vulnerability to depression, that doesn't mean that their child will get it, for they have another parent from which they gain half their DNA. However, when both parents have it, your chances are much slimmer. For Barbara, that means that the apple will probably fall damn close to the tree.

Depression sufferers often exhibit "an inability to sustain reciprocal cooperation." They lose the capacity to compromise or cooperate, leading to problems in relationships. Furthermore, those with clinical depression don't recognize a square deal, even when an offer is moving more and more in one's favour. On a neurobiological level, the regions of the brain that handle these kinds of social exchanges do not activate. They can't see what's fair. They can't see what's unfair. It all feels the same. This phenomenon appears in *The Mexican*. Early in the film, a scene between Julia's character Samantha and her boyfriend Jerry results in yelling and throwing of objects. From her hotel room on the third floor, she tosses down his belongings to the street, enraged over the circumstances of their delayed vacation in Vegas, finding that he has to work instead. She feels that it's not fair, a typical depressive behaviour, while he feels that she's overreacting. Samantha bellows, "Don't do that! Don't you do that! Don't diminish my needs." As Jerry tries to reason with her, her mind jumps around until she begins talking in psychoanalytical jargon, telling him that he's "blame-shifting." The audience realizes that Samantha is well acquainted with the shrink's couch.

Later, despite being taken hostage, Samantha connects personally with a henchman named Winston "Leroy" Baldry. As time goes on, she discloses more and more about herself, describing her "psychosomatic insomniatic manifestations." Stumbling over her words, Samantha elaborates, stating she requires "sunshine to grow." All of these statements ring of clinical depression: the labelling of her disease as "psychosomatic", which implies a mind-body connection, as which depression and a host of other mental illnesses can fittingly be described; the mention of insomnia, a sleep disorder that plagues many depressives; and, of course, the need for this so-called "sunshine to grow", a sense of happiness that feels unattainable and the sense of stagnation until it reappears in one's life. It doesn't take a genius to sense what's going on.

In *The Normal Heart*, Julia plays Dr. Emma Brookner, a wheelchair-bound specialist on "gay cancer." Emma moves around in a motorized wheelchair and examines homosexual men without discrimination. She tells openly gay writer Ned Weeks that it's an immunity problem; she thinks it's sexually transmitted, but she can't prove it. Emma asks Ned to tell his readers, predominantly gay men, to cease all sexual activity. Ned raises funds and awareness as he watches his friends and acquaintances dropping like flies. No one is taking it seriously, though, including the gay community it is tearing apart.

Julia's character Emma is a fast-talking no-nonsense doctor. The audience learns of Emma's past, starting with her childhood when she contracted polio. She wasn't expected to live past twenty-four hours and yet she did. She survived. She lived. Her social life took a toll, separated from her classmates and peers her own age. She describes herself as "the holy terror in a wheelchair." She becomes accustomed to their fear. She decides that she doesn't need love; she's hard and cold and emotionally detached. People with physical disabilities are routinely more likely to suffer depression, especially those who have suffered a spinal cord injury resulting in mandatory wheelchair use for mobility. Depression, in and of itself, is disabling, its impairment described as "equal to that attributed to cardiovascular disease, and greater than that caused by other chronic physical disorders such as hypertension, diabetes mellitus, and arthritis." Unfortunately, pharmacotherapy for depression, not just in spinal cord injury patients but for everyone, only began to advance in the fifties, years after Dr. Emma Brookner started suffering from it, years after she was put in a wheelchair. Those with long-term spinal cord injuries are more inclined to withdraw from the community; this poor social integration and lack of social pursuits only adds to the problem of depression. It is this attitude, though, that allows Emma to work so feverishly in the field of AIDS research. She doesn't cry; she copes, turning angry and asocial instead. Julia exhibits her depression in a different way, as a tough and wintry woman.

Meanwhile, Roberts imbues the role of Snow White's stepmother with aggression in *Mirror Mirror*. She's a temperamental woman that's gotten her own way for far too long. When Snow White, turning eighteen, begs on her knees to attend the ball her stepmother is throwing, the Queen's reaction is a quiet outrage. She scolds her for even suggesting it, violently tugging on her hair and slapping her cheeks.

Aging is the Queen's main anxiety. Julia plays her as a vain woman, self-critical about her "crinkles." Unfortunately, her criticisms are materialistic, never examining the rotten soul beneath her skin. Instead, her deteriorating looks bother her and distract her from her single focus: leading a luxurious life as the ruler of the kingdom, paid for in full by the citizenry's tax dollars. Boiled down, though, Julia's character's motivation isn't looks but money. When the cash-poor monarch faces the possibility that the years-junior prince may fall instead for Snow White, she puts a hit out on her. Her violent tendencies rear their ugly head. She turns vicious and homicidal. Anyone who crosses her needs to be fixed. This short-tempered aggressiveness is typical of someone suffering from clinical depression.

But the plot trudges on. Not above using black magic to enchant her new groom, she plots and schemes her way into a proposed joining of the kingdoms to fill her coffers. Told explicitly that there would be "a price", she gambled on. She felt invincible, a powerful woman dabbling in the dark arts to get her way. When she uses a potion on her prince, she doesn't even read the label, a show of hasty carelessness on her part. That's not to mention the risks she takes to keep her sex appeal. Sex is her weapon, a tool in her arsenal to nab her fifth husband with an M.O. akin to a black widow. All of this doesn't bring her down, though; it fuels her, egging her on. The magic queen isn't depressed; she's plain old evil.

At first, I concluded that *Mirror Mirror* was an outlier on Julia's downward spiral. The symptoms – the feelings of guilt, the poor concentration, the loss of appetite, the sleep disorders – weren't presenting themselves in the typical way. Still, unlike Julia's earlier career, in this role she does not die. She just ends up miserable and alone, ashen and shrivelled, a deserved fate for her wickedness. It came to me only then that her depression is in the epilogue. The film ended just before revealing the signs. Her cheeks are sunken, evidence of significant and, as magic may have it, sudden weight loss. With nothing but time, her decrepit body will surely withdraw from society and immerse itself in a bubble of introspection, forced to deal with feelings of guilt and regret.

Nowhere does Julia Roberts showcase depression more than in the role of lost and alone Elizabeth Gilbert. Based on the bestseller, *Eat Pray Love* tells the story of newly divorced writer Elizabeth Gilbert and the voyages she takes to Italy, India, and Indonesia to indulge in the food, find inner peace, and rediscover love, respectively. At the start of the film, Elizabeth wakes from her slumber and falls to her knees to pray. She doesn't want to be married anymore, a decision that seems to come out of left field. She loves her husband and they seem to live the life of Riley, travelling the world together as a job perk. And yet it's divorce time. Questions pop up for me. If a person can get up one night and, out of nowhere, decide she no longer wants to be married after eight years, then what are the chances she'll find satisfaction in anything for more than a fleeting moment? Will she constantly be seeking happiness, never content with the person she is and everything she has? One must ponder these things as Liz trots from country to country for a year in search of fulfilment.

Another sign of depression is overeating. Liz eats excessively compared to those around her, not just in Italy where the food is a major pull factor, but in India, too, where she earns the nickname "Groceries." She experiences significant weight gain at one point, buying a new pair of jeans to compensate for her expanding heinie.

Major depressive disorder can sometimes be accompanied with sleep disorders, whether it's a problem getting to sleep or, conversely, a problem getting out of bed. Liz begins *Eat Pray Love* with the incapacity to rest, waking in the middle of the night. Let's jump halfway around the world. There she travels to an ashram in India where now she falls asleep sitting up during meditation. Every morning, she wakes to her alarm and the audience can see her temptation to hit the snooze button. Liz just can't handle sleep.

She also can't seem to meditate. Her mind is bombarded with a thousand meaningless thoughts a minute. Her poor concentration is evident to everyone but herself. "If you can't master your thoughts, you're in trouble forever," warns Richard, a fellow devotee at the ashram. "Why don't you just let it be?" Later, after she's travelled to Indonesia, Ketut, a Balinese healer, describes the Liz he knows. "You have too much worry, too much sorrow," he says. I don't know about you, but that sounds like a diagnosis of major depressive disorder from two different sources. Sure, the phrasing may be simplistic and non-medical, coming from, first, a no-nonsense Texan, and then, a holistic Balinese frame of reference, but their points are identical. No need for a third opinion.

Withdrawal from social situations is a typical symptom of depression. While in Indonesia, Liz is invited to a party on the beach to which she tries to politely decline, based on a knee injury, but her excuse is invalid when it heals swiftly. This isn't the first time she's dodged social interaction. Richard asks her to come with him, but she uses the excuse of tiredness. Then, sitting atop a roof in India, Liz hallucinates conversations with her ex-husband Stephen. Going around the world for a year devastates a number of her ties back home, including both her protective editor and best friend and her new and much younger boyfriend. Interfering with relationships is another sign of depression, something she doesn't seem to mind nearly as much as one would anticipate. In fact, this is one of the few things Elizabeth doesn't spend her time dwelling upon. Her impulsive globe-trotting trip takes precedence over her loved ones. It's as if she's suffering a mental illness...

In *Closer*, Julia Roberts plays photographer Anna Cameron. From the get-go, it's obvious that Anna is depressed. She's separated from her husband and engaging in a flirtation with Dan, a man already attached to another woman. She stays up until four in the morning reading Dan's book; from the bags under her eyes, it's possible that she's struggling to sleep at night. Anna spends most of her free time at the London Aquarium observing the fish, withdrawn from sex and social interaction in general. Then, she meets Larry, a dermatologist; they start dating each other steadily. Eventually, she marries, but while Larry's away on business, Anna carries on an extramarital affair with Dan that lasts a year. In a study investigating the link between depression and infidelity, infidelity was labelled a humiliating marital event, the kind of which threatens to dissolve marriages. It was found that an extramarital affair increased the likelihood that the married parties involved would suffer a major depressive episode, even after controlling for marital discord in general and both family history and pre-existing bouts of depression. How much more likely were they to suffer depression? Six times more likely.

Contrary to popular belief, it is not always the gregarious extrovert who engages in extramarital affairs; in fact, depressed people are often the type to do so. Those who suffer from clinical depression often must combat self-esteem issues and fear of rejection; timid and unassertive, they struggle with intimacy and believe they are inadequate, so they compensate with quantity, not quality, of relationships. (That's not to say that all who cheat are shy and depressed, but many are, and that's what's important here.) Anna is obviously a quiet person, suffering in silence. You can see the tears in her eyes as she sits up late at night, sad and tired and, of course, depressed. Eventually, she tells her husband Larry that she's leaving him. "You're leaving me because you think you don't deserve happiness," Larry tells Anna. He's a doctor and he's reading the signs. He may be a dermatologist, not a psychologist, but he's not far off. It isn't until months later that Anna sees Larry again, this time to sign the divorce papers. Her heart aches and her eyes are gloomy. She even admits that she feels guilty to Larry. And shortly thereafter, after slipping back into Larry's bed, Anna returns to her husband permanently. She dumps Dan who is distraught over her betrayal. Dan visits Larry at his office to beg him to let Anna go, to let her be happy. But Larry sees the confused Anna for what she is, a "depressive." He tells Dan that depressives, in his opinion, "want to be unhappy to confirm they're depressed. If they were happy, they couldn't be depressed anymore. They would have to go out into the world and live, which can be depressing." He perfectly encapsulates the cyclical trap that is depression, the interminable recurrences just as one gets back on one's feet.

Each character Julia Roberts has played is unique, a person in its own way. They all differ and yet so many are tied together. The first bunch were spared by death but only narrowly. And after *Brockovich*, it seems Roberts only played people with clinical depression. It's an odd coincidence, I'm sure, not something that she or her agent actively sought to do. But it also brings to mind the many faces that the second half of her career has, a large set of people who all encounter symptoms of depression. We look at the first half of Roberts's work as the ones closest to death, but what about the second half? Depression is no joke. In their darkest hour, those who suffer from this illness are closer to death than any Darby Shaw or Vivian Ward. Depression can make life excruciating with the combination of physical and emotional symptoms. Those who fight it don't beat it and call it a day. It's like an uphill battle that finally relents, flowing into a valley that then hits a wall. They're there for the long haul. Not everyone can handle this endurance test regrettably. When it all adds up, compounding daily until it becomes too much, depression leads to suicide. It's a disease that literally kills. It may not look as electrifying onscreen, but conquering depression is more death-defying than any stunt.

Bachelor Number Two:

How Love Triangles Push Us Towards the Wrong Person

The more, the merrier. That's the old adage that has steered us all into the ditch. We often feel that having more selection, more choices, more flavour, offers more value and lets us get what we want. We think we're in control. In reality, the opposite occurs. In general, variety confuses human beings. The more options we have, the less satisfied we are with our choices. Often, this dissatisfaction is because of poor decisions, getting overwhelmed and choosing something we didn't actually want, simply because it was there. In other cases, we get so inundated by options that indecisiveness takes over and we opt out entirely, choosing in essence not to choose. And still, there are those who would otherwise be satisfied with their choice, if they weren't thinking about the other options, the ones they didn't choose, what they could've had but didn't.

In terms of fulfilment, making choices as a consumer, picking out a brand of jeans or a jar of jam, is no different than selecting a mate. The more options you have, the more likely you are to choose the wrong one. It's a scary fact, considering that, while picking Levis when you wanted True Religion certainly may bother you when you wear them, tying your soul to another's seems a bit more grand in scale.

So how do you gauge what is the best decision when it comes to picking your soul mate? The science of love is weak at best with often contradictory results; there isn't one formula for matters of the heart. Nonetheless, there are a few things on which relationship experts have come to consensus.

Dr. Helen E. Fisher of Rutgers University has examined love from a neurological frame of reference. She concluded that the brain has biological responses toward love. In fact, there are three systems: the lustful sex drive motivated by the production of estrogen and androgen hormones; the passionate attraction system, characterized by the neurotransmitters dopamine and norepinephrine and a fall in serotonin, which causes one to crave their partner, constantly thinking about them and feeling exhilarated by their presence; and, finally, the companionate attachment system caused by the neuropeptides oxytocin and vasopressin that encourage one to stay and build a life with another, building a home together and rearing children.

The second system, the brain's attraction system, is the one at play during love triangles and thus worth examining. It is often referred to as infatuation or romantic love and is evident across the universe. This system usually activates in response to novelty, a new lover arriving. The majority think of little else, over four-fifths of their conscious time spent daydreaming about their wonderful honey-bunch. We're energetic and bubbly. Suddenly, the world is rose-coloured and our lover farts rainbows. Our brain chemistry changes; this is scientific fact. Eventually, we transition from the attraction to the attachment system, forming a monogamous bond that, for some, lasts a lifetime.

But a poor few get trapped in limbo, never leaving the attraction system. They become absorbed with another person. This stagnation leads to stalkers or victims of suicide after thinking of nothing else but their unrequited love. That transition in the brain is important.

One study published by the Royal Society found that, when it comes to choosing a mate, "*variety* and *number* of options are not substitutable." In other words, it's not the more people at your disposal that limits your satisfaction and willingness to engage in a relationship, but rather the more unique the people are from each other. For example, a cheerleader picking from three jocks is more likely to be happy than a cheerleader choosing from a jock, a goth, and a nerd. Please forgive the trite stereotypes used to elaborate the point, but, on the surface, the second set of potential suitors has too much variety, although both sets have the same number (three).

Three has always been a bit of a magic number. Three has stability, as in a tricycle or a tripod. Three seems sufficient and effective, such as how we perceive the world through three dimensions. Three seems honest and believable, as proven by the religious reliance upon the Holy Trinity (Father, Son, and Holy Spirit) and the Hindu Trimurti (Brahma, Vishnu, and Shiva). We've learned of the magic of three since childhood with the three little pigs, the three little bears, and the three blind mice. Even the sports world recognizes three strikes in baseball. These trichotomies are so numerous in philosophy that one could fill many volumes with examples. Orator Cicero declared "omne trium perfectum", which translates from Latin to "everything that comes in three is perfect."

Except for love triangles. The love triangle is a cultural touchstone. Everyone has heard of it, our protagonist divided between the affection of two, often polar opposite, lovers. Taking the idea of greater dissatisfaction with greater variety to a whole new level, love triangles often have us rooting for the wrong guy, the less desirable partner in the end. Sure, one may have breathtaking looks, adventurous aims, or that feistiness in the bedroom that can't be tamed, but often it is that one who couldn't care less for our hero, the one who will likely commit adultery or remain self-centered after the credits roll. Yet we still want them to be together. There is always a better choice, but neither the character nor the audience wants them to be chosen. Again, with more unique options comes more dissatisfaction.

The world of film is full of love triangles. For every Betty, there must be a Veronica, just to give Archie a romantic subplot. Let's examine some of the more popular ones.

In the *X-Men* franchise, there is a love triangle between Hank McCoy, Erik "Magneto" Lensherr, and Raven "Mystique" Darkholme. It reveals itself first in the prequel *X-Men: First Class*. Erik interrupts the potential first kiss between young lovers Raven and Hank. It's 1962 and the government has wrangled together the more cooperative mutants they've encountered. Hank has prehensile feet and a beautiful mind. Raven is cobalt in colour and a shape-shifter by nature, disguising her blue skin under the façade of Jennifer Lawrence's face and body. Both Hank and Raven possess physical mutations whereas Erik can manipulate metal. His powers don't mar his external appearance. He doesn't understand them; they're teenagers whose bodies are being gawked and ogled by scientists and G-men. Still, Erik shares his two cents, boldly reminding Raven every chance he gets that, if he were her, he would never disguise his looks. How would he know? He may be a mutant, but he's not that kind of mutant.

However, what they do share is a common bond of mistreatment. Although he doesn't divulge too much, timid Hank seems to have been bullied for his differences. Erik is the opposite, proud to announce who he is and from where he came. Orphaned by the Holocaust, his deep-seated rage always gets the better of him, his powers manifesting most strongly in these intense emotions. Hatred, rather than love, drives him. Raven falls somewhere betwixt the two. She was abandoned as a child, but she found a true friend in Charles Xavier, a young telepath her age born into the bejewelled clutches of an affluent and largely absent family. They've all had their fair share of tragedy.

Hank and Raven are closer in age, revelling in their youth in spite of their situation. Erik, more mature, is bent on revenge and frowns upon their juvenile happy-go-lucky behaviour. Raven looks to Erik for validation, her self-worth hinged on his approval. She jokingly dubs him "Magneto", but he seems disinterested in her childish games. The more he shuns her, the more it spurs her on. Simply put, Erik is too old for Raven, and even if he wasn't, his interests lie in his own selfish causes. At first, Erik desperately wants to kill the Nazi who killed his mother. Alas, it doesn't end there. Immediately after, Erik turns his threatening glare toward the human race as a whole. As he sees it, non-mutants are "united in their fear of the unknown." He'll never be satisfied with just the love of another. This does not a stable relationship make.

Thrown together in the midst of the Cuban missile crisis, Raven seems to grow more and more in love with Erik, pulling away from Hank. In fact, people who meet in dangerous situations tend to have higher than normal dopamine levels in their brain. Dopamine grows as tasks become increasingly precarious. It's not like adrenaline, which encourages us to fight or flee from danger. No, dopamine encourages us to run towards danger, rather than away from it. Those on dopamine highs like the risks; they like the danger. Unfortunately, dopamine reuptake also reinforces feelings of doe-eyed attraction and passion, according to Dr. Helen E. Fisher. Those relationships borne in risky environments often depend on chemical imbalances in the brain, synapses awash in dopamine. Raven is literally intoxicated by her own neurotransmitters, leaving her adoptive brother, Charles Xavier, lying shot on the beach just to stand beside the power-hungry Erik.

Then, *X-Men: Days of Future Past* confirms what we knew all along. Not once but twice Magneto turns the gun on Mystique. And what does Hank do? He dives at Magneto, sending the bullet off track. After being wounded, Mystique hunts down Magneto, but he softens her again, like putty in his hands. He manipulates her. He plays with her heart to get what she wants. She's not a person, but a plaything. In contrast, Hank lets Raven be, loving her from afar and contemplating if this is just "who she is." Because of Erik, Raven is determined to live a life where it is always kill or be killed.

Fly forward into the twenty-first century. In *X-Men: The Last Stand*, Dr. Hank McCoy is all grown up. He's now Secretary of the Department of Mutant Affairs, a minister in the President's cabinet. Homeland Security is tracking Magneto, but instead captures Mystique when she is caught imitating a government official after breaking into the FDA. Again, Mystique's imitation is literal; she is a lithe blue shape-shifter, able to take any form she desires, literally becoming anyone's doppelganger in seconds. Hank nods knowingly; you sense a history there. "You think your prisons can hold her?" he says more than asks, smirking.

Hank listens in on the security feed of her holding cell. Raven's interrogator pleads with her to tell them Magneto's location. She is, after all, his right-hand woman. She won't answer their questions, refusing to respond to "Raven Darkholme", convinced that it's her "slave name." Her heartbreaking history is given in spurts and spouts. It's revealed that Raven's family tried to murder her, presumably because of her blue appearance. Her interrogator grows more impatient and hostile, calling her Mystique, a name she prefers and to which she'll respond. And respond she does, kicking herself out from behind the table, making quick work of the guards and strangling her interrogator with the chain that links her wrists together.

Hank warns the President that holding Raven will "provoke" Magneto. He seems eager to enter negotiations with him, but the President brushes the matter aside and asks Hank instead to promote a mutation antibody vaccine, a "mutant cure", in a positive light. (In the prequel, Hank developed his own cure, a combination of chemicals and Raven's unique DNA, and injects himself with it. At first, it works and his feet normalize, but seconds later, it backfires. Hank grows a thick layer of blue fur and earns the label "Beast", a moniker that even Raven uses.) No one – not Magneto, not Mystique, not McCoy – feels this is a good idea, but it's approved anyway. Magneto, a Holocaust survivor, immediately jumps to conclusions. In his mind, it's a mass extermination, uttering the word "genocide." First things first, though. He must rally his troops, demolishing the maximum security convoy transporting Mystique cross-country, along with a select few mutants with equally threatening abilities. But when a guard manages to load his gun with a bullet containing "the cure" and points it squarely at Magneto, Mystique jumps in the way, taking the bullet herself and thus losing her mutant powers. Lying naked and vulnerable on the floor, Raven turns to Magneto, weakly begging for his help, but Magneto shuns her, showing no sympathy. "You're not one of us anymore," he says. In no time flat, he replaces Mystique with Jean Grey, his new ingénue. Clearly, Magneto's love for Mystique was conditional.

Meanwhile, once Hank learns of Mystique's fate, he is certain that this vaccine is "a slippery slope." He's angry about the involuntariness of it all, Mystique's forced inoculation weighing on his mind. He expresses his ire in the dignified fashion typical of a diplomat by advising the President against it. Not once does Hank leave the mutants by the wayside. He stands strong with the X-men, waging war against the Brotherhood, Magneto's makeshift albeit mighty anti-human army. In the end, the X-men save the day and McCoy becomes an ambassador, rewarded for his efforts that went above and beyond the call of duty. Raven picked the wrong horse.

Staying within the context of mystical fantasy creatures, I turn my eye to *Harry Potter*. Woefully unhealthy but dreadfully romantic, the Severus/Lily/James love triangle is often overlooked, but perhaps one of the best examples of which one suitor, the snubbed suitor, is head and shoulders above the other. To understand the predicament, first a little background information: Voldemort, the big, bad evil that permeates the series, is gaining ground in the final film. He is the dark to Harry Potter's light. He wants to use the Elder wand, a powerful tool in his arsenal if it would only respond to his touch. Upon learning that it is attached to the hand of Severus Snape, the potions professor at Hogwarts School of Witchcraft and Wizardry, Voldemort draws blood from Snape and then orders his pet serpent Nagini to "kill." Harry Potter rushes to Snape's aid as soon as the coast is clear. Bleeding from the neck, Snape's last words to Harry are, "You have your mother's eyes." Through use of the many enchanted devices at one's disposal at Hogwarts, Harry learns of Snape's connection to Harry's mother.

Harry's mother, born Lily Evans to a family that bullied and ostracized her for her magic powers, found a friend as a young girl, a boy named Severus Snape. Labelled "a freak", Lily doubted herself, but Severus encouraged her, telling Lily that she is "special" and it's the green-eyed monster that made her family cruel. Severus and Lily would sit for hours on the river bank, but upon arriving together at Hogwarts, they are swiftly separated by the Sorting Hat – if you don't know what it is, don't ask – into different Houses, she into Gryffindor and he into Slytherin. Still, they remained friends, despite James Potter's increasing proximity to Lily as a Gryffindor and, in contrast, Snape's ever-growing distance. After a bullying incident in which James Potter disarms Severus Snape of his wand and taunts Severus as he sends him into the air, things are never quite the same. He watches as Lily and James come together as a couple. However, and most importantly, Severus acknowledges that Lily is growing and changing as a person. He sees that she is not the same girl that sat with him on the riverbank. She's not ashamed of being a witch and he no longer needs to comfort her in that regard. Instead of diminishing his interest in Lily, Snape's fondness for her grows with the years, now from afar.

Decades pass. Lily marries James and has a son, Harry Potter. For most men, the love would cease. Not so for Snape. Knowing that Voldemort thinks that Lily's son Harry will halt his rise to power, Severus concludes that Voldemort will try to kill anyone in his path to get to Harry. He begs his boss, Hogwarts headmaster Albus Dumbledore, to "hide them all." Emphasis on "all." He cares for Lily, of course, but in order to guarantee her happiness, he knows that she'll need her husband James whom Snape never liked, as well as their baby boy Harry. A lesser man would selfishly save only the woman he loves in the hope that she would forget her old family and start a new one with him. Not Snape. Despite his reputation as a gloomy and spiteful loner, he understands all too well the human heart and the effects that love has on it. Try as he might, neither he nor Dumbledore could save Lily and James, but Harry miraculously survives with only a lightning bolt-shaped scar as evidence.

Heartbroken, Snape is ordered by Dumbledore to protect Harry, convinced that, while currently extinguished, Voldemort's powers will re-emerge and endanger Harry. Snape agrees under the condition that no one is to know that he's watching over Harry, Lily's child with Snape's rival. Dumbledore describes this side of Severus Snape as the best of him, putting himself forever at risk to safeguard "the boy." As the years pass, he grows to care for Harry, but he never lets on. Because of his love for Lily, his love for Harry exists against all odds. No truer love exists than one that lingers after the physical sense of the person is gone. And no matter how many years pass, Severus never wavered. His heart was hers "always."

This love triangle differs from many others. For one, it is horribly one-sided in physical intimacy. Severus and Lily never danced together; never embraced; never kissed; certainly never made love. She had all that instead with James. But who is the one who picks up her books when James and his rambunctious friends knock them out of her hands whilst running in the hall? Severus Snape was wholly devoted to Lily, from start to finish in both her life and his own. If the shoe was on the other foot, would James Potter have tried to save Severus and Lily Snape's child? I have my doubts.

In recent years, no love triangle has incited so much vitriol between its partisans than that of Team Jacob and Team Edward fighting for the affection of *Twilight*'s Bella. The love triangle doesn't truly emerge until the second film, *New Moon*, but once it does, it is nonstop, incessantly causing fights onscreen and feuds off. Spoiler alert: Edward wins Bella's heart and Jacob falls by the wayside. But I feel it's time to take a second look at why this choice may not be in Bella's best interests.

First of all, vampires control people's minds, and although part of the narrative claims that Bella is one of the few humans who can resist this influence, she seems awfully fixated for someone who hasn't fallen under the vampire spell. But that requires us to make assumptions, so let's put that aside for a second to examine the evidence presented in the films that most strongly exhibit the triangle.

In *New Moon*, Edward reveals the faults in his glittering façade. Let's start with the first and most obvious: he is a vampire and she is not. She is at constant risk of being eaten by his family, whereas Jacob's family, a pack of werewolves, are already friends with Bella's family. There's a mutual history there. Bella's father tells her that she needs "to learn to love what's good for [her]", referring to Jacob. When Bella discovers Jacob's true nature, Jacob informs Bella that werewolves only kill vampires, not humans. The type of creature that consistently tries to kill Bella is a vampire, whether intentional (the malevolent Laurent and Victoria) or accidental (the benevolent but weak-willed Jasper). Bella is convinced that she cannot be with Edward without being a vampire, too, and part of that is superficial. She feels that, as she ages, he will no longer be attracted to her, which is a convincing argument that their relationship isn't love but rather skin-deep lust. Edward is 109 years old but appears seventeen. Bella turns eighteen and immediately becomes concerned that she will turn into a desiccated old woman. Jacob turns eighteen, too, though; he ages just as a human would, werewolf or not, and his feelings appear to be more than just physical attraction. Furthermore, if it's not enough to take actions for meaning, if it has to be spelled out, Edward himself tells Bella quite plainly: "You can't trust vampires."

There are more subtle signs of relationship troubles brewing, although subtlety is not the strong suit of the *Twilight* films. Maintaining relationships outside of the romantic is vital to maintaining a sense of self and keeping all aspects of one's social and love life happy and in balance. While Jacob retains the connection to his "tribe" and encourages Bella to do the same, Edward isolates Bella from her friends and on occasion her family. Edward romanticizes death and suicide, waxing on about the beauty of the Romeo and Juliet relationship. Overbearing and clingy, Edward tells her where to go and what to do. When he leaves, he tells her to stay, like she's a puppy, not a person. He creates feelings of inferiority in Bella while simultaneously abandoning her. After Edward disappears without warning, Bella suffers night terrors and depression. Toying with someone's emotions isn't Jacob's modus operandi, though. Now gloomy and self-destructive, Bella seeks out dangerous activities in order to feel the same "rush" she experienced when dating Edward. As aforementioned, the neurobiological implications are that Bella is unable to transition from the attraction system to the attachment system and is suffering from dopamine overload. Regardless, Jacob wants to be with Bella and leads her towards productive behaviour. He draws her out of her depression and brings Bella a sense of happiness and normalcy. Jacob helps her rebuild a motorcycle and steers her away from peril without exerting dominance over her. The few times she does venture too close to the sun, Jacob is present to help her, saving her twice, first from a menacing vampire named Laurent who is preparing to kill her and again from drowning as she dives recklessly off a cliff. Edward is nowhere to be found during both of these incidents, having fled months prior. When Edward finally returns, his disdain for Jacob is plain and the feeling is mutual. However, when Edward interrupts Bella, overriding her every word, Jacob tells Edward not to "speak for her." Edward's response is anger. The altercation turns violent with Jacob and Edward rushing at each other with snarls and snaps. Bella dives between them to stop the tussle and, despite everything indicative otherwise, she decides that Edward is the one for her.

In *Eclipse* (the follow-up to *New Moon*), more of the same continues. Charlie Swan, Bella's father, doesn't particularly like Edward. He guides his daughter away from him, asking her to "get some separation from him", but Bella ignores his advice, of course. After forcing his daughter to stay home, Charlie relents, asking her then to spend some time focusing on her friendships, but when Bella tries to visit Jacob, Edward disables the starter in her truck. Edward insists that Bella visit her mother, but when she does, Bella's mother worries about "the intense thing" that Edward has for Bella and expresses concern that her daughter "make the right decisions for [herself]," not what Edward desires. Bella is so wrapped up in Edward that everyone can see it but herself.

When she returns from her visit, Bella learns that problems have been brewing behind her back, events that Edward kept from Bella through lies of omission and outright deceit. Jacob feels it is wrong to force her into the dark, that Bella has "the right to know" when the shit hits the fan. Jacob treats her like a human being with the mental capacity to make decisions. Edward doesn't, treating her like a ward that he cares for, wielding authority over her.

Jacob isn't perfect, though. At his lowest, he tells Bella that he thinks it would be better for her to be a corpse than a vampire, which is surely an idea ingrained by his fellow werewolves. But with Jacob, nearly in tears, it feels as if there's a depth, a second meaning, to this statement; what Jacob intends to say is that he would rather Bella be at peace than in harm's way and suffering the soulless life of a vampire. His choice of words was all wrong (he's eighteen, so let's not be too judgmental), but his intention is important, whereas Edward provides a stark contrast, all sugary sweet statements with ulterior motives behind them. And although Jacob persists mostly because he is in love with Bella, he still opens himself up to rejection on the grounds that she doesn't throw her life away on a bad decision. Yes, Jacob knows he is the better choice over Edward and tells Bella the advantages of a life with him, laying his points out in a neat and orderly way; he tells Bella that she doesn't have to change or leave behind her entire social circle to be with him. But when push comes to shove, Jacob still identifies that Bella is rushing into a lifestyle, vampirism, that she can't take back, an irreversible decision that will change her life forever. And as the valedictorian address at Bella's graduation points out, eighteen is not the best age for "hard-and-fast decisions."

Taking Jacob out of the triangle as a likable alternative, Edward alone isn't too appealing. Sure, Bella may be enticed by him, but they couldn't be more different. For some, a wedding symbolizes the strength of a relationship, celebrating a couple's love. As a vampire, Edward's been around awhile and his notion of marriage isn't the modern-day norm. He doesn't believe in premarital sex or kissing without her father's permission. He comes from the days of chaperoned picnics and strolls along the boardwalk. Bella tells him his views are, in her words, "ancient." Yet after this discovery, he proposes marriage and she accepts. Bella is a modern woman with values that fit contemporary society. She even insists she'll hyphenate her surname. Edward is far more traditional, though, and once married, one of the factors that drives newlyweds to divorce is disagreement about expected spousal roles.

In addition, in-laws play a major role in relationship success, both before and after marriage. As aforementioned, Charlie doesn't like Edward and, faraway and oblivious of the goings-on in her child's life, Bella's mother still seems anxious about the control Edward has over her daughter. As for Edward's parents, they are nonexistent; what he calls his family is just a brood of vampires that he refers to as his "family" due to their shared thirst for blood. Now, there are two reasons why what Charlie thinks matters. The first is obvious: parents who like their child's choice of mate will be more supportive and give the relationship a greater chance of success. The second reason, though, is that parents tend to disapprove for a reason. If they don't like Edward, which they don't, it is because they recognize a problem on the horizon. These problems are present regardless; it's just that Charlie, who isn't blinded by love, saw them first.

Let's deal with something divisive before continuing onto the next few love triangles. Class is a major factor in the success of a marriage. Put down that chair and let me explain! Yes, it sounds horribly Victorian, but there's a reason why the rich tend to marry the rich and the poor the poor, and it has little to do with old-fashioned snobbery. No, the real reason is culture. While heritage and good social standing were the strategy in obtaining a marriageable partner once, the name of the game is having a similar culture from which to draw, a substantial platform from which both spouses understand one another. Speaking in terms of cotillions and capital stocks is lost on one who has to scrimp and save to buy bread and butter. Plus, those from the same culture tend to have the same values in regards to religion, parenting, and the roles in the marriage itself. The rules are already established. It may not be romantic, but it's easy, and easiness works to one's benefit when trying to have a successful marriage. True, the jarring effect of something new for both parties might ignite passion at first, the rough-around-the-edges blue-collar boy and the out-of-his-league daughter-of-a-doctor girl, but when reality sinks in, they have nothing in common. That's not to mention that the impoverished tend not to marry and often split apart while the privileged marry and remain married. It's controversial, I know, but the facts sometimes are cold and hard.

Now, let's look at *Dirty Dancing*. Frances "Baby" Houseman and Johnny Castle are so beloved by fans that many forget Baby's other suitor, the resort owner's grandson Neil Kellerman. Let's compare them, shall we? Kellerman's is a summer resort in the Catskills. There are two types of people at Kellerman's: the rich who stay there and the staff who work there.

There is a slight differentiation made between the staff: the lowly entertainment staff are working for the pay cheque while the waiters work to pay their tuition at Harvard and Yale. For example, Robbie Gould is a waiter who catches the eye of Baby's sister Lisa, but Johnny Castle is a ballroom dancer and instructor. While the Housemans approve of Robbie, a medical student, Johnny seems a hopeless cause, a man-child without ambition.

But I digress. Neil is introduced to Baby through her father's friend Max Kellerman, the resort owner. He brags to the Housemans how Neil is at the Cornell School of Hotel Management. Baby will be an undergraduate majoring in "economies of underdeveloped countries" at Mount Holyoke, a women's college, that upcoming autumn. Not only are Neil and Baby enjoying a higher education and all the benefits it bestows upon them, but if a relationship is to bud and bloom between them, there's only a few hours between their respective schools, his in Ithaca, NY, and hers in South Hadley, MA. Then, there are their hopes and dreams. Note that *Dirty Dancing* is set in 1963. Baby is interested in helping third-world countries and plans to enter the Peace Corps, equal parts feminist and activist. This picture Baby paints appeals to Neil, as he confides in Baby his own unorthodox plans; he intends to take off to Mississippi with a few busboys to be freedom riders, fighting segregation in the South. These are not the actions of the spoiled and ignorant. They may be rich and of high social standing, but neither Neil nor Baby are brats. Instead, they share interests and have similar family values.

Enter Johnny. Baby is in marvel of him and his dance partner, Penny, a former Rockette. Enticed by their provocative style of dance in an era of modesty, Baby follows Billy, Johnny's cousin, to the staff quarters where the dance staff grooves to pounding tunes. There, Johnny pulls Baby aside and dances with her. Brief as it may be, the dance leaves a lasting impression on Baby long after Johnny disappears into the crowd. It is interesting how limited Baby's proclivity for dance was prior to meeting and dancing with Johnny. Afterwards, she stares intently at him, ignoring Neil's advances. Still, Neil shows confidence and skill in running the hole, acting as an apprentice to his grandfather at the resort he will surely inherit in due time. Neil has a plan for his future. Neil has looked two steps ahead to navigate around obstacles to his goals. He's also self-aware of his position, telling Baby that he's been labelled the "catch of the county", not for who he is but for the "two hotels" he's rumoured to possess. His interest lies in Baby, though.

Unfortunately, Baby is googly-eyed for Johnny who pays no attention to her whatsoever until they need a favour. Eager to help at every turn, Baby first finds $250 (that's $1,929.34 in today's money) to pay for Penny to have an at-that-time-illegal abortion; then, she offers to fill in for Penny the day of the procedure, learning complex choreography instead of vacationing; then, in the middle of the night, she wakes her father, a doctor, and begs him to save Penny when her abortion is botched; and finally, she provides an alibi when Johnny is accused of a theft he didn't commit, admitting to spending the night with him in front of Neil; his grandfather Max, Johnny's boss; her befuddled mother and sister; and, worst of all, her disappointed father. Johnny's reaction? He mocks Baby for being a daddy's girl, naïve and unaware of all those working around her. He loses his patience and berates Baby as they work through dancing basics, like timing, holding the frame, distributing weight in her feet, and following his lead. He rushes her. He belittles her intelligence. He insults her skills. She bends over backwards nonetheless. In the end, he uses her as she tries to "save [his] ass when what [she] really wants to do is drop him on it."

Why does she do it? Lest you've forgotten, they have nothing to share with each other. Baby and Johnny are from different walks of life with no common ground. He's not eager to communicate with people of higher social standing in any meaningful way. He feels that they've kept him down, halting him from pursuing his dreams of becoming a professional dancer. He has ideas and is full of creativity, but he doesn't want to share it with "these people" because, through his eyes, "they are rich and they're mean." But he's all too happy to take their money and sleep with their wives. A subplot slid into *Dirty Dancing* is that Moe Pressman pays for his wife to have "extra dancing lessons" while he plays cards; his wife parlays these dancing lessons into sex. Johnny is happy to use his body, too, for prostitution, not just dance anymore. He does it for the money. He can't afford to support himself, never mind Baby whose dreams are larger than life. Through his harsh attitude towards his employer and unwillingness to compromise, Johnny is likely to end up in a union job painting houses, like his uncle, far from the dance floor.

And if you're compelled to mention dance as something that generates a bond between them, think again. Although Baby learns to dance, she doesn't seem especially thrilled by it. She does it initially because it's part of her altruistic nature to help someone in need. She continues to dance afterwards to stay close to Johnny. Even the soundtrack echoes that sentiment, with lyrics like "Do you love me / Now that I can dance?" from "Do You Love Me" by The Contours and "Oh, won't you say you love me? / I'll make you so proud of me / We'll make them turn their heads every place we go," from the film's opening track "Be My Baby" by The Ronettes. She's grasping at straws to keep him close to her. And that's the problem.

The only motivation for them to be together is pure animal lust. If you'll notice, she never glanced twice at Johnny until she danced with him. Physical attraction can be confused for true love easily, especially in the early days. What's more is evidence that sweat plays a role in confusing a yearning body for a yearning heart. The smell of fresh sweat contains a male pheromone called androstenol that has been found to arouse female sexual response. A shirtless Swayze means that the sweat probably won't oxidize, keeping that aura of fresh sweat that is oh-so-appealing to the ladies, and, of course, Baby is always in close range, less than the maximum foot and a half required to detect androstenol. They are constantly one-to-one, no other men in her field of vision as she shimmies to and fro. And since the effect is mutual with androstenol affecting both men and women, Baby is, to some extent, doing the exact same thing to Johnny. Take a closer look: Baby glistens with an ever-present sheen and Johnny needs a towel to his brow ninety percent of the running time. They spend all of their time dancing together, a perpetual perspiration misguiding them.

Want to hear the real kicker? Neil is interested in dance! He's no chump when cutting a rug and he even mentions closing out the summer season's show with a racier dance called the pachanga, which Johnny shoots down. The problem is simply that Baby was never close enough to Neil to smell the sweat. If they'd spent a little less time taking leisurely walks and a little more time throwing around the pigskin, they'd be engaged.

One after the other, love triangles always lead us astray. Many teenage love stories have conclusions that are embarrassingly faulty. Impatient and entitled, Blane McDonnagh in *Pretty in Pink* chases after Andie because of a fleeting attraction. He dates her, but they have nothing in common and he feels nothing but shame. He's embarrassed that Andie makes her own clothes and works at a record store; Andie feels inferior and doesn't want Blane to see where she lives. She never meets his parents and he never meets her father. In contrast, Duckie is reliable and respectful of Andie. Duckie's been her friend forever and even tells her father that eventually he wants to marry her. He fears that Blane will break her heart. He fights to defend Andie's honour. And, to put it bluntly, Duckie and Andie are from the same tax bracket. They lead similar lifestyles and communicate well. Andie just needs to open her eyes, for it's plain to see that Duckie is the right fit and Blane is a flash in the pan.

A similar problem arises in *The Notebook* in which Allie can't figure out which man to pick. Allie obeys a rigid schedule day-to-day. She decides everything with "Mommy and Daddy." That includes her future where she'll receive a promising college education and marry a respectable boy. Her life is cherry-picked from the best of all options. But things go awry when she spends one summer roughing it in a small town where she meets a boy named Noah Calhoun, a startlingly different person than she. Allie is reserved and Noah is not. Even their meet cute displays how vastly incompatible they are. At a carnival, Noah asks his buddy, Finn, about Allie, a friend of Finn's girlfriend. "She's here for the summer," Finn says. He adds as a warning: "Her dad's got more money than God."

Allie expresses no interest in Noah who works down at the lumberyard. Noah wants her attention, though, so he climbs the Ferris wheel and hangs off the bar until she agrees to a date. Allie doesn't want Noah's blood on her hands. But after their date by coercion, they become a package unit moving everywhere as one.

When their story is recounted decades later, they're described as having no "regard for consequences." Their life is fancy-free and they don't deal with the woes of normal folk. All they do is eat ice cream and swim. Finally, it comes to a head when Noah goes to Allie's house for lunch. At forty cents an hour, Noah isn't what Allie's parents were looking for in a son-in-law. Allie intends to attend Sarah Lawrence in New York, faraway from Noah. The flurry of passion subsides and Noah realizes that he doesn't fit into Allie's carefully designed life plan. Her parents label him as "trash" and Allie struggles to choose between her family with whom she was once close and Noah with whom her future is unpredictable. Considering the vision Allie has for her destiny, Noah isn't the piece that'll make the puzzle whole. This intense summer should be but a blip on her radar, for her life holds so much more than this boy that shares none of her interests.

Allie goes off to school as war is declared and decides, in her third year, to volunteer as a nurse. There, she meets an injured soldier, a Southern gentleman whose personality isn't bound to a healthy vigour; his name is Lon and he asks Allie out, which she laughs off. But in no time flat, Lon has healed. The Southern gent asks her out again and, this time, she agrees. Allie falls in love with Lon and is endlessly happy. She can afford to do whatever she pleases and Lon wants to do whatever Allie pleases. And, above all, Allie's parents approve, a factor that would prove a hitch in any plan involving their beloved daughter. Lon jokes with Allie and knows her well; he can sense the friction between her and her parents. But in spite of how fond her parents are for Lon, she agrees to wed him anyway, grinning ear to ear and nodding without hesitation. Allie experiences no hardship with the necessities. Lon is "old money" and buys them a beautiful place of their own. Their forthcoming nuptials are reported upon as "the social highlight of the season."

Meanwhile, Noah returns from the war with a GI bill that can scarcely afford him his dream house, the Windsor Plantation, but through the altruism and faith projected from his father's willingness to sell the family home and pool the funds with his son, Noah is able to buy the ramshackle place and rebuilt it to his liking. Once it's restored, Noah asks an obscene amount for the house but never wants to give it up. Every bid is too high or too low, always too… something. Depressed and hung up on Allie, he dreams of a life he never had. If he ever had her, it would never meet his expectations. Clouded with thoughts of her, he succumbs to alcoholism and engages in a purely physical relationship with a widowed neighbour that is unfair to her messy emotional state. He's not a good guy; he's a man obsessed with a fantasy image.

When Allie learns of Noah's whereabouts and sneaks off to see him, Lon finds the hotel she's at and telephones to check that she's all right. Knowing where Allie lives, Noah only writes for a year, never visits when he receives no reply and certainly doesn't search the phone directory for her number. When met with a dead end, Lon persevered. When met with a dead end, Noah built a house and imagined an alternative universe. To be in a relationship that succeeds, you have to participate. I declare Lon the better of the two, but Allie sees it differently.

But both boil down to high school romances. Let's focus on something more life-and-death. In Paris at the turn of the century, tuberculosis is running rampant. Infectiousness in cities closed in at a rate of close to one hundred percent. The working class were dying and poverty from industrialization received the blame. The sanatorium became the place to go, a quiet and clean area where the sick could breathe fresh air. But staying at one of these facilities wasn't an option for the penniless; no, they proved too costly. And this is the setting of *Moulin Rouge*.

The story goes a little something like this: Satine is a courtesan at the booming burlesque house, but her glamourous feature act is becoming too difficult to perform. Unfortunately, Satine has tuberculosis. She's prone to passing out and coughs up blood; if something isn't done soon, she'll die. Through her good fortune, she is matched up with the Rich Duke, a wealthy investor who wants to make her famous. He's inclined to spend the rest of his days with Satine, lavishing her. And considering Satine's line of work, she should be rather pleased that it's not another one-time customer. "Being on the street is terrible," she declares. "A girl has got to eat." And in her case, a girl has got to get to a sanatorium lickety-split. Antibiotics won't be available until the forties, so this is her best shot at survival. The only way she can afford such a stay is through the generosity of the Rich Duke. He is genuinely enamoured with her. I think he wants her to live.

Unfortunately, Satine meets the poor playwright Christian. He can barely feed himself, so he can't afford her healthcare. And if we add in the argument that love is the magnet that pulls them together, I beg to differ. Satine is paid to appear lustful and, though she may feel something for Christian, her career is based upon sleeping with other men for money. If she wanted to be with Christian, she'd quit her job in a heartbeat, but she's rather the money. It hurts, but the Moulin Rouge is priority one. But Christian isn't willing to share Satine, so instead of ending it amicably, he becomes a disgruntled ass. He shows up at the premiere of her play and throws money at her to degrade her before she takes to the stage. He knows Satine's unwell, but that doesn't stop him from chasing and overwhelming her. He is cruel and forceful. He calls her a "whore" and tells her how little she means to him. Satine is heartbroken and embarrassed, wheezing for breath on the stage as the audience stares and gasps. His response to their break-up is evidently to be an utter prick. That'll win her back.

And, unfortunately, it works. Through a mixture of sweat and tears, Satine rushes into Christian's arms. The Rich Duke is distraught, ready to storm out of the theatre. Irate, he even points a gun at Christian. But he doesn't pull the trigger. He's knocked aside and that's the last we see of the Rich Duke who cared for Satine. Then the curtain falls and, worked up by the whole ordeal Christian's put her through, Satine collapses and dies prematurely while everyone watches and no one does a thing to help her. She may have had more time, had Christian not shown up and worked her into a lather. The Rich Duke who fancied her may have helped her live, but no, that didn't fit into Christian's little "story about love." Her untimely demise offered him a sense of closure and he wasn't happy until he received it. Even if the Rich Duke and Satine didn't last, anything was a better alternative than the self-centered Christian.

I am barely scraping the surface. Love triangles have been around for eons. Romantic comedies dripping with sentiment have affected views of how relationships should be. An Australian poll found twenty-five percent of those in romantic relationships think they have to be psychic in order to please their partner because that happened in a movie one time. People chase "the warm and fuzzy feeling" and forget what true love really is. Expectations are unreal. It's time to realize that films end with credits and we never see what happens after the fireworks. Real relationships have to endure so much more than a sprint through an airport. So, let's get with the program. Don't look at life and treat it like a fiction. Perhaps love does

mean having to say you're sorry from time to time.
And maybe then you'll have what she's having.

The Razzie Dazzle:

How to Win The Golden Raspberry For Worst Picture

We all have different tastes. What one likes, the other won't. That's why we have the authority of John J. B. Wilson.

John Wilson graduated from UCLA with a degree specialized in motion picture and television studies. From there, he held jobs in show biz as a publicist, writer, director, producer, and creative consultant, shoulder to shoulder with big names like Disney and Fox. He even worked for the Academy Awards where the best of the best hob-knob for one special night as the world watches. But being amongst great talent didn't mean that Wilson didn't see the flops, too. Spending his life in the biz, he has seen over five thousand films and, as an expert on "all things that suck on the big screen", he decided to found the Golden Raspberry Award Foundation. At first, it was just a parody in his living room, serving as the antithesis of the Oscars on the same night of its international broadcast. But surely, it grew and grew as the years passed, and today, news coverage reaches an estimated billion people. The Razzies will celebrate thirty-five years in early 2015, handing out once again their Worst Picture award.

So what does it take to be considered the worst? Sure, you can be pretty bad as countless nominees are, but what puts one film beyond the rest? What will get you that glorious Razzie?

All it takes sometimes to make a movie go from poignant to pretentious is a bad review. Panned by the critics, your film can fall rapidly from grace to the bargain bin. A high majority of the Razzie nominees are certified "rotten" on the critical aggregation website, *Rotten Tomatoes*. But wouldn't you figure the lowest scores, the zeroes and one percenters, would nab the Razzie? Common sense says that, at least according to the Roger Eberts and Elvis Mitchells of the world, these films are the worst, but here we have a curious case. Only seven – *Movie 43*, *Gigli*, *Battlefield Earth*, *Wild Wild West*, *Bolero*, *The Lonely Lady*, and *Can't Stop the Music* – of the Worst Picture winners are critically considered the worst amongst their nominees. Both *Battleship* and *That's My Boy* ranked worse than *Twilight: Breaking Dawn, Part 2*, but Bella and Edward got the trophy. *Bucky Larson: Born to Be a Star* failed harder than *Jack and Jill*, but the latter reigned triumphant. Everyone recalls how awful the aptly named *Disaster Movie* was, far more than the less memorable *Love Guru*, which won the Razzie nonetheless. *Caddyshack II* is worse than *Cocktail*. Who wins? Why, *Cocktail*, of course. And so the trend marches on. Therefore, it is safe to conclude that the worst film according to critics does not guarantee the film will win the Razzie; in fact, it actually works less in your favour.

We've determined then that the critics don't matter when it comes down to the nitty gritty. Perhaps it's the audience that does. There's little way to track word of mouth, but we do have the means to check how often people searched a film's title on the almighty Google. Using Google trends to compare Razzie winners to their nominees, one finds that the patterns are horribly inconsistent. In fact, in the month prior to the Golden Raspberry ceremonies, the film that wins is only the most searched amongst its nominees 27% of the time. (Note that Google only provides information on search results as far back as January 2004.) Knowing this, prevalence in the web community is no indicator of prevalence at the Golden Raspberry ceremony.

So what is it then? Is it the money? Is a huge loss what takes a film from being a bad picture to Worst Picture? According to the numbers, it certainly helps. Razzie winners simply don't earn back their money. They average a budget of $49.67 million and a U.S. box office, when rounded up to the nearest tenth of a million, of $49.5 million, which accounts for a loss of $170 thousand for every Razzie given out. And that's the average! Only eight – *Twilight: Breaking Dawn, Part 2*; *Transformers: Revenge of the Fallen*; *Indecent Proposal*; *Cocktail*; *Star Trek V: The Final Frontier*; *Bolero*; *Rambo: First Blood Part II*; and *Mommie Dearest* – managed to turn a profit and, of them, half were part of major franchises guaranteed to draw in audiences regardless of the quality of the picture. The others used the promise of sex and star power to sell tickets. That means that twenty-six of the winners didn't break even. No one is rushing to see the Worst Picture winner.

Knowing that money plays a factor, we should logically follow the scent. The studios monitor the monetary situation and yet it makes little difference which studio it is. A quick tally reveals that Paramount Pictures has released the most stinkers that have won the Razzie at a whopping six, followed close behind by Warner Brothers and Sony Pictures with four each. But considering how many other film companies (Universal, Buena Vista, Touchstone, and TriStar, to name a mere few) have received the same honour (dishonour?), it becomes evident that the studio responsible plays a trivial role.

A common thread linking a slew of these films is that they are instalments in some franchise. The ongoing joke is that studios keep making the same film over and over. If they manage a hit, a sequel is in the works before the box office closes on opening weekend. And yes, as I said before, there is a pattern amongst the Golden Raspberry nominations and sequels. But when it comes to winning, it's a whole different ballgame. Only the first sequel (that's the second movie in a series, as in *Basic Instinct 2* and *Transformers: Revenge of the Fallen*) and fourth sequel (that's the fifth movie in a series, as in *The Twilight Saga: Breaking Dawn, Part 2* and *Star Trek V: The Final Frontier*) has ever won the Razzie. Over twenty-two percent of the Worst Picture nominees are sequels, but that's still less than a quarter over thirty-something years. (FYI: It's hard to keep track of the many offshoots of the original *Scary Movie* franchise to determine where *Disaster Movie* falls, so we'll just ignore its presence for this tally of the sequels.) Being a bad sequel isn't enough to merit the title. Statistically speaking, being a sequel will only get a nomination at best. At worst, your movie just sucks.

Maybe there's something about the creation of a film. The cast, the crew... Can one bad egg screw it up for everyone involved? Using the three strike rule to predict a bad trend, the following performers show one of two things: Either they hand in poor performances or have a manager who fails to find them the right roles. Unfortunately, there are a load of these dishonourable mentions that have been in at least three stinkers: Respected names like Talia Shire and Marlon Brando are a surprise to see next to court jesters like Eddie Murphy. Comeback kid John Travolta managed to spread out his embarrassments, acting in a Worst Picture nominee approximately once a decade. Bo Derek can blame her late husband John for directing her in three consecutive howlers. Also at three, Sharon Stone and Halle Berry (coincidentally, both worked together in *Catwoman*) stand alongside Ryan O'Neal and Jon Voight. There's room for Taylor Lautner and Ben Affleck – in his pre-*Argo* beefcake days – upping the ante to four. Beautiful blondes Uma Thurman and Madonna hold court with four themselves. It's a shock to see Oscar royalty like Al Pacino and Liam Neeson in this company, but they each have their own regrettable decisions, again four each. Remaining at four, action stars Burt Reynolds and Bruce Willis and dramatic actor Dennis Quaid fall behind Kevin Costner, Demi Moore, and Rob Schneider, an eclectic bunch with only one thing in common, that they were in five Razzie-nominated flops. But alas, they are still not the worst. No, they are far from it. In one corner we have an action star that rose to fame with a Best Picture Oscar. In the other, we have a guy using his hand and his armpit to make flatulent sounds. We know them all too well. Please ready your pies for Rocky Balboa and Billy Madison.

Adam Sandler has been a bit of a laughingstock as of late. He managed to spend his early years unscathed, but as time wore on, he teamed up with the same dozen people to make movies and, boy, do they ever suck. Critically considered a joke but commercially satisfied, Sandler worked his way up from *Big Daddy*, *Little Nicky*, and *I Now Pronounce You Chuck and Larry* to more crude and obnoxious fare, like *That's My Boy* and *Grown Ups 2*, until he finally netted himself a Worst Picture Razzie for *Jack and Jill*. The smell of Sandler is the aroma of the Razzies.

But the turd in the toilet has to be good old Sly. Sloppy sequel after sloppy sequel, the *Rocky* franchise grabbed two Worst Picture nominations for the fourth and fifth instalments. (*Rocky IV* is one of my guilty pleasures, but don't spread that around.) The same goes for his *Rambo* series; the second and third films received two nods. But then there are the standalones, a string of no-name unmemorable films that have held Stallone's face in the mud like one of his opponents from either *Rambo* or *Rocky* (take your pick). No, it is films like *Rhinestone*, *Cobra*, and *Lock Up* in the eighties followed by *Cliffhanger* and *The Specialist* in the nineties that have taken their toll on the voting ballot. Sprinkle a few twenty-first century mistakes on top, à la *Driven* and *An Alan Smithee Film: Burn, Hollywood, Burn*, and it's not hard to see how he can be considered the actor with the worst luck when it comes to picking 'em.

But actors have no say in the other aspects of film production. They do what their directors tell them to do. There are some easy targets in this respect; I can think of a few. Directors Uwe Boll, George Lucas, and Prince got a lot of flack for each being nominated twice for Worst Picture, but there are far worse culprits. There are a handful of triple-timers, such as the aforementioned John Derek (*Tarzan the Ape Man*; *Ghosts Can't Do It*; and *Bolero*), John G. Avildsen (*Rocky V*; *The Karate*

Kid, Part III; and *The Formula*), Renny Harlin (*The Adventures of Ford Fairlane*; *Driven*; and *Cliffhanger*), and Hal Needham (*Stroker Ace*; *Megaforce*; and *Cannonball Run II*). But there still remains a trio of truly disgraceful auteurs. All three are household names, each defined by their own little niche. One likes big spectacles, heavy on effects gunfire and marked by lens flares and three-second shots. The second prefers loud and obnoxious comedies using the same actor over and over to shill fart and poop jokes to the masses. And the third was once beloved for an interesting film filled with subtle symbolism leading up to its surprise ending, but now he is renowned for his forced plot twists, ineffectively used to tie together a broken narrative that always seems to involve a male lead and an especially sensitive or supernatural youth. These three are Michael Bay (*Transformers: Revenge of the Fallen*; *Transformers: Dark of the Moon*; *Pearl Harbor*; and *Armageddon*), Dennis Dugan (*Jack and Jill*; *I Now Pronounce You Chuck and Larry*; *Grown Ups 2*; and *Big Daddy*), and M. Night Shyamalan (*The Last Airbender*; *Lady in the Water*; *The Happening*; and *After Earth*). Any of those three at the helm of a film can guarantee at least a nomination.

So my guess for this year's Worst Picture? It's tough to call. *Tammy* bored me and *Sex Tape* felt like an R-rated Apple commercial. But you've got to do worse than that to win a Razzie. A few films rise above the rest like buoyant flies in a soup of sewage. Both directed by Michael Bay and distributed by Paramount Pictures, *Transformers: Age of Extinction* is the fourth instalment in its series and, with an 18% critical rating on *Rotten Tomatoes*, it's got everything going for it – or nothing, depending on how you look at it. Don't forget *Blended*. Certified "rotten" at 14% on the Tomatometer, *Blended* is another Adam Sandler tale of debauchery with his team's fingerprints all over it. This is a film where an elderly woman flies off an ATV into a cactus and our sides are supposed to be splitting with laughter. Yet both the new *Transformers* and *Blended* made back their budget and then some, profiting tens of millions apiece. So I'll bet on the dark horse and say *Men, Women & Children*. Sitting beside *Blended* and *Transformers 4*, it may not look like much, but *Men, Women & Children* satisfies the checklist quite well. Though it doesn't have Dennis Dugan behind the camera, it does contain Adam Sandler. Check. It shit its own pants at the box office. Check. Its critical score on *Rotten Tomatoes* is 31% and I'm confident that it will sit beside films with worse scores than that, but as we now know, just because the critics think it stinks doesn't mean Razzie voters will bestow upon it the Golden Raspberry. In fact, it more often goes the other way. Check. And when compared to other flops like *Blended*, *Tammy*, *Sex Tape*, *Transformers: Age of Extinction*, and *Teenage Mutant Ninja Turtles*, it doesn't receive an overabundance of web attention. Check. And yes, it's distributed by Paramount. Check.

By the time this essay is published and read by you, my dear friend, you likely already know who won the Razzie. There's a chance you're nodding in amazement. There's an even greater chance you're smugly smirking at how dreadful my psychic powers are. Oh, well. It's the Razzies. Crazier things have happened. But if I'm right, oh, if I'm right, I'm buying that lottery ticket.

It's The End of the World As We Know It... ...And It's Rated G:

How Pixar Sends A Dubious Message

Fairy tales are kids' stuff. At least, that's how it used to be.

The argument that once promoted the reading of fairy tales to children, the idea that it provided a moral education by instilling good values, is actually the argument used against it today. As anyone who read *Little Red Riding Hood* can tell you, these values are delivered in a cautionary style, enforcing social norms through fear. Stay on the path you know and don't talk to strangers. Child psychologists weren't as prominent in the olden days as they are now, so we didn't have their hue and cry to warn us against Mother Goose and Humpty Dumpty. Now, we're being told that these tales don't teach morality as much as they scare young children into behaving in a certain way (often a socially conservative way, to boot). This conditioning isn't considered educational or even ethical anymore as it doesn't help kiddies understand the ever important "why." Why should little Bobby choose to act that way? Bobby doesn't know; Bobby's just afraid of being punished by the Big Bad Wolf to misbehave or even question the so-called rules.

Yes, parents disapprove of fairy tales for using these sadistic scare tactics and turn elsewhere for their children's story-time fun. In this politically correct culture with great sensitivity for the alleged delicate sensibilities of their little ones, parents reject the traditional fables of Hans Christian Andersen and the Brothers Grimm. Almost a fifth are concerned that they are too frightening for their children. So, where do they turn? Why, the pretty colours of Pixar, of course!

Our culture is increasingly multimedia. Technology is integrated in the classroom from a young age. Children now know more about their digital devices than they do about books. If that's the case, then it won't hurt to send a cultural message via this generation's preferred communication channels. Why not deliver a moral education on Blu-Ray?

With everything from accusations of lewd imagery to complaints about poor role models, the once-beloved Disney has received a great backlash from parents. Pixar became a favoured alternative. Even Pixar seemed to hate Disney a few years back. Talk of a split became buzz-worthy news, a rumour that never came to fruition as reality. Pixar films have long been considered acceptable for all ages. The majority of the oeuvre is G-rated; only *Brave* is rated PG for some scary action and rude humour. It makes sense then that Pixar would serve the needs of that ever-so-impressionable five-to-nine age group who allegedly quake in fear from the likes of *Snow White* and *Rapunzel*.

So, let's have a gander at the sacred Pixar collection, blessed by family-friendly advocate group Common Sense Media as acceptable programming for the kiddies. We'll start at the beginning with *Toy Story*. Woody, the cowboy with a pull-string speaker box, is the leader of the toys. Responsible and fair, Woody leads them through meetings, ensuring everyone is content and partnered up before the big move. Despite being his owner Andy's favourite toy, he neither brags nor belittles the others, and yet he is replaced by a space ranger toy called Buzz Lightyear. Woody swiftly becomes envious of the attention young Andy pays to Buzz, and when Buzz grows in favour with the other toys, too, Woody determines that Buzz must be eliminated. And what better way to nullify him than knock him behind Andy's dresser?

Unfortunately, Woody's plan is full off hitches resulting in Buzz's fall through the window into the front bushes. When Andy takes a trip to the pizzeria, he begrudgingly takes Woody. Unbeknownst to Woody, though, Buzz has made his way out of the bushes and over to the car in the front yard. He climbs up to the sunroof and leaps into the backseat next to Woody. The two toys brawl and fall out of the car onto the parking lot of the gas station and are ultimately left behind. Buzz and Woody eventually end up at Andy's neighbour's house, a vicious brat named Sid who torments his younger sister and hybridizes toys using various body parts. The nightmare-inducing scene in which Sid's toys are introduced – "cannibals", Buzz calls them – is sure to frighten small children. Before long, Sid straps Buzz to an explosive labelled "The Big One" and sets his alarm for Buzz's demise. What more evidence is needed to prove that not knowing your place is bad behaviour with harsh consequences? *Toy Story* is a cautionary tale warning children of the dangers of ambition. Whether it's a futuristic spaceman yearning to fly or simply yesterday's toy trying to regain popularity with its owner, attempting to be something more in the world earns a first-class ticket to terror and torment.

Toy Story 2 then abuses fear of abandonment to frighten children. Abandonment is the number one fear for children who are dependent completely on their parents or guardians. Trauma in this respect at a young age can carry through to adulthood. Children blame themselves and internalize the grief, damaging their fragile psyches. They feel that they are somehow responsible.

To what end does *Toy Story 2* exploit this fear? Again, to show the importance of knowing one's place. Woody receives a tear in his arm and is shelved by Andy. On the shelf, he meets a dust-covered penguin named Wheezy (he's obviously been forgotten) and suffers a series of nightmares concerned that he'll get thrown away. When Andy's mother holds a yard sale, she takes Wheezy but leaves Woody safely in Andy's room. Because of his own phobia, Woody is determined to save Wheezy and he does just that, climbing into the 25-cent junk box and fishing him out. At this point, Andy's Slinky Dog observes Woody from the window and, misunderstanding why Woody is diving into the 25-cent box, expresses disgust that Woody thinks he's only worth a quarter. In this world of make-believe, toys have value but not all are valued the same. There is a caste system in place ranking them. Unfortunately, Woody is spotted by a toy collector who steals him from the yard sale. The message is this: When Woody decided to retrieve Wheezy, he disrespected the established hierarchy of toys, and for that, he must pay the price.

What are the consequences? Woody is kidnapped and held hostage in the apartment of the toy collector. When Woody meets fellow merchandise, he is described as "valuable property" and is informed that he'll be shipped to a Japanese museum, far away from Andy. There's an entire subplot here that highlights the fickleness of children, showing that kids outgrow their toys and abandon them. Even Buzz is abandoned on his journey to find Woody, stuffed and sealed into a box by the floor model of a new Buzz toy. Everything is about abandonment. Even when his friends come to rescue him, Woody is so suspicious of Andy's loyalty that he decides he is of a different class of toys "for display only." Fear can be used to keep children in their place as they watch their favourite toys do the same.

Toy Story 3 is more of the same, only this time it's the rest of the toys that feel they can strive for more than Andy's abandonment. "Masters of our own fate" is the resounding theme of *Toy Story 3*. As donations to a daycare, Andy's toys conclude that having no owner is the best possible option. The alternatives are collecting dust in the attic or getting crushed in a trash compactor. Daycares are perpetually revolving doors of children of a certain age. As one batch grows up and leaves, the next lot come through the door. The toys decide to disobey Andy's wishes and jump into the box for daycare donations. Unlike the previous films, Woody doesn't try to overrule Andy's authority. He's learned his place and now he does what he's told.

Unfortunately, the daycare isn't the wondrous place it seems. The preschoolers are rambunctious and messy, throwing the toys around with a complete disregard. They abuse Buzz, Jessie,

Slinky Dog, Mr. Potato Head, and the rest of the toys. This is their punishment for trying to fulfil their destinies as playthings. And when Buzz shows "leadership" and "initiative" amongst the older daycare toys, their chief, a teddy bear called Lotso Hugs, penalizes Buzz by resetting him to his default factory setting. His personality, the thing that makes Buzz unique, is gone. Now Buzz is no different than the rest, blindly following the crowd. And although this hostility towards hope and aspirations is perceived from the words and actions of the film's villain, its message is reinforced when Andy resumes ownership, only to thrust the toys into the hands of a little girl named Bonnie. She's in charge now. And they'll dutifully obey her as they watch Andy drive away.

Children respond to the social cues of Andy's toys; they are, after all, the heroes, the good guys, and so their message rings clear. *Toy Story 3* tells the toys to stay in line and stay put, never striving to do anything other than what they're explicitly told to by their "owners." Ambition is a crime in the toy world. And if the toys say so, the children will listen.

Similarly, *Finding Nemo* uses fear to ensure obedience. The only offspring of a widower clown fish, Nemo yearns for some freedom. On his first day of school, his unadventurous father swims him to school, lecturing him on how dangerous the sea is. His overprotective nature has become too much for Nemo and, in an act of defiance, Nemo swims over to a boat and thumps his fin on its bottom. Instead of facing a stern talking-to from his father, Nemo is immediately captured by a scuba-diving Australian dentist who thinks the ocean is his own personal fish tank. Parental separation is scientifically proven to terrify a child; this fear is used to enforce the film's point, that everything is Nemo's fault because he did something his parents told him not to. The message is a dangerous one: Always listen to your parents without exception, kids, even if they're overbearing or worse.

In Nemo's case, his father thinks Nemo shouldn't learn independence because he fears for his son's survival, but what happens when your parents aren't looking out for your best interest? There are situations in which rebelling against parents isn't just necessary but preferable. Take, for instance, the children of cult members. There's no finer example than the Peoples Temple in Guyana. The members of the Peoples Temple gave birth to thirty-three new human beings, thirty-three innocents led astray by their parents, thirty-three new cult members kept in the nursery. Three hundred children lived there, too, children whose parents signed over their custody rights to the Peoples Temple where cult leaders would discipline them by hanging them "head-first into the well late at night." But the Peoples Temple ended dramatically. In an act referred to now as drinking the Kool-Aid, cyanide was forcibly "squirted down the throats of little ones" as parents watched on. More than nine hundred children died; almost three hundred were shot. We now call Peoples Temple by another name: Jonestown.

From the sixties onward, another cult popped up. Initially called the "Children of God" but a decade later changed to "The Family", adherents would often molest their children. Many were offered up to the cult leader. Various cases of incest and child abuse were brought against the group. Again, children led astray by parents spouting the greatness of something not-so-great.

And these things still happen today albeit to a lesser extent. In remote North Korea, young children are taught to hate America with indoctrination and propaganda at every turn. At one national festival meant to celebrate the country's founder, thousands of second-graders joined the Korean Children's Union in a militaristic vow of pro-war patriotism. Their parents and other adults, including veterans, encouraged this ritual, instead of teaching them to fight against xenophobia and look towards a more peaceful future.

And closer to home, there's scientology. Scientology has long been accused of brainwashing its believers. There is also much warranted ado over physical violence and infringement of civil rights within its church, some of which included rumoured attacks on members ordered by senior executives and the equation of homosexuality with perversion. The rules of Scientology force "disconnection" from its critics and skeptics. In other words, a former Scientologist can not speak to his or her family if they remain part of the church. And this is a group that educates children in compounds. Many parents enrol their children in Sea Org where they may "sign contracts for up to a billion years of service." The children would then perform manual labour and are charged exorbitant amounts of money if they choose to leave in adulthood. Some Scientologists urge their children to enlist in Sea Org, allowing and approving of a new wave of child slavery to emerge.

All of these groups may feel like extreme examples, but the same attitudes apply to everyday prejudices. Racism, sexism, and homophobia are no different; children raised by people who utter "faggot" and "kike" will often repeat it. Kids learn by example. Bigotry births bigotry, if children don't fight against it; they must disobey their parents to be tolerant of a diverse world.

So, to be good for a developing mind, Nemo needs to touch the boat and swim back to safety, just to know that he can. But that doesn't happen. And there's the rub. There's no question that *Finding Nemo* scares children into behaving, and so, it performs the same function as the fairy tales that parents don't wish their kids to hear.

The Incredibles has an obvious message: You cannot be yourself. Let's put aside that superhero stories have long been gay allegories in which men in tights with secret identities stand in for closeted homosexuals. No, I look past this trite symbolism to something even triter, something best known as conformity. You have to be normal. Average is likable; unique is aberrant. Do everything by the book. Colour inside the lines. Punch the clock. Do as the Romans do. Mr. Incredible spends his days stifling his superhuman strength as Bob Parr and everything remains a-okay. He truly is Parr, as in "par", the golfing term for "average". The second that Mr. Incredible tries to do something other than be Parr results in a major mess. He gets fired, to start. He follows that up by taking off to a volcanic island where he is hunted by an evil machine. And finally through his actions, he endangers not only his life but also the lives of his entire family who arrive to rescue him. The villain in *The Incredibles*, Syndrome, decides that he must always be himself at the expense of others. The Parrs contrast as people who feel obligated to fit in at the expense of themselves. Although they use their powers for good, the *Incredibles* family still feels the need to hide. We're telling children that to be you is to be bad. These are our heroes, for Pete's sake. Their message to the generation of the future? Be average. Settle for normal.

Cars is another cautionary tale, intent on scaring kids into knowing where they rank in comparison to others. The hero of this story is Lightning McQueen, a souped-up race-car. Accidentally abandoned when travelling cross-country, our hero destroys the road in the small town of Radiator Springs. When they ask him to clean up the mess he made, he complains ad nauseum about how he is a "precision machine" and can't do the work. He even tries to speed off, running away from his problems. Clearly, he's too talented for consequences.

When he finally reaches the speedway, Lightning envisions the big race as "one winner, two losers." But after suddenly embracing an empathetic attitude, he goes on to lose the Piston Cup to an arrogant competitor who plays dirty. Effort is not recognized in *Cars*. Effort does not matter. In a preliminary race, completely mangled vehicles are towed off the racetrack, one of which begs not to be towed away and insists that he can still race. This scene implies that weaker competitors can never work their way up, and unless you're the best of the best, unless you're Lightning McQueen, perhaps you shouldn't even try. I suspect this message isn't the kind parents want to pass onto their children.

The same can be said for *Ratatouille*. Remy the rat believes in renowned chef Auguste Gusteau's claim that anyone can cook. While Remy is certainly a great cook, one born with talent and a palette like no other, he never needs to practice to keep it up. He is, after all, a rat. Opportunities to be in a kitchen are limited and often life-threatening. But put him in front of the pots and the pans, and Remy leaps into action.

Compare Remy to sneaker-clad fledgling Chef Linguini. Despite the ample practice he receives working in the gourmet restaurant Gusteau's, Linguini cannot cook. No matter how much time he devotes to the craft, he will never match Remy's skill. When he opens a restaurant of his own, Linguini still needs Remy to do all of the cooking. The lesson remains the same as *Cars*: The greats already have it and don't have to work hard to keep it. But if you don't possess that *je ne sais quoi*, you never will, no matter what you do.

Cars 2 takes a more violent turn. Good behaviour, as in trying to do the right thing, a value taught to children from the start, gets you killed in *Cars 2*. The number of innocent vehicles blown up, shocked by electricity, or otherwise murdered in this film is far too great and, in a film aimed at children, that number should be zero. Even the childlike tow truck Mater is endlessly chased by gunfire. While the other Pixar films scare children into behaving, *Cars 2* just scares children for very little purpose at all. And then there are the contradictions. For instance, Lightning McQueen goes head to head in a race with his bully, an Italian car named Francesco who intimidates and humiliates Lightning. Please note that this character is our hero, the role model for the kids. "Lemon" cars, like Pacers and Gremlins, have been bullied for decades and thus they take a stand and demand respect. But they're considered villains. With its mixed messages that serve only to confuse children,

Cars 2 seems to frighten for the sake of frightening, but scrape away and you'll find a grim message. When standing up against bullying is villainized, the door is open to let bullies be the victors. That is the message *Cars 2* sends to little ones.

Would you want your children to think that deceit is reassuring? Would you allow your children to read a fable that reinforces lying as a viable option when things don't go your way? If your answer is no, then you should reconsider *A Bug's Life*. According to the film's narrative, a colony of ants spend their harvesting season gathering food not for themselves but for the cloud of grasshoppers that threaten and intimidate them. But when inventive Flik drops his newest contraption too close to the pile of seeds and berries they've amassed, the entire collection slips into the water nearby. The colony is furious. They are warned by the grasshoppers that they only get one second chance and must risk starvation to feed their bullies. (I am not going to delve into the implications of how creativity kills; frankly, the way they react to Flik's ingenuity speaks for itself.)

To rectify the situation, Flik suggests that he voyage off the island to find help. The royal council agrees, merely to get Flik out of their antennae. And so off Flik goes, searching for "tough warrior bugs" to fight the vicious grasshoppers and scare them off for good. After witnessing their performance in a bar brawl, Flik is certain he's found them: a scrappy male ladybug; an eloquent stick bug; a psychic praying mantis and his beautiful moth wife; twin pill bugs who only speak a foreign tongue; a black widow and her beetle buddy; and a very hungry caterpillar. Flik drags them back to the island and convinces the ants that these bugs are the answer to their problems. When the truth comes out that the bugs aren't literally going to "knock them dead," that they are circus performers with no combat skills whatsoever, Flik decides to keep it hidden. He is certain that the colony will feel better being lied to, so the circus bugs keep up the act and reap the praise and benefits. Of course, they are discovered and met with disappointing frowns. But instead of suffering major repercussions for their ruse, Flik and the other bugs save the day and fall back into the graces of the colony. Apparently, children should be raised to fib their way out of their problems.

As aforementioned, abandonment is a frequent weapon in Pixar films. *WALL-E* is no exception. Alone on Earth after pollution levels have grown too elevated for life, WALL-E is a robot who cleans up trash. His only companion is a Twinkie-loving cockroach. WALL-E longs for love, the kind he's seen in the movies he's scavenged, but when he finally finds it in an advanced technology robot named EVE, he is abandoned once more. What brings this about? Well, WALL-E is a curious robot who obsessively collects objects left behind by the former inhabitants of Earth. He has everything from forks and spoons to iPods. He begins to show EVE his collection of gadgets: his whisk; his Rubik's cube; his light bulb and lighters; and, finally, the last bit of vegetative life. And that's where the trouble starts. Poor WALL-E is unaware that EVE has been sent to find evidence of sustainable life by the humans sailing through space. Upon discovery, EVE takes the sample and powers down to protect the plant, but WALL-E doesn't understand what's happened to his friend. Once a fiery personality, EVE has become unresponsive. This is his punishment for discovering the world around him. Curiosity killed EVE. So, mind your own business, children, or lose your only friend.

Up doesn't fare much better. It teaches children that the outside world is dangerous and thus exploration of it is immoral. After the loss of his wife Ellie, Carl Fredricksen is left alone, his house amidst a construction site. The only time he leaves his house is to grab his mail from the box just outside his fence. You'd think he's lead a rather calm existence, but you'd be wrong. One day, while fetching the mail, he attacks a construction worker after they damage the mailbox. This incident goes to court and Carl is ordered to leave his home and enter a retirement community. This is what adventuring gets you, even if it is only to the edge of the yard. And that doesn't include the mayhem he encounters as he literally moves his house to South America, floating it away on the buoyancy of balloons.

Meanwhile, Russell is a little boy, but more importantly, he's a Wilderness Explorer. He's been collecting badges for awhile, building up his wilderness skill set. Russell is one badge away from becoming a Senior Wilderness Explorer, and that badge is helping the elderly. He sets his sights on Carl Fredricksen, but Carl just wants to be left alone. Russell is hell bent on that badge, though, and the day that Carl decides to attach thousands of helium balloons to his house to fly away is the day that Russell gets trapped on Carl's porch soaring high above the city. His own sense of adventure brings him nothing but trouble as he's transported with an old curmudgeon to a different continent without his consent. He'll have a hell of a time explaining this one to his mother, especially the part where he dangles helplessly miles above ground. What an anecdote.

And then there's Charles Muntz, an explorer whose brain is addled with the desire to capture a rare bird species, a task that has kept him tucked away in South America for decades. His need for adventure has left him with only one type of companion: dogs and lots of them. They're all equipped with bark-to-voice technology, collars Charles invented to allow their thoughts to be translated into English speech. The few times humans have crossed his path, Charles was so distrustful that he killed them, suspicious that they're after the same exotic bird for which he's searched the region many times over. And so, he goes after Carl and Russell in the same bloodthirsty fashion. Exploration doesn't facilitate learning. In the case of *Up*, a sense of adventure corrupts.

Which brings us to *Brave*. *Brave* centers on Merida, a rambunctious lass, miserable with her lot in life. She wants to shoot arrows and climb mountains and ride her horse through the trees. Born a royal, she is forced into a traditional position of nobility, told what a princess does and does not do. The rules are laid out for her in a matter-of-fact manner. A princess is well-spoken, enunciating and projecting every word across a large room. A princess knows her own backyard, aware of her kingdom and its every anecdote. A princess is cultured, knowing her arts and music. She can't doodle, chuckle, devour her food, or sleep in. She has to be full of compassion and caution. The highest priority, Queen Elinor tells Merida, is that she must "strive for ... perfection." An unattainable goal, if I've ever heard one, surely setting poor Merida up to fail from the get-go.

Brave dwells on the concept of destiny. There is no free will but some succeed because "some are led." In other words, if you're not a princess or born into a similar position, then sorry, kids, you're screwed because it's not in the tarot cards or whatever the Scottish equivalent to tarot cards is. Merida's mother Elinor, the Scottish queen of Dun Broch, tells her folk legends about the will-o'-the-wisps, blue ethereal fairy-like spirits that inhabit the woods. She tells her daughter they "lead you to your fate." Fast forward a handful of years and Elinor is holding a competition for her daughter's hand in marriage. Merida is outraged that the winner of some game will be her husband, her future king, her fate, but Elinor insists that this event is where her life's preparation has led. Elinor treats the idea of betrothal with one of the sons of the clans as ideal, but when Merida throws a fit, Elinor tells her marriage is "not the end of the world" with the sort of blasé attitude reserved to whether or not you want jam on your toast. So which is it? Is marriage the end-all-be-all or is it just another day? And if it's not important, why force her to do it at all? Surrounded by a boisterous father and prank-pulling triplet brothers, Merida only has one female role model in her life and that's her polite-to-a-fault mother. It is especially vital that Elinor set the right example and encourage Merida to be the best she can be, rather than marry the best she can get.

After making a big show of her own prowess at archery, belittling all of her suitors and disobeying her livid mother, Merida runs off, fleeing the castle for the woods where she follows the will-o'-the-wisps to a woodcarver's house. Merida quickly discerns that this whittler is, in truth, a witch. She bargains with the elderly sorceress for a spell to change her ... mother. This scene has played out once before, back in 1989, in Disney's *The Little Mermaid*. A redheaded princess visiting a dubious conjurer to change one's fate and spite one's parents, all to do with a boy (or, in Merida's case, three boys), is not a novel concept. This action never ends well, always holding a catch that leads to dire consequences. You could say its mere inclusion in the story acts as a cautionary tale, a scare tactic that inspires impressionable minds to listen to their parents no matter what. Never question Ma or Pop, even if it goes against everything for which you stand. Never venture out and seek a solution to your problems because everybody is suspicious and untrustworthy. Just do as you're told or your mother will be turned into a bear.

Monsters, Inc. and *Monsters University* are two films that, within their narratives, literally economize fear. The power supply for the monster population is generated by the screams of children, and, in one climactic scene in *Monsters University*, the screams of adults, too. Fear is currency. Horrifying is their business. Their goal is to frighten children. Creepy shadows and bumps in the night are par for the course. These films don't teach children not to be afraid; they teach them that it's inevitable, an ongoing trade for this fantasy world just outside their reach.

But that's not why it's dangerous to the impressionable. No, something further menaces beneath the surface of *Monsters, Inc.* Disguised as a buddy comedy, *Monsters, Inc.* utilizes performance anxiety as more than just a narrative tool. These monsters are Scarers who, as aforementioned, must frighten children in order to power their society. As Scarers, they have to stay on top of their game at all times. They must be their best. What happens when you're not performing optimally? Let me paint you a word picture. Say you do everything right; you scare the kid and the kid's shrieks fill your canister to the max. You're walking tall. But on the way out, your furry foot grazes a stray sock. It sticks to you. You close the door behind you and you're greeted not with encouragement but an embarrassment of agents in Hazmat suits. This exact thing happens to one monster, George Sanderson. At the sight of the sock, his assistant, who considers him a brother, belts out in a panic, "2319! We have a 2319!" In seconds, George is tackled to the ground. You see, children are toxic in the monster realm and anything they touch is akin to a poisonous contagion. A contaminated monster is one that made a grave blunder and deserves punishment. With a thorough shaving and a cone around his neck, George Sanderson knows this all too well.

One of the film's villains, Randall, is too competitive for his own good. He's not satisfied with breaking the scare record. His sole motivation is to take over the whole industry, so he develops a cruel torture device to extract more screams from children. And Randall's obsession is no anomaly. A tertiary character named Roz never lays off the protagonist's silly sidekick Mike Wazowski for not filling out his paperwork. Her warning? "I'm watching you, Wazowski. Always watching…" Mike shudders; Roz terrifies him. There's nothing quite like performance anxiety to cripple a Goliath, but anyone who has suffered from it knows that being watched only exacerbates the problem.

What's the worst that can happen, though, if you don't perform well? The consequences can only be so harsh, right? Well, in the *Monsters, Inc.* universe, you're only…banished to the Himalayas! It's all right to be achievement-focused, but making mistakes is part of learning. Being afraid to err is what *Monsters, Inc.* preaches, though, and that is detrimental to a child's delicate psyche.

From the scathing assessments above, you'd think I hate Pixar. Quite the opposite; I love them. I think their work so far has been mostly consistent and original. Equally entertaining for little tots and the parents who take them to the cinema, I applaud Pixar for making films that I personally feel are suitable for all ages. My point is, then, that the preciousness with which some parents shield their children's eyes is getting out of hand. There is no evidence that fairy tales are going to damage the youth of today. Pixar isn't the alternative because no one needs an alternative. If you like *Toy Story*, that's great, but don't use it as the 'I Can't Believe It's Not *The Lion King*' substitute entertainment. I watched *Snow White and the Seven Dwarves* and grew up to be a feminist. I read about Rumpelstiltskin, Goldilocks, and the Three Billy Goats Gruff and never went to therapy. You can remove the safety lock off the toilet seat now. Everything will be okay.

Stirring The Pot:

The Real Hegemony of
Litchfield Federal Prison

Everything I've learned, I've learned from film and television.

Children are sponges. The brain's first five years are the years of greatest potential, working twice as much as an adult brain and maintaining far more connections than an adult does before the brain rewires itself to those neural pathways it uses the most. Yes, the circuitry changes as we age, but during this period of development, each brain cell has the capacity of a minimum fifteen thousand synaptic links to be made to our billions of other neurons. Stimulate the brain while it's young and it stands a greater chance of acquiring that factoid, storing it in the brain bank seemingly for life.

Yes, children are sponges. They learn from everything around them and parents – whether they care to admit it or not – tend to plop their babies in front of the TV. It starts from a young age. According to findings by the Kaiser Family Foundation, children five and younger spend an average of two hours in front of a screen every day. I was no exception. I remember things today that I saw decades ago on television. I credit *Sesame Street* with teaching me the alphabet. My first word stemmed from an animal segment with Elmo. *Animaniacs* taught me the Presidents in order (that is, up to Bill Clinton) and some basic American geography, outlining every state capital plus

Washington, DC. Yakko, Wakko, and Dot taught
me how to multiply two double-digit numbers; they
provided me with plain-English interpretations of
Shakespearean passages and historical lessons on
the explorer Magellan's unsuccessful search for the
East Indies. *The Simpsons* gave me lessons in
Roman numerals and the Pythagorean Theorem; it's
through Bart and Lisa that I understand interest
rates. Education doesn't stop at childhood, though.
In a way, all television and film can be educational,
if you give it a chance. I learned what a sedative
was from my first horror movie, *Misery*. I got my
first dose of legal jargon from *Legally Blonde*.
Through repeated viewings, I familiarized myself
with *mens rea*, the "vicious will" needed in one's
mind for a criminal to be tried as sane. I discovered
what an Episcopalian was from a reference made to
Charlotte's Christian behaviour in an episode of *Sex
and the City*. I also found out that the *mikveh* is the
bathing ceremony that marks the official conversion
to Judaism from *Sex and the City*. Basically, any
religious education I have was extracted from *Sex
and the City*. It's clear that we retain and recall
more from the boob tube than we ever do from the
classroom.

However, some learning experiences are far
from normative. For example, how many people go
to prison? (In fact, more than we think, but more on
that later.) I learned about the prison experience (not
for the first time, but for the first time *thoroughly*)
through *Orange Is The New Black*. As a woman,
when I go to jail, it's not going to be like *Oz* or *The
Green Mile* or *The Shawshank Redemption*. No, if I
ever found myself heading to the clink, it would be
Orange Is The New Black all the way for me. This
is the first time I've ever witnessed the female

jailbird tale told so passionately and vividly. The only other films I can envision that tell this kind of story are seventies-style sexploitation flicks, pseudo-pornography of nymphomaniacs in black-and-white-striped jumpsuits gyrating for the director's scopophilic gaze. That is not the case in *Orange Is The New Black*. The first season (the one in which this essay will focus exclusively) introduces prison newcomer, Piper Chapman, a Mary Sue figure shaped to mirror real-life writer, non-profit activist, and series consultant Piper Kerman. The season deals with Piper's transition to the new way of life on the inside.

As a rule, there are no rules to prison. Women's prison is no exception. As Nicky Nichols so eloquently implies, there is no way and no reason to study for prison. You just have to learn as you go. There are regulations, sure, ones found in the handbook administered to each inmate the day they arrive. No running in the yard. No cell phones. No physical contact of any kind. These rules can be manipulated and outright ignored, enforced only by the strictest drill sergeants who haven't had their morning coffee; other times, you catch a break and the violation magically wasn't seen, an unspoken agreement by an officer who just wants the weekend to start early. These are not rules. They're arbitrary and oft-forgotten guidelines.

The unwritten rules that do exist are embedded in maintenance of power dynamics, parameters set not by the correctional officers but by the inmates. The COs couldn't give less of a shit about their job. At the end of the day, they just want to go home. If that means buying a replacement for a missing screwdriver and declaring it found, that's what a CO will do to keep the magic ball bouncing.

However, as outsiders continue to remind the ones trapped within the walls of a penitentiary, "prison is a fishbowl." Unfortunately, this advice doesn't help those who have no control over whether they stay or go. So, instead, the inmates build their power structures from within, controlling what they can.

You may not come to power easily. A long sentence isn't enough; otherwise, Yoga Jones would be making offers they couldn't refuse. No, there's an art to it. One must first play by the rules, and once power is bestowed, one gets to write the rules. The irony is not lost on me that the centre of power in Litchfield's women's prison is the kitchen. For all the fights for power in the various waves of the feminist movement, when we're all tossed in a jail-shaped box, the strongest women still float to the kitchen. That's not to say anything disparaging about the ladies who run the kitchen in *Orange Is The New Black*. The Warden's assistant, Joe Caputo, describes the position of head cook in the kitchen as "queen bee." Used like a reward by the COs and tossed from one "tribe" to the other, the women who run the kitchen – not work in it, but run it – are anything but meek. They are fighters. They use their power for good, not evil. They expose drug rings. They protect innocent pregnant girls. They try to make the lives of their peers a little bit easier. Compare this to one CO's fight to close the track and bribe a handful of prisoners with doughnuts to keep quiet. Compare this to the unbridled sexual harassment spread by another CO. One thing's for sure: the kitchen is the domain of power, not the staff lounge.

Now, what are these vitally important rules? They are numerous and informal, learned by living it, not by any handbook. At Litchfield, they include but are not limited to the following:

One, do not ever complain about the food. Humans need only a few essentials to survive. They need shelter, air, and nourishment. The people who control the kitchen control your life. You don't make an enemy of the chef or you might as well say sayonara to meals altogether. Nicky Nichols, the protégé of the Russian chef at Litchfield, lovingly nicknamed Red, asks Piper as they eat mediocre bologna sandwiches at a picnic table if she likes her lunch. "I'm not complaining," Piper replies. "You learn fast," Nicky smirks. You don't break this rule twice. Food is fundamental. When you bitch about it, that's someone's work you're shitting on, and since the kitchen is the centre of power, you're shitting on the clink's CEO.

Two, if you need something, you find out what other people need. Although bartering is officially prohibited, the inmates know otherwise. You trade your way up to what you want. Facing her first real foe in prison, Piper discovers that her nemesis suffers from chronic backache. Piper knows that, if she doesn't appease this rival, she's going to run into far more trouble than she bargained for. So Piper gets to work, trading this for that until she has the ingredients for the jailbird's equivalent of Bengay. The snipers are called off. Balance is restored. And Piper's not the only one. When a fellow prisoner Mercy's sentence comes to its end and she readies to leave, Mercy's girlfriend, Tricia, asks Miss Claudette, a ten-years-in lifer, to bake her signature coconut cake as a bon voyage treat. Miss Claudette refuses, but Tricia insists, "I'm going to find something you want." You find out what other people need. That's just how prison works; from the nineteen-year-old with three years left to the salt-and-pepper-haired post-menopausal OG, everybody knows it.

Three, never sell out your inmates to a CO. The guards aren't on your side. Frustrated at the hand life has dealt them, they like to exert their power by exacting revenge upon the vulnerable incarcerated ladies within. Piper hands in a cell phone to her counsellor at his request, but she refuses to give the name of the inmate to which it belonged. She pleads ignorance, claiming that she found it abandoned in the trash, but her explanation is not enough to satisfy the CO. "The way these inmates treat snitches – it's ugly," he says. Even he knows the rules. When Nicky divulges to CO "Pornstache" Mendez the methods Red uses to smuggle in toothbrushes, pantyhose, pore-cleaning nose strips, and other so-called luxury items, Nicky upsets the status quo at Litchfield. Something crumbles and, in the end, inmates pay. Those who break this rule face the wrath of someone.

Four, if you can't find out what someone needs, then handle your own business. COs don't like prison drama. They don't care enough to deal with death threats between prisoners, so you're going to have to handle your own homicidal fundamentalist zealot with a penchant for crystal meth. If you don't, you're more likely to be thrown into solitary confinement "for your own protection." And when you get out, she'll know you ratted. You can ask for help from trusted inmates, but at the end of the day, you learn to handle it on your own.

Five, either be gay or be straight. There's no room for the Kinsey scale in prison. Lesbianism is not a part-time activity. Morello tells everyone how she is engaged to a man named Christopher, a man who never visits her in jail but whom she loves anyway. She plans their wedding and their honeymoon and every detail of their married life, but she's not exactly heterosexual. Desperate for someone's warm embrace, she turns to her gay friend Nicky Nichols, diving into her arms and accepting her love. The same applies to Piper whose romance years before with drug importer Alex Vause is the reason she's in prison in the first place. Piper and Morello are both bisexual women, but that doesn't fly in Litchfield. The reality of bisexuality has no place when there are hardcore gay women who want to know if you're either on the playing field or you're not. And if you're merely gay for the stay, don't flip-flop. Your choice is binary. Gay or straight. Take your pick and stick to it.

Six, stick to your race. "It's tribal," Piper is told when she realizes that skin colour divides the jail into little pockets. White girls bring white girls toiletries. Latinas help each other thread their eyebrows. Black girls support their Nubian sisters. It's racist but prison isn't politically correct. This informal rule is obvious to the administration, so much so that the Women's Advisory Council (WAC) is divided into each colour. WAC, the prisoners' body of representatives who communicate with CO Sam Healey to request items and services for the inmates, are elected by the inmates themselves. However, it's not your standard election. No, Piper learns that "you can only vote within your race", loosely defended that only someone of that race can decide what people of that race may need. Sure, Taystee and Piper can be friends, but when you boil it down, you stick to your tribe.

Seven, don't take drugs. This is one of those few rules enforced by the COs, too. No one is faithful when they're addicted and everyone must pledge fealty to someone when they're behind bars. The junkie gets a bull's eye on her back, a sign that says they can't be trusted. And when loyalty is your bargaining chip and your word is your bond, as it is in women's prison, then you don't want your reputation to be soiled. Just say no, kids.

Eight, if you help anyone with legal correspondence, you better be prepared to help everyone and their cousin. Everyone is innocent. She "wasn't even in Jersey when that shit went down." They allegedly didn't do the crime and they sure as hell don't want to do the time. So, your offer to assist someone writing an appeal letter will apply to all inmates at an alarmingly fast rate. Good for one, good for all… or good for nothing.

Nine, know when to shut up. A chatterbox is a problem. For most, it's merely annoying. Morello's babbling about floral arrangements and wedding cake toppers is a nuisance to Red and Nicky, both visibly rolling their eyes. But that kind of talk is innocent. It's only bothersome, a problem to inmates with a migraine and a temper. However, for some, talk is dangerous. If you're going to yammer on about the food, please refer to rule number one. Furthermore, a secret shared with the wrong person can break ties, shift power, and get someone's face good and ruined. In a women's prison, you fight with words more than fists. You know who's never in trouble? Norma Romano, the mute sous-chef at Litchfield. I don't consider that a coincidence. In the end, it's best to bite your tongue before someone rips it out.

And so on and so forth. This is just a sprinkling of the unofficial rules of Litchfield. There are many more buried beneath layers of nuance and forced social interaction between groups who don't understand each other and groups who don't care to. These don't include the host of faux-pas behaviours that, while not a broken rule per se, will result in snorts of derision and changes in public perception. Suddenly, you're the dirty girl who sleeps in the bed instead of on top of it. Who wants that?

I'm sure many more little doctrinal joys perk up as occasion strikes. But Litchfield is just one prison. Perhaps the rules are specific to each institution. Perhaps they're all the same. Who knows? If I'm lucky, I never will. And it seems, to some extent, it is luck. As CO Susan Fischer says to inmate Piper Chapman, "The only difference between us is, when I made bad decisions in life, I didn't get caught. It could've been me here in khaki, easy." In recent years, the United States has been throwing every Tom, Dick, and Harriet behind bars. Not only has the American incarceration rate quadrupled since the peace-loving late-sixties to early-seventies era, but also the majority are often impoverished minorities who, through lack of a system that gives even the slightest shit about them, don't have an adequate education, enough to know how to get out of the criminal rut. Approximately three-fifths are black and Hispanic; in fact, a black male born today has a greater chance of incarceration than completion of his studies for a four-year college degree. That's not to say they are the only ones who deal with their department of corrections. No, in fact, approximately one in every hundred American adults goes to jail, no matter their colour, adding up to a population of 2.2 million adults in prison, the largest statistic of this kind in the world. If you take every inmate on Earth, about every fourth person could sing you "The Star-Spangled Banner." America loves to lock up its people, and, considering that about one in every four prisoners is American, *Orange Is The New Black* reads less like entertainment and more like a documentary. So, I don't know the rules and I don't know just how factual the chronicles of these Litchfield inmates are. What I do know, though, is not to traffic thousands of dollars of drug money to Belgium.

Alas, we are all in a fishbowl, whether we're in orange or otherwise. We are no different from the nonviolent repeat offenders of *Orange Is The New Black*. One inmate Taystee is a repeat offender not because, ooh, she loves the life of crime. No, she intentionally goes back to jail because she needs the structure. In Litchfield, she knows what to do. It's organized and gives her purpose. Her release is more punishment than her capture. People need rules – all people, not just the incarcerated – and we will make them up as we go along, making our own lives a touch more complicated just to keep walking in the right line. Having rules is a certain kind of freedom, an ability to be free to know the routine, what to do and what not to do. It's the instructions to walk the tightrope in the circus that is life. (And I'm sure prison life is quite the circus.) Sometimes, we have to chain ourselves to these rules, women and men alike, just to keep ourselves happy. Without them, we're all prisoners.

The Lucrative Lore of Lorre

Chuck Lorre must love *The Odd Couple*.

The Odd Couple was originally a play by Neil Simon, adapted into a film in the late sixties. The film opens on Felix Ungar. Felix wanders into the Hotel Flanders asking for a room, saying he won't be staying for any serious length of time. His separation from his wife Frances is fresh, a wound still stinging. It's a wound he's sure will heal over soon, one that he hopes is just a nightmare he'll wake from, one that may kill him if he doesn't kill himself first.

Meanwhile, the mood is much lighter at Oscar Madison's place. The guys gather to smoke cigars and play some cards. Oscar insists that his friend Murray should lend him a twenty for the game, only to be abruptly told that he owes all of his friends some money. Evidently, Oscar's a big spender, whether he has it or not. His accountant, Roy, another poker buddy, carps that Oscar takes nothing seriously, an easygoing guy who never sweats. Life's too short for Oscar not to enjoy it. Life's also too short to clean up. Oscar's house is a bit of a mess on account of his slovenly habits. If he spills beer, his friends mop it up because they know he won't. Oscar has a broken refrigerator that sits for two weeks unrepaired, its contents becoming an increasing gamble.

Oscar is different than Felix. Felix is neurotic, overwrought with thoughts of his looming divorce. He's melancholy over his wife, sobbing forever and a day, but Oscar's failed marriage is a joke to him by this point. When his short-fused poker buddy complains about the smell of rotten food from the fridge, Oscar merely replies, "If I wanted nagging, I'd go back with my wife."

Oscar doesn't want to change. About forty minutes in, the two sit on a park bench, discussing what once was their married lives. Felix is crying about how impossible he was to live with when Oscar begins to crow about his lot in life. This speech encapsulates Oscar's character: "I've been one of the highest paid sportswriters for the past fourteen years. We saved $8.50 in pennies. I'm never home. I gamble. I burn cigar holes in furniture, drink like a fish, lie to her every chance I get. […] I still can't figure out why she left me."

Even after hearing this, Felix wants to move in with Oscar, a man whose personality couldn't be more different than his own. They clash straight away. Felix Ungar is neat, uptight, and neurotic. He can't seem to enjoy things, including the loose Pigeon sisters that Oscar serves Felix on a platter. No, he's simply not that kind of guy. He's more cerebral, too in his head for that kind of thing. He's a "smart guy." In contrast, Oscar Madison is sloppy, dishevelled, and hedonistic. He's a gambler and a sports guy who lives in a poorly kept house and likes it that way. He spends without care but seems to enjoy his life. He doesn't really think. He's a "stupid guy." In the end, *The Odd Couple* boils down to two mismatched men living together who don't particularly get along. The humour is in the juxtaposition.

Chuck Lorre is the creator of many hit shows, most notably *The Big Bang Theory* and *Two and a Half Men*. He took the basic principles – two men, one "smart" and one "stupid", and not ideal roommates at that – and applied them for what's commercially proven as comedy television gold. In a 2003 featurette about the making of *Two and a Half Men* called "Two Adults, One Kid, No Grown Ups", series co-creator Chuck Lorre confesses, "They're kind of archetypes, you know. They're twisted Jungian archetypes. […] You have the eternal boy [played by Sheen] and Cryer plays the character who is more everyman. I'd like to think of him as Job, you know. He's trying to live a good life and he's being punished." Jon Cryer continues to spill behind-the-scenes secrets, such as the fact that Alan was supposed to be a neat freak, much like Felix Ungar. In a self-referential bit of wit in the seventh season, Alan refers to the premise of *The Odd Couple* as implausible. This comment exposes the mirror image Lorre has presented. The authorial intent is revealed in a tongue-in-cheek way and likewise defended when Alan adds, "It would be different if they were related." After eight seasons, that excuse is invalid. But more on that later.

In the *Two and a Half Men* pilot, the first scene in which the audience is introduced to Charlie is noteworthy: About to jump into bed with one woman, he receives a phone call from another woman, one that watchers can deduce has slept with Charlie based on her affectionate pet name for him, "Monkey Man." Nevertheless, she has a hostile tone, angry that he hasn't returned her phone calls. Charlie chooses to ignore the call and, despite overhearing the message, this new woman about to jump in the sack does the same. She has no fear, confident that she won't suffer the same fate. That poor myopic girl.

Meanwhile, in the next scene, Alan is summed up. He states how he thought he had a strong marriage. He spouts on and on about how he was always faithful. Alas, their two views (specifically their views on women) are what will always separate them. Take, for instance, this conversation between Alan and Charlie after Alan's wife Judith has kicked him out:

ALAN: Look, okay, this is just until things settle out. A couple of days max. She will come to her senses.

CHARLIE: (sarcastically) Yeah, that's what women do.

In other words, Alan feels that women are reasonable people that think matters through, given enough time, and then draw conclusions based on logical grounds. Charlie belittles Alan as he believes the opposite, that woman are irrational beings with which he desires no long-term commitments, not to any of them. Since Chuck Lorre tends to portray women in the worst light possible (if not frightening, then vapid; if not vapid, then dense), Alan is ultimately wrong about his wife but that doesn't take away the validity of his position on women as a whole. He believes in people and, to Alan, women are people.

In the pilot, Alan Harper is introduced as a successful doctor (in fact, Chiropractor of the Year in San Fernando Valley), placing him firmly in "smart guy" territory. Charlie Harper, on the other hand, got lucky. He has no skill set whatsoever… except for a modicum of musical ability. He uses that talent to write TV jingles (not full-fledged songs but twenty-second compositions to shill Maple Loops). In a speech identical in tone to Oscar Madison's monologue, Charlie describes his line of work best: "a lot of money for doing very little work." The poster boy for instant gratification, Charlie burns through his money on alcohol, cigars, and fancy cars. One of his more serious ex-girlfriends Lisa, played by Sheen's then-wife Denise Richards, describes Charlie Harper as "a grown man who can't even commit to long pants." He is the "stupid guy."

According to the eighteenth episode of the first season, "An Old Flame With a New Wick", Charlie has only been blind-sided by a break-up once, a devastating incident since he is the love-'em-and-leave-'em sort; being dumped is outside of his realm of experience. He rarely considers the feelings of anyone involved when he wants a woman. At one point, Charlie risks a malpractice suit against Alan's divorce lawyer Laura (played by Heather Locklear) while Alan is fighting his ex-wife for custody of their son Jake. For what? To bed her, of course. Then, in the third season, Charlie exploits his eleven-year-old nephew Jake to get closer to Mia, an attractive ballet teacher. Charlie Harper has no compunction when it comes to getting women in the sack. Everything is fair game.

Unfortunately, the audience witnesses the decline of Alan to Charlie's level. In the first season, Alan watches Charlie place Jake's belongings around the house in order to impress and seduce a child-friendly woman. This exchange follows:

ALAN: You know, Charlie, if you took half the energy you put into manipulating casual sexual

150

encounters and used it to actually build a relationship, you'd be a lot happier.

CHARLIE: Hard to imagine.

Fast forward to 2011. In the ninth season opener, Charlie Harper has died. His beach house, left to his brother Alan, is mortgaged thrice over and Alan can't even pay the property taxes. They have to sell it. Here is where Ashton Kutcher is introduced as Walden Schmidt, a techie billionaire swiftly inserted into the Charlie Harper slot in the hopes that he will deftly fill the "stupid guy" role. However, Walden is broken-hearted. He's woefully still in love with his wife and high school sweetheart Bridget who is seeking a divorce. He stumbles into the late Charlie Harper's beach house after being kicked out of his own. Does this scenario sound familiar?

Walden is not Charlie. In fact, he is nothing like him. In no time, we learn that Walden doesn't care for alcohol and doesn't watch porn. Instead he wants to learn to bake. He is sensitive, faithful, and somewhat effeminate. While Charlie drank excessively to deal with his family problems, Walden admits that his parents' divorce made him angry, but he converted that anger into a passion for computer programming. Charlie Harper took the destructive path, the path of the "stupid guy", while Walden channelled his energy into something more constructive, in the typical "smart guy" fashion.

Role reversal aside, someone has to be the "stupid guy." So, the roles switch for two: Once Felix, Alan now becomes piggish Oscar, and Walden is instead a diluted version of Felix, a pseudo-Felix if you will. This is Alan's progress, if we dare refer to this development as progress. Prior to Walden, Alan was reduced to a schlubby divorced dad. Without the diminishing effect from Charlie's presence, though, Alan can evolve (or, more accurately, devolve) into a carefree dude and move on. Walden buys the beach house in a desperate need for the love offered by Alan who, despite financial dependency upon his new roommate, manages to oftentimes look down upon Walden. That's right: The "stupid guy" looks down upon the "smart guy."

It's not unrealistic for Walden to accept the role as resident smarty-pants. He is a twenty-first-century kind of guy, tech-savvy in a technological world. It's a natural progression that the "stupid guy" Charlie Harper, a songwriter for television commercials, is replaced by a "smart guy", Walden, a web-based entrepreneur. This is, in essence, art imitating life as the world evolves around *Two and a Half Men*. The series is forced to follow in order to stick with the times. It is no more evident than in the ninth season episode, "The War Against Gingivitis", in which Alan fails to recall his password and is baffled when Walden graciously walks him through a routine password reset. Keep in mind this was once the self-reliant man who insisted on fixing the satellite himself in the third season premiere.

Enter Jake, the so-called half-man and an interesting element in the shifting dynamics of the so-called "smart" and "stupid" guys. In the presence of his son who always imitated and worshipped his uncle Charlie, Alan loses his status as the laidback Oscar-type. He must accept responsibility and, to do so, he must revert to neuroticism, morphing into his Felix persona. He's forced back into the role of the "smart guy", the geeky dweeb picked upon by the "stupid guy", who oddly enough is Jake Harper, a diminutive version of Charlie Harper. He shrinks back to his original form in his brother's shadow. Like the schoolyard bully, he forces the geek to compromise his dignity. Alan is therefore not a full-blown "stupid guy" if he can bounce back and forth with such ease. In fact, these changes show off an interesting aspect of *The Odd Couple* dynamic that Lorre imitates. The character of Jake makes stupidity, and thus the opposite side of the coin, intelligence, entirely relative. Everything is circumstantial.

The question remains, though, whether it is better to be "smart" or "stupid" in Lorre Land. Will you receive more success as a dummy? Will it be the right kind of success? In a ninth season episode, Alan's reading material consists of *How To Hypnotize Women And Make Them Your Slaves* and *Ten Minutes a Day to Incredible Wealth*, thus implying that Alan's definition of success is strictly in terms of money and loose women, particularly lots of both. Monogamy is no longer what Alan desires, not as a "stupid guy." As the series progresses, success seems to be hinged not as much on financial gains, but rather achieving a supportive and loving relationship, one that offers fulfilment like no other area of their life.

However, relationships grow even more complicated when observed as a dichotomy between the "smart" and the "stupid." The uptight former has always been paired with the laidback latter to showcase how neuroticism destroys one's sociability. Seemingly, the "smart guy" is just terrible with women. They have no aptitude for it. Meanwhile, the "stupid guy" loses any sense of sentimentality and proceeds to care less and less about others, leading the masses to be inextricably drawn to them. It's counterintuitive. By not giving a hoot about others, one attracts others. There's a sense of selfishness attached to this blasé attitude of self-fulfilment. You only care enough to not make your own life suck. Don't piss off the people that matter; don't engage anyone longer than you must. In exchange, take what you want when you'd like. And that includes women.

The once positive outlook towards relationships that Alan blasted at his brother Charlie has vanished. Alan is a self-interested pessimist now. When Walden asks for advice, Alan parlays a bit of truth-telling into living rent-free. Charlie saw his brother as a burden, not a buddy, in the second season premiere, and this relationship is mirrored with Alan and Walden. Funnily, Alan often implies Walden as the burden. Alan impedes Walden's relationship with his girlfriend Zoey and feigns a second heart attack (after suffering a real one) in a desperate attempt to stay in the beach house. He literally preys on Walden's social good will and views Walden's happiness with Zoey as a burden to his own happiness. Alan explicitly states that he can exploit Walden's guilt and determines that Zoey (who sees through Alan's tactics) has to go. He doesn't look out for his so-called buddy Walden; Alan is out for himself. As for women, Alan scams on them every which way, while Walden is the one who wants a long-term commitment. In contrast, Walden worries about the sexual needs of the woman with whom he is besotted. He even frets over a premature 'I love you' (his, of course, not hers). Walden declares, "I want to be in a relationship, with romance and intimacy and commitment." This man is no Charlie Harper.

Meanwhile, in "Frodo's Headshots", a ninth season episode, Alan literally thinks he is Charlie Harper, imitating him in both dress and behaviour. It's an in-your-face plotline that highlights all of the aforementioned changes in *The Odd Couple* dynamic. To say the least, Alan no longer cares. Alan admits to his girlfriend Lyndsey's face that, until she agreed to do a threesome with him, he "didn't care if [she] lived or died." Again, Walden is the opposite, as aforementioned, and remains unrewarded for his efforts.

The only person who seems to love the "smart guy" is his mother. In one sixth season episode, Evelyn Harper (played by Holland Taylor), Charlie and Alan's mother, raises her glass in a toast to her younger son on his birthday. "You were always the good son," she says to Alan. "Of course, your brother didn't set the bar very high." Yes, it seems the "smart guy" is always mommy's favourite, while the "stupid guy" is treated with disdain. Alas, as the series goes on and Alan becomes the "stupid guy" and Walden "the smart guy", Evelyn Harper's attitude changes. By the ninth season, upon hearing from Walden that Alan suffered a heart attack, Evelyn proclaims, "I don't know what I would do if anything happened to him. I've already lost my good son." Evelyn even has, as she puts it, "carnal designs" for Walden. Walden, the new "smart guy", is adored not just by Alan's mother but his own, too. Walden's mother Robin affectionately refers to Walden as her "brilliant son." Robin takes such an interest in Walden that he's forced to lie about the collapse of his relationship. Upon hearing of the split, Robin worries about Walden and suggests an intervention. This isn't the first time Chuck Lorre has shown this relationship, the "smart guy" beloved by his mother alone.

Before Chuck Lorre involved women in the plot of his hit show *The Big Bang Theory*, Sheldon and Leonard were Alan and Charlie equivalents, respectively. In the hyper-intellectualized world in which Leonard and Sheldon live, Leonard is, for lack of a better word, the "stupid guy." Sheldon openly mocks Leonard's Princeton education, implying its inferiority, while Leonard refers to Sheldon as "the smartest person I've ever met." Sheldon himself knows just how clever he is. He self-proclaims that he has "the kind of mind that comes along once, maybe twice in a generation." It's easy to see that, in this pairing, Leonard is "stupid" and Sheldon is "smart."

As such, the same pattern emerges. There are the little things. For example, Felix honks his nasal passages to fix his "sinus condition", reflected in the hypochondriac Sheldon. When Felix first shows up on Oscar's doorstep, he tells him how he can't sleep until he tidies the place up a bit; Sheldon is similarly a clean freak, breaking into his neighbour's apartment in the middle of the night to dust, polish, fold, and organize. More importantly, though, the male-female interaction dynamics are identical. Just as Charlie was beloved by babes in spite of his bad behaviour, so too is Leonard. Over the course of four seasons, Leonard beds at least seven women, including his neighbour Penny, North Korean spy Joyce Kim, physician Stephanie Barnett, cosmological physicist Elizabeth Plimpton, attorney Priya Koothrappali, wealthy widow Mrs. Latham, and fellow colleague and physicist Leslie

Winkle (twice – once in the first season and a confirmed second "booty call" in the second season). He even manipulates his girlfriend into watching the movies he likes and having sex with him at work by playing on her sympathies in the seventh season.

Meanwhile, Sheldon, the "smart guy", admits that he doesn't "know the first thing about women." To describe Sheldon's romantic status as complicated is a gross understatement. When his neighbour Penny asks about his sexual orientation, she learns that his social circle only ever considered that "he has no deal", that he's a strictly asexual being. His only relationship is with Amy Farrah Fowler, a neurobiologist with whom Sheldon shares a companionate and passionless dynamic, one with little to no physical intimacy.

At least, though, Sheldon is intensely adored by his mother, Mary Cooper. She takes a healthy interest in Sheldon without becoming overbearing or judgmental. She asks Sheldon to go with her on a Christian cruise in the fifth season, which is further evidence that she likes spending time with her son. (Spoiler alert: He doesn't go with her.) She handles his idiosyncrasies and instils in him a sense of manners and social customs, proving she is one of the few people who could get through to him when it comes to interpersonal interaction. In the first season, Mary rushes to Sheldon's side to help his recovery after getting fired. Then, again in the third season, after experiencing personal betrayal and professional humiliation, Sheldon runs back to his mother in Texas where she welcomes and feeds her son a home-cooked meal while encouraging him to talk out his problems. She even invites over his friends to facilitate this communication. In spite of her devout religious beliefs, she still tries to relate to everybody, no matter quirk or creed.

Unfortunately, Leonard's mother Dr. Beverly Hofstadter isn't so affectionate. Leonard reveals that Beverly wrote a book about him called *The Disappointing Child*, full of observations from when she subjected a young Leonard to social experiments that scarred him for life. For example, Beverly performed electroencephalograms on her son as he potty-trained. She also refused to celebrate Leonard's birthday because "being expelled from a birth canal was not considered [an achievement]." And it's not just how she used to treat him. She maintains this arctic demeanour with her adult son. She voices how unimpressed she is with Leonard's professional work. Her constant derision during her visits sends Leonard down a booze-addled road of self-medication. Beverly even prefers communicating with Sheldon over her own son. While Sheldon's mother Mary couldn't care less about science and infuses her son with love, Leonard's mother Beverly has a cold detachment when dealing with her son, a former test subject in her eyes. If he was only a little bit smarter, a little bit more Sheldon-esque, maybe she'd love him.

Two and a Half Men's Charlie shares the same complications with his mother. As much as Evelyn Harper frowns upon her son Charlie, he reciprocates, referring to Evelyn as a "toxic she-devil." Charlie has deep-seated issues with his mother. When he becomes romantically entangled with a woman decades his senior, Angie, both he and his brother Alan compete for her attention, just as the two did as children for Evelyn's attention. Charlie's psychiatrist (played by Jane Lynch) insists that his problems stem from the emotional deprivation from his mother in his formative years, but Charlie points to Alan as "the needy one," once again deflecting the negative attention. Despite the intellectuality that marks their counterpart, the "stupid guy" finds a way to assert his superiority somehow.

Despite all of their positive traits, the "smart guy" still idolizes the "stupid guy" for having the one thing they can't: the love of another. In the tenth season premiere, Walden begs for the reciprocation of love from his significant other. "Saying yes to someone who loves you more than life itself," Walden declares, "is not complicated." She denies him, leaving him broken-hearted. The idolization of the other guy, the "stupid guy", who lives without care of love is near inevitable. This is a mistake, though, for love is a two-way street. The "smart guy" knows this deep down, buried below the never-ending rejection. The "stupid" ones are adored and lusted after, but they aren't capable of sustaining healthy romantic relationships. Evelyn Harper looks comparatively at her two sons and determines that Alan "at least aspires to normalcy, tries to have meaningful relationships with women." Rose offers Charlie Harper the unconditional love so desired by a "smart guy", but it remains unrequited. The lives of "stupid guys" are deprived yet satiated by other excesses. Just as Felix admired the view from Oscar's apartment twelve floors up, so does Alan, looking out at the beach vista from Charlie's porch. But where does this kind of life lead? It leads to getting pushed in front of a Parisian train.

Before piano-playing Charlie and cello-playing Leonard, Chuck Lorre created another show back in the nineties called *Cybill*. Unlike *The Big*

Bang Theory and *Two and a Half Men*, *Cybill*'s American television ratings in its four-season run never broke into the top twenty. Yet, Lorre stayed true to his formula from the get-go. Look no further than protagonist Cybill's two ex-husbands. Her first ex-husband, Jeff, is a baseball-cap wearing Hollywood stuntman who "gets thrown from a speeding train with [his] head on fire" for a living. He's a bit of a laissez-faire wild thing. If that doesn't sound like Oscar, I don't know what does. After Jeff comes Ira, Cybill's nerdy second ex-husband, a man who is desperate for his ex-wife to take him back. I hear echoes of Walden and early-series Alan Harper, our true-blue Felix fill-ins. These two drastically different ex-husbands, a major focal point of *Cybill*, are juxtaposed intentionally, a real odd couple.

Let's take a brief moment to examine how timeless the idea of an odd couple is. These men are down and out, not exactly living ideal lives. They wanted different things and led different lives which shaped their different personalities; neither got their wishes and now they're lumped together, the same but different. What does that say about the American dream? If Guy A can do everything right and Guy B can do everything wrong and both of them end up in the same circumstances, the purveyors of manifest destiny have been fibbing. Through pursuit of their own individual versions of happiness, their paths have crumbled and met at a conjunction that was never part of their plan. The same applied in 1968, the year of the original *Odd Couple*, as it does in the here and now, pertaining to the sitcom gold of the twenty-first century. It's time to call a spade a spade and a sham a sham. Our hearts may believe in the rags-to-riches romanticism, but in the Lorre world, it so often goes the other way. The American dream has become the American nightmare.

One final thought: Why exactly are these shows centered on men? Why are women pushed into the background, sometimes as set dressing and other times as weapons? It isn't because they can't write women well. No, it all comes back to Felix and Oscar, the crown princes of Lorre Land. In the presence of a woman, there can be no "smart" one and "stupid" one. All women become Felix, more pensive and cerebral than their Y-chromosome-possessing compatriots. (This is not necessarily reality, mind you; rather it's the law of Lorre Land.) Bombshells leave these men picking their jaws up off the floor. Shrews leave them cowering in the corner. As Charlie's girlfriend Michelle describes it, "You love her and yet she scares you." One way or another, the men become goobering idiots in their presence. In the end, gals cannot be part of Lorre's lore. Their interactions don't follow the rules of his Neil Simon-penned bible: *The Odd Couple*.

A Blue-Collar Blue Ribbon:

Why Roseanne is The Best TV Mom

Parenting has become a thing. There are a seemingly infinite number of schools of thought on how to raise your children, differing on an equally infinite number of issues. Everybody is sure their way is the right way. But this is all conjecture. No one knows for certain what to do. A child comes with no definitive instruction manual.

For eons, television has been infiltrated with the nuclear family. We've built our expectations of what home life should be from these depictions. As such, one of the most timeless and socially recognized characters is the TV mom. Mothers on television have been a mainstay, but their role has changed throughout the years. Television mothers used to be seen and not heard, wearing pearls and smiles. But slowly reality seeped into TV programming and the mothers became increasingly rushed off their feet, trying and often failing to do it all. In that line of thinking, it is easy to see that happy housewives, June Cleaver of *Leave It To Beaver*; Laura Petrie of *The Dick Van Dyke Show*; and Carol Brady of *The Brady Bunch* don't compare to grown-up hippie Elyse Keaton of *Family Ties*; oblivious single mom Joyce Summers of *Buffy the Vampire Slayer*; and the nineties mama with the blue beehive and the furrowed brow, Marge Simpson. The progress continued with increasingly realistic depictions, like Debra Barone of *Everybody Loves Raymond* (what TV mom hates her in-laws more?) and Claire Dunphy of *Modern Family*. The TV mom is always evolving and will likely continue to evolve.

None of these women can compete, though, with Roseanne Conner. Voted upon by more than a million Americans, ABC News and People Magazine declared Clair Huxtable their favourite TV mom just two years ago. June Cleaver, Carol Brady, and the intrusive Marie Barone were inexplicably runners-up. *Au contraire*, folks: Roseanne may have not received the votes but she is better than Carol, June, Clair, and all the rest of those classic clean-cut mothers and the raunchier newbies, too. The simple fact is that, unlike *The Brady Bunch* or *The Cosby Show*, *Roseanne* was based in reality.

According to a 2010 survey conducted by the Pew Research Center, the majority of Americans identify as members of the middle class. The middle class family is one that encourages education for their children and believes in the values of home ownership and job and retirement security. *Roseanne* centered on the Conner family, a middle class bunch that dealt with matters the way the middle class would. Roseanne Conner wasn't able to press a button and have dinner appear like Jane Jetson.

And she wasn't living the upper-middle class life of the Huxtables. According to the wage indexing series published by the U.S. Social Security Administration, one would earn on average $19,334.04 in 1988. Compare then, the cost of homes. Everybody needs a place to live. The cost to buy a house in Chicago in 1980 was $65,000. Construction on a few vacant lots provided new houses in the city, but most new residences cropped up in the suburbs. So, that's where Roseanne went. Her family lived in the suburbs of Chicago where housing was cheaper and thus more affordable, a middle-class attitude shared by many in the same financial position. Meanwhile, Brooklyn, New York, offered a higher price tag than something more Midwestern. By 1980, the cost of a new home in northeastern United States was $69,000. The New York housing market boomed throughout the eighties. Half of Brooklyn saw prices triple and then some. Even during the downturn of the early nineties, Brooklyn fared well, experiencing smaller decreases than other New York boroughs and the rest of the country. Most middle-class people simply could not afford to live in a brownstone in New York.

Clearly, the Huxtables weren't living the average lifestyle, financially speaking. Cliff Huxtable is described as a doctor who "makes a tremendous amount of money" and that income is supplemented greatly by Clair Huxtable's profession as a lawyer. The firm even makes Clair a partner, to boot. I can't imagine they ever struggle with a budget. When times got rough for the Conner family, though, they had to make sacrifices. They take out a second mortgage to buy a motorcycle shop, which goes under during the recession. They're left jobless, months late paying two mortgages on one house depreciating in value but gathering interest nonetheless. They usually have no job security, unemployed on and off throughout the series. Everybody they know is "just getting by." Out of work but not out of ideas, Roseanne, her sister, and their friend decide to pool their funds and go into business together. Without experience or collateral, they're unable to get a start-up loan to fund their restaurant. Roseanne has to fall on her sword and turn to her judgmental mother who will only give her daughters the money if she can become a silent partner. What else can they do but accept? In the interim, they choose to pay the water bill and lose their electricity because they can't afford both. This is a family that saw their fair share of final notices. The Huxtables never did. Not everyone can live the Cosby lifestyle. Giving children a financial education is vital. Mothers need to teach their sons and daughters the value of a dime or otherwise risk sending them hurdling face-forward into a mountain of debt.

But it's not just who you are and where you live but what you do that makes you a truly great TV mom. Let's take the time machine and warp back to the seventies when *The Brady Bunch* epitomized the happy family. The bubbly blonde TV mom portrayed by Florence Henderson was far from ideal, though. No, Carol Brady didn't know her ass from her head. When her youngest child, Cindy, comes home visibly upset, Carol doesn't recognize that anything's wrong. Her inattentiveness to her child continues throughout the day. She doesn't even ask Cindy her troubles until her eldest daughter, Marcia, spells it out to her at dinner. Then, when her stepson, Peter, is bullied at school, Carol encourages Peter to punch him if necessary, rather than alerting a trusted adult on school premises, like a teacher or schoolyard guard. She completely bypasses this option as if it doesn't exist. But the most obvious fault I can find in Carol Brady is that her children don't trust her much. In a different episode, Carol's eldest stepson, Greg, succumbs to peer pressure, smoking with three other boys in a rock band. Upon learning of this bad behaviour, Marcia feels more comfortable divulging her secret to Alice, the housemaid and cook, than her mother. Then, in another episode, Carol is fully aware that Marcia has fallen in love, but when Marcia finds that her crush isn't interested, Carol sits idly by eating pot roast while Alice gives the advice and dabs the tears. The facts are in: Alice the maid acts as a better mother than Carol does.

And this isn't the first mother who's been snubbed by her children. Perpetually vacuuming in pearls, Barbara Billingsley personified the classic perfect mother stereotype as June Cleaver in *Leave It to Beaver*, but June found in the first few episodes of the series that her youngest son, Theodore "Beaver" Cleaver, is afraid of her. When Beaver's new teacher Miss Canfield gives him a note for his parents to read, Beaver concludes that he's been expelled from second grade. Instead of passing the note on, he falsifies her signature on a forged note saying that his parents have "whipped him", a suitable punishment for expulsion. Little does he know that it's a request that Beaver perform in the fire prevention pageant. When his mother agrees to a parent/teacher meeting to sort out the confusion, Beaver skips school and scrounges together change in an attempt to take a trip somewhere far-flung, like Mexico. In another episode, Beaver loses $1.75 given for him to visit the barbershop. Without the money, he is unable to get his hair cut before the Christmas play, so he asks his brother Wally to give him a haircut. When it looks awful, Beaver conceals it beneath a stocking cap. June tells her husband Ward, "It certainly is your fault and mine." She blames herself for frightening her son since Beaver is too scared to tell his mother anything. These episodes are exhibitions of the obvious lack of trust

June's children have in the lady who raised them. Decades later, in *Everybody Loves Raymond*, when Debra Barone discovers that her daughter Ally's failing grade is due to distraction by a boy named Tommy in her math class, it comes to light that Ally confided in Debra's sister-in-law, Amy, about her swoon-worthy crush. In other words, Ally trusted her mother less than she trusted her aunt. June Cleaver and Debra Barone, meet Carol Brady.

Carol Brady is guilty of other lows in television motherhood. When Carol's daughter Marcia learns that her crush loves bugs, Carol encourages her daughter to change who she is, spending time testing her on the names of cicadas and beetles. The only thing Marcia and the object of her affection now have to bond over is insects, which Marcia couldn't care less about. After much pretending on her part, the boy Marcia adores asks her to "go steady", but Carol tells Marcia that she must first ask her husband and Marcia's stepfather, Mike, for permission. That's right; Carol Brady needs not to consult but to ask Mike for permission on how to raise her own daughter. Clearly, Mike rules the roost and Carol allows it, which instils anti-feminist notions in her impressionable daughters' minds, not to mention those of her stepsons who already isolate themselves to talk "man's business." For shame, Carol.

Fast forward to *The Wonder Years*, in which the protagonist Kevin's mother is Norma Arnold. Norma exemplifies the typical sixties housewife, especially in how she deals with grief through food, cooking the perfect ham and moulding the perfect gelatin dessert. As a TV mom, Norma caters to her husband over her children, asking them to keep "the equilibrium" by trying to not make their stressed father "crazy." She is more a wife than a mother. When her son gets in trouble, she doesn't defend him, opting to take the other side, the one that is scolding him no matter whether or not he can justify what he did. She doesn't give Kevin the slightest chance to explain his actions. Even Carol Brady believes her stepson, Greg, when he says he doesn't smoke, which is a far worse offense than Kevin's sassy mouth. In fact, mouthy adolescents are actually found to be those who show a greater probability of rejecting peer pressure. That sassiness is a show of responsibility and independence. As long as they feel they have their parental support network, teenaged sassiness is an indication of good things, not bad. All three of Roseanne's children are sassy, always quick with a witty comeback, further evidence of a warm and secure upbringing. Furthermore, joking with children helps set them up for social success. It encourages creativity, sociability, and stress management skills. Being stiff, stern, and serious is way worse than having a laugh with the kids. And Roseanne sure gave everyone the giggles.

Part of what we love about TV moms is their unique connection to their young children. It tends to pull on the heartstrings. But what happens when the children go to kindergarten? What can be done when they go to their first slumber party? And worst of all, where do you turn when they decide to leave the nest? Will this precious connection be irreparably severed? In an early episode of *The Dick Van Dyke Show* entitled "The Sick Boy and the Sitter", Laura Petrie starts off on the right track as a calm and collected mother caring for her son who has a slight fever. However, Laura swiftly becomes agitated when her husband, Rob, insists that she attend a work party with him; she's hesitant to leave the little tyke with a temperature under the care of a fifteen-year-old babysitter. She starts off with a reasonable level of fretting, but when Rob convinces her to leave against her better judgment, she becomes an overprotective worry-wart, going over every last detail with the babysitter until her husband lifts her up and throws her over his shoulder. And after everything, when she comes home, her son is safe and sound. The reality is that smothering is not mothering. There's a line that Laura crosses that turns her from a good watchful parent to that loathsome helicopter mama. Even modern TV moms, like Gloria Pritchett on *Modern Family*, can become overbearing in their need to protect their children. This mistake can last a child's lifetime. In fact, when children mature and decide to leave, parents should let them go. Overprotective parents create anxiety and fear of new experiences in their children. In the sixth season of *Roseanne*, Roseanne shows her chops as a mother as she decides to let go of her second-born, Darlene. Roseanne lets Darlene leave home for art school before she's seventeen because Roseanne knows that, not only is art her daughter's calling, but also that Darlene's ready to fly the coop. Roseanne is a good mother, raising her daughter right until it's time to let her go into the world on her own.

What makes a TV mom better is the presence and actions of the underpublicized TV dad. Ideally, families should co-parent with a division of labour, not just of child-rearing duties but all household chores. If both parents contribute in some respect, then both parents can be the best they can be with neither burned out by their individual workload. In *The Dick Van Dyke Show*,

Rob Petrie spends countless late nights working close to a beautiful actress and his wife, Laura, grows jealous. She also has an endless series of errands to match her cluttered mind that's ill at ease. Eventually, their son begins to ask questions, too, asking if this actress is "more beautiful than Mommy." The cheating rumours may disappear by the end of the episode, but Laura just goes home and does it all without Rob picking up the slack. The same goes in reverse, too, when Laura gets a job dancing. Rob who never does his share of the housework is thrust into the role of primary caregiver, forcing him to cook and do laundry, both of which are foreign. His homemaking skills are noticeably inferior to Laura's. For example, his son yearns for "regular food" and complains that his mother's bananas are better than his father's. Meanwhile, Laura comes home late and exhausted. She doesn't help out with the house and, more importantly, she doesn't see her child. Some fathers have no interest in helping out their wives, as is the case with Debra's husband, Ray Barone, on *Everybody Loves Raymond*. After complaining about reading a book to his sleepy children, Ray gets a dressing down from his brother, Robert. Robert tells Ray that he's unwilling to co-parent with poor put-upon Debra because Ray's relationship with his own father is best described as "strained." Through no fault of her own, Debra has to suffer, running around and doing it all for her kids at a mediocre level, rather than sharing half the work with her husband and being at her absolute best. And it's not just her children but the entire family that burdens Debra alone. In the sixth season, Debra's young son, Michael, writes his own story, but the entire family is insulted and humiliated when Michael weaves an unhappy tale entitled "The Angry Family." At first, Debra compares herself to those around her and decides that they are "a normal family, comparatively." But during her conference with Michael's teacher, Debra breaks down and tells her that she is "in no position to judge" as she doesn't have to deal with the "truckload of their insane family dreck." With a husband who never supports her and refuses to accept some responsibility of domestic life, Debra is on the verge of a nervous collapse. Even the much-admired Clair Huxtable of *The Cosby Show* felt harried. She worked the second shift when she came home from work at the law firm to a house where "people are crying" and "somebody's drinking bubble bath." Co-parenting was attainable here, too, but Cliff simply didn't cater to the children's individual needs as Clair did. Instead he made jokes and kept them each in one piece; occasionally, he would even cook. Beyond that, Clair was on her own. To some TV moms, accepting all parental responsibility has become the norm. In the pilot episode of *Modern Family*, Claire Dunphy, mother of three and wife of sixteen years, proclaims that she's "done our job"; she says this as she sits beside her husband, Phil, who isn't responsible because he aims to be "the cool dad", memorizing the soundtrack to *High School Musical* to relate to his children. He struggles to discipline his children and Claire frequently becomes fed-up of being the "bad cop", but co-parenting is a two-person job and Phil is unwilling to be seen as anything other than his kids' friend. Then, on shows like *Buffy the Vampire Slayer*, in which the TV mom is a divorcée, co-parenting becomes nearly impossible. For single lady Joyce Summers, no one helped her out when

Buffy got out of hand. She remained blissfully unaware of her daughter's position as a vampire slayer for several seasons, probably too busy keeping the house tidy to actually parent her teenage daughter. Cut to *Roseanne*. As the matriarch to be reckoned with, Roseanne emphasizes the significance of co-parenting to her husband Dan, asking him to do his part rather than tiring herself out doing all of the childcare. Both Dan and Roseanne had jobs. Neither could do it all without the help of the other. Again, co-parenting is better for the children as it not only improves the interrelationships and dynamics within the family but also because neither parent is overworked in respect to their kids and thus Roseanne and Dan can both bring more of themselves to each of their three children, Becky, Darlene, and DJ.

So far we've seen a checklist of what Roseanne doesn't do compared to the behaviour of her fellow mothers of the small screen. What about what she does all by herself? In the series pilot, "Life and Stuff", Roseanne exhibits her maternal strengths. She teaches autonomy to her daughter, Darlene, by encouraging her to find her own textbook and deliver school correspondence on her own, something children should manage to do independently. She also teaches her children the value of a dollar and respect for their belongings. When her eldest, Becky, complains about her schoolbag, Roseanne jokes that she'll be using it until she's thirty. Miffed as Becky is, Roseanne's teaching her children not to be wasteful, something needed more than ever in the nation responsible for the greatest waste generation in the world.

Roseanne's not done, though. In the pilot alone, she also shows that she addresses issues if they're ongoing, not the passing problems typical of growth and development. When Darlene's history teacher points out her childish ruckus as an example of "an aggressive manifestation of a deeper internal problem", Roseanne brushes it off. Sometimes it's just a kid being a kid.

But what if it isn't? What if it's something more? Well, she's able to distinguish that, too. In a fourth season episode, Darlene falls into a depression. It's more than just adolescent doldrums. It's more serious and Roseanne identifies that before anyone else does. Darlene quits her extracurricular activities and mopes on the couch. She gives monosyllabic responses and refuses to socialize. "She just isn't into anything," Roseanne remarks. As a mother, she addresses it, asking without interrogating. Darlene wants to be left alone to contemplate matters, so Roseanne decides that they as a family should observe and support her but not meddle. Simply put, Roseanne knows her children. She takes note of their interests and can distinguish their personalities. She moves with ease from teasing her popularity-obsessed eldest daughter over her excessive phone usage to calming her injured middle child by painting a mental image of the demolition derby. Adjusting parenting techniques to suit individual children was confirmed as the best method of child-rearing by the Journal of Abnormal Child Psychology in 2011. Every child is unique, and thus, parenting should be, too. Roseanne knows who they are and lets them become their own people. Roseanne shapes not who they are but how they act, focusing on courtesy and hard work, not pretension and fitting the mould.

That being said, respect is important. There's a difference between playfulness and waywardness. A good TV mother knows where to draw the line. Early in the ninth season of *Everybody Loves Raymond*, Debra's thirteen-year-old daughter, Ally, is respectful and obedient to her father, Ray, but not so to her mother. When Ally receives an F in Mr. Putnam's math class on her otherwise pristine report card, Debra becomes concerned about her daughter's lack of respect. Her mother-in-law, Marie, tells Debra that "you can't expect to impose discipline on children that have never had any," implying that Debra never gave Ally consequences. Two seasons earlier, when Debra tells her twin boys to clean their room, Michael and Geoffrey ignore her and look to their more lenient father to get them out of it. This exemplifies the lack of respect all three of Debra Barone's children have for her.

And she's not without company as an unheard mother. Laura Petrie of *The Dick Van Dyke Show* again fails in this regard. Rob and Laura's son, Richie, never listens to his mother's instructions. She tells Richie to turn down the television. He doesn't listen. She tells Richie not to touch the hors d'oeuvres. He doesn't listen. But being the happy housewife, Laura never raises her voice. Instead, she looks to her husband, asking him "to do something" when their son disobeys her. And as time marched on, TV moms still lacked the chutzpah to tell their kids off. No, they would bend and ask their husbands to do it. Nearly a decade after Laura Petrie first graced the small screen, Edith Bunker of *All in the Family* appeared, still asking her husband to do her thinking and disciplining for her. It's called self-respect, dingbat.

Let Roseanne show you how it's done, Edith. Roseanne didn't have a problem being the

bad cop. When she needed to reprimand her
children for bad behaviour, Roseanne didn't use
cheap tactics. Dan, her husband, made a fool of
himself, describing frightening scenarios that have
no effect whatsoever. When Darlene was caught in
a white lie and her dad waxed on about how liars
lead a lonely and desolate existence, even Roseanne
dismissed it. Instead, the matriarch reminds her
children why it's wrong, which instils values in
them far more than fear-mongering ever could.

She's a reasonable TV mother, too. Facing
an early bedtime, Darlene tries to buy more time,
arguing that her friends get to stay up later than she.
Roseanne doesn't budge, enforcing the idea that
doing what your peers do isn't necessarily the best
thing for you. She reckons with each of her
children's debates and suggestions on an individual
basis. If she thought Darlene could handle it, she
would ease off. That's not speculation. In the next
episode, Roseanne accepts change when her
daughter, Becky, asks to babysit. At thirteen, Becky
feels she's old enough, citing her friend, Cindy
Clark, who has babysat since she was nine. At first,
Roseanne is hesitant and wants her sister Jackie
watching the children, but after deliberating and
concluding that Becky is mature and responsible
enough to handle the job, she agrees to a half-night
trial, with their Aunt Jackie showing up an hour or
so later.

Compare to the lady voted the most admired
and respected mother by the Mother's Union in
Britain (she received a quarter of the votes, a
landslide win), the iconic blue-haired Marge
Simpson. Marge's daughter, Lisa, asks if she can
babysit. Lisa is clearly not ready. First of all, she's
only eight years old; she still has to stand on a chair

to reach the microwave. "Parents need to be sure their sitter can handle anything that might happen," Marge says. "That's why they hire teenagers." Lisa claims she is responsible, often mistaken for a year older, but she proves inept in emergency situations. But when Marge is offered an opportunity to attend a waterfront party, she'll be damned if she lets a little thing like parental obligation stand in her way. Instead, she wantonly leaves Lisa to watch over her older brother Bart and baby sister Maggie. And what happens while they're gone? Baby Maggie is wired from eating caffeinated ice cream, hanging off the shower rod and playing in talcum powder, while Bart acquires a dislocated shoulder from tumbling headfirst down the stairs. That doesn't include the impromptu bachelor party in her living room and the delivery of a $225 vinegar-drenched submarine sandwich, followed by visits from the paramedics, a military officer addressing a reported UFO sighting, and a limousine driver responding to a call from the Ghanaian ambassador, all of which Bart ordered in a series of crank calls. By the end of the night, Lisa puts her restless sister in a pet carrier and her injured brother in a wheelbarrow to transport them to a second-rate doctor. This entire incident could easily be avoided if Marge had hired a reputable babysitter or at least phoned to check in.

And that's not Marge's first faux pas. Four seasons earlier, when her husband, Homer, decides not to attend church on Sunday, Marge becomes concerned. Homer says he sees no point in dragging himself out of bed to be told all the ways he may go to Hell. Homer feels he is a good person and connects to God in his own way, but, for Marge, that is not enough. She intends to "raise these children right" and feels their father is a bad influence if he expresses his religiosity inwardly rather than attending a place of worship. For not living in accordance with a religion, Marge tells the kids that their father is "wicked." This label sends the message that a godless person is a bad person, a horribly intolerant idea that damages their open-mindedness. And it's not as if Homer's attendance at church has had any substantial effect on his moral character; he sleeps through the sermons and can't recall any of the scripture or teachings. What does Marge hope her husband will gain by going? More importantly, what does she hope her children will learn?

Children's religious involvement does not translate to good motherhood. Some believe that teaching them some form of faith will have a constructive effect, but I beg to differ on several grounds. For one, the concept of hell and damnation is traumatic to children; the mental damage it causes far outweighs any benefits that religion may play in the lives of youth. And it's not just hell. Ally, Debra Barone's daughter on *Everybody Loves Raymond*, was raised with the idea that we are all God's children and go to heaven when we die, but the implications that we must stop first on earth before we ascend to heaven baffle her. She is left more confused by her religious education than she would have been without it. Then, there is the morality aspect of religion. Morality is being able to discern what is right from what is wrong, not being able to memorize commandments. Being told what is and what is not acceptable means that the child never learns critical thinking skills and is more likely to be swayed by peer pressure, simply because someone told them to do something. Their brain was developed in an environment encouraged to give into the sway of the religious masses; the same tactics can be used to convince someone to smoke, drink, rob, or even kill.

Another unfortunate facet of religion is sexual shame. The dogma of churches, mosques, and other religious institutes overvalue the virgin. Because of their worship of such saintly figures, religious authorities and devout parents tend to teach children to be uncomfortable with sexuality. They create an aura of guilt about normal parts of human growth and development. These functions are healthy, but are treated with such disgust that children become embarrassed of their own bodies. Their self-esteem drops as the majority of children succumb to the emotional impacts of their reprimanding parents.

Even when it made her feel a touch awkward, Roseanne was always sex-positive with her children. Her first daughter, Becky, trusts her mother enough to confide in her about her sexual habits and asks for birth control "just in case." Faced with the alternative, Roseanne realizes, "I can do this," and takes her daughter to visit the gynaecologist for a full examination and a prescription. Jackie, Roseanne's sister, reminds her of the risky sexual behaviour they engaged in when they were teenagers and commends Roseanne for being "such a wonderful, progressive, open-minded mom that she can talk to about that." Ultimately, Roseanne would rather her daughter trust her for information rather than "Johnny Hormone." Then, the middle-child, Darlene, shows she is comfortable talking about sex with her mother, having a frank discussion about losing one's virginity. Roseanne listens when Darlene speaks and answers her questions honestly. There's no judgment, just

positive communication. Finally, there's
Roseanne's youngest and only son, DJ. She insists
that Darlene hold off on the jokes during his
masturbation phase. She struggles to understand
how her little one who still wears dinosaur pyjamas
can be going through puberty, but she tries to
maintain a sex-positive attitude. She encourages her
husband, Dan, to speak to him, something Dan's
parents never did with their son. Roseanne knows
he'll be more comfortable discussing these matters
with his father, just as their daughters were more
comfortable talking about their periods with their
mother. Roseanne emphasizes the importance not to
"traumatize" him. She wants DJ to know that what
he's doing isn't bad; it's natural. She wants to be a
sex-positive parent, making her son feel that the
lines of communication are open "if he has, you
know, any questions about sex."

But Roseanne stands alone. Norma Arnold
of *The Wonder Years* isn't just reluctant to discuss
sexuality with her children, ranging from her eldest
daughter's choice to purchase birth control to her
youngest son Kevin's choice of reading material.
Upon realizing Kevin is becoming curious about the
birds and the bees, Norma's response is a
combination of rage and embarrassment, thinking
he found the book *Everything You Always Wanted
to Know about Sex but Were Afraid to Ask* in her
personal library. They don't resolve the matter,
choosing to stay mute; in the Arnold household,
there's an unspoken embargo on frank discussions
of sexuality. The same can be said of *The Brady
Bunch* with the word "sex" only being uttered once
in the context that Carol has a problem talking about
it.

Being sex-positive is an important part of being a good mother. Parents want to protect their children and having conversations throughout their life involving sexual topics is key. Responding to questions about sex with a negative attitude creates a wall between children and their parents. Children no longer want to have open discussions with them if the dialogue will be one-sided and full of shame. The trust is gone. No, the fact is, almost all children will eventually participate in some form of sexual activity, so blocking them from understanding about reproduction and sexual rights is detrimental to their growth. Sex talks are not single occasions, but rather an ongoing series of "teachable moments." For this reason, sex-positive parents are available to their kids, ready to listen when they need an ear and ready to answer when they need a voice.

What's the alternative? We're living in a world where there is no medical definition for virginity and yet the emphasis for daughters especially is on protecting and preserving it. Jessica Valenti, author of *The Purity Myth,* explains that "sexual intimacy should be honored and respected, but that it shouldn't be revered at the expense of women's well-being, or seen as such an integral part of female identity that we end up defining ourselves by our sexuality." In other words, a daughter's moral character – it's rarely a son's reputation damaged if he boffs an entire county – is not tied to an intact hymen, and reinforcing such notions is only damaging to her own self-worth.

And just because girls get a lack of flack doesn't mean that boys get off scot-free. No, by all means, boys need to learn about sex just as much as girls. Unfortunately, the characteristics of stereotypical masculinity don't jibe with the vulnerability of learning, especially sex education. To learn, one must first admit that they do not know. Boys trying to be men would rather be considered ignorant than emasculated, rather macho than informed. But there's a great deal of risk when you're unaware. Since boys are often overlooked regarding the sex talk, misogyny is allowed to run rampant. Lack of information breeds ignorance, and so uninformed boys educate themselves and each other when no one with unfiltered and accurate answers arrives to save the day. They need to be told to look at sex as a "joint responsibility", especially in regards to condoms and overall pregnancy prevention. Yes, we must address males as well as females; otherwise, the world is divided on gender lines, sending half the troops one way and the other half another. A sex-positive parent like Roseanne knows that. She insists her son be treated no different than her daughters. Her maternal instincts are keen, even when the conversation may be awkward.

But I digress. Let's return to the idea of a religious upbringing. Only two percent of Americans say that they don't believe in any god. Seventy percent believe in the afterlife; the same portion believes in horoscopes. Half of the U.S. subscribes to the belief that psychic powers exist. Almost one in every three Americans admitted that they believe that the stars and their location in the night sky affect their lives. One in every five Americans is convinced that aliens may be coming for them. As a reader, I'm sure some of these beliefs seem plausible, but most sound ridiculous. And yet these are the religions bestowed upon children.

It doesn't matter whether they're the Judeo-Christian teachings or the mystical leanings of the

New Age movement. Nicholas Humphrey, a secular
humanist who supports open dialogues and debates
on religion, has compared the religious education of
children to body mutilation. He argues that a parent
is forcing a child in both cases to be a different
shape than they would naturally become on their
own, the former deforming the brain and the latter
deforming the body. I won't dare tread so heavily;
instead, I will look to verifiable science. There is
physical evidence of religion and its effects on the
human body. Faith reduces stress, which would be
great news for believers if it weren't actually a
symptom of brain dysfunction. The regions of the
brain that should react to mistakes simply tune out
as religious belief increases. Judgment is impaired;
consequences are no longer comprehended. Since
there's physical evidence of changes in the brain's
frontal lobe, changes that indicate issues with error
awareness, along with a shrivelling of the memory-
processing hippocampus, I don't consider forcing
religion upon developing minds a smart decision.
The TV moms who refer their children to the Bible
for answers may be doing more harm than good.
Roseanne never taught religion to her children.
There was never any need to bring these notions to
her offspring. They were able to think on their own
and needn't pray to fix their woes.

And there we have it. Roseanne does what's
right and doesn't do what's wrong. And above all,
Roseanne would never try to be Carol Brady or
Norma Arnold, Claire Dunphy or Clair Huxtable.
She wouldn't do what I have done here, detailing
the differences between her and other matriarchs.
Comparing yourself to other parents and striving for
impossibly perfect standards of childcare is a major
no-no. The best mothers do their best and go to the

beat of their own drum. It reduces stress and builds self-esteem, making one a better parent than if one kowtowed to the pressures of other mothers. No, Roseanne would always be Roseanne, the best damn mom on television, no home-baked pies or pearl necklaces required.

T-Rex Infested Waters:

The Synonymy of *Jaws* and *Jurassic Park*

I loved both *Jurassic Park* and *Jaws* as a kid and still do today. I was introduced to *Jaws* through my mother, an avid fan, but like every kid my age, I saw *Jurassic Park* because it was the thing to see. I could see in my parents' eyes the same excitement watching *Jaws* as I had watching *Jurassic Park*. It was identical, the thrill at watching something so intricately part of who we were. When someone walked heavily past the dinner table and my water glass trembled from the impact, I was instantly taken back to *Jurassic Park*. And I'm sure my mother questioned how safe it was to get back into the water after *Jaws*. A generation apart but the connection is the exact same.

The nature of the "beast" is similar in both films. The monsters are vicious products of nature, albeit science plays a role in breeding lost species in *Jurassic Park*. They aren't merely vicious, though; they're smart. "They're extremely intelligent," game warden Robert Muldoon explains of the raptors. "When she looks at you, you can see she's working things out." He adds that, although the fences are electrified as a safety precaution, the raptors cleverly tested different areas of the fences for weaknesses and recalled which areas they'd attacked and which they hadn't. Although there is far less observation of the shark in *Jaws*, the same can be said of it. The shark is clever, trying to flip the boat and rarely falling for the usual tricks. It almost manages to outwit three grown men, one of which is an experienced shark killer.

Speaking of which, there's something to be said about the people in both of these films, but before all else, we must know where our cast of characters are. Both films are set in family-friendly tourist locales; *Jaws* unravels in the beachside town of Amity and *Jurassic Park* is the dinosaur-filled theme park on Isla Nublar, an island 120 miles west of Costa Rica. Both films open with an attack where you don't see the monster. It is left to the audience's imagination what horrific creature is behind the curtain. In *Jaws*, police chief Brody wants to close down the beaches during Independence Day after a girl is killed by a shark, but the mayor is hungry for tourism and its resulting cash flow into Amity and convinces Chief Brody not to do so. In *Jurassic Park*, the theme park owner, John Hammond, cannot legally open Jurassic Park without the approval of the lawyer representing the park's investors. In order to get that approval, he drags a group of experts over to the island to observe the park and essentially give their consent to its opening. It is "a serious investigation of the stability of the island", which owner John Hammond insists is safe, even after the initial dinosaur attack that kills one of his employees.

So, we'll return to that earlier question: Who are these people? And do they have anything in common? I'll answer the second question first with an unequivocal yes. Despite the differing titles, the characters going after the "beast" in *Jaws* and *Jurassic Park* are virtually identical. In *Jaws*, Quint is a professional shark hunter, rough and ready, and Matt Hooper is a by-the-book intellectual specialized in marine biology. In *Jurassic Park*, abrasive palaeontologist Dr. Alan Grant is an intellectual absorbed in his field, much like *Jaws*'s Matt Hooper, while the Quint equivalent is a combination of two characters in *Jurassic Park*: The ever-eccentric chaos theorist Dr. Ian Malcolm shows the unconventional side of Quint, the side that gets Quint laughed out of town, and the friendly and enthusiastic palaeobotanist Dr. Ellie Sattler mirrors Quint's tenacity.

The protagonists of both films – Dr. Alan Grant in *Jurassic Park* and Chief Brody in *Jaws* – show a complex relationship with children. Brody is a father but he spends only short bursts of time with his children as he's preoccupied with protecting the town as sheriff. When a child dies in Amity, Chief Brody is to blame. He does have a soft spot, though, for his sons, asking the youngest for a kiss "because [he] needs it." Meanwhile, Dr. Alan Grant doesn't have children because they're too costly and loud. In general, he doesn't like them, but he's never been acquainted with one that shares his interests. When Dr. Grant arrives at the park, owner John Hammond's grandson, Timmy, idolizes him. Timmy loves dinosaurs. He read Dr. Grant's book. He knows everything there is to know about him. Much like Chief Brody, Dr. Grant never had enough time to focus on kids because his career consumed all of his time. Not that either of them are complaining – no, both characters seem happy to work their days away. But Dr. Alan Grant finally gets the opportunity to connect with a child through the turmoil that throws Timmy and him together in the park.

Note also that both films lecture against a disregard for the safety of others. Since the Mayor is the employee of the town who fights against public safety in *Jaws*, I would call him out as the secondary villain, behind the shark, of course, and so it would seem that park owner John Hammond is also fighting against public safety in *Jurassic Park* by virtue of the fact that he's trying to open his dinosaur-ridden island death trap as a theme park attraction. But it's not John Hammond to blame, for Hammond genuinely thinks Jurassic Park is safe. He's not intentionally trying to endanger people for a quick buck. No, that honour goes to a second employee at the park, an IT security administrator named Dennis Nedry. In exchange for 1.5 million dollars, Dennis agrees to steal viable dinosaur embryos for a rival company. In order to do so, Dennis has to shut off the security system, thus endangering everyone in the park, including owner John Hammond. Safety first is the name of the game. He who endangers becomes the big, bad wolf.

Enough about the story they tell. Put aside the film's narrative. Go on, put it aside. Now, look at what remains behind the scenes. There's even some similarity there. For example, Steven Spielberg's involvement is noteworthy. Spielberg directed both *Jaws* and *Jurassic Park*, and, of course, Spielberg's usual suspects worked on both projects, including composer John Williams. Both films are based on novels, and each film produced a number of sequels. After the original *Jaws*, there were three sequels. After the original *Jurassic Park*, there were – drum roll, please – three sequels, and there's about to be a fourth as of June 12, 2015. If we boil away the details, *Jaws* and *Jurassic Park* might as well be the same film.

So why are they so beloved? The biggest complaint today seems to be that Hollywood keeps making and remaking the same films. Nothing is original. Yet these films are the same, made two decades apart, and still get all the love. And they do get all the love: *Jaws* and *Jurassic Park* both have ninety percent approval ratings with audiences and even greater critical scores, 98% and 93% respectively. People love these films.

I'll venture a guess. It's because these films are original iterations. They are overcoming the monster, yes, just as *King Kong* did and a host of other films before it. But *Jaws* and *Jurassic Park* bottled a spark, a little something-something that no one else had. Spielberg and the rest of his team came together in a perfect storm of creativity and managed to net lightning. They didn't set out to copy. They set out to do something different.

So we can rule out the director, the crew, the cast, and the rest of the production team. We have a new culprit then with the thrifty money-makers we call the studios. Why then do film studios keep making the same old? That one's easy. Because we keep watching them. The latest *Hunger Games* and *Transformers* sequels received the top ten highest box offices this year, along with a remake of a remake with this year's *Godzilla*; a sequel to a remake, *The Amazing Spider-Man 2*; and a re-imagined *Sleeping Beauty* remake, *Maleficent*; but those films opened without critical acclaim. Middle-of-the-road or worse films make a pretty penny. Meanwhile, decent films don't net a cent. Almost all of the top fifteen best films, critically speaking, released this year didn't make it into the top eighty at the box office. There are only two exceptions; for those who are interested, the exceptions are *The*

LEGO Movie and *X-Men: Days of Future Past*, a film based on merchandise and a sequel to a prequel, respectively. Studios don't dare risk their spare change on a medium-budget creative project when they can pump out a sequel of something mediocre or worse that is at least familiar and thus reliable at the box office. This trend is not new. Back in 2011, the top seven films at the box office were sequels to already proven financial successes: a *Harry Potter*; a *Transformers*; a *Twilight*; a *Hangover*; a *Pirates of the Caribbean*; a *Cars*; and a *Fast and the Furious*. We've been buying into it noticeably for several years now and perhaps at a less perceptible level for decades. So the fault is ours. If you're fed up of the same tired remakes and sequels populating your cinemas, I have a not-so-novel approach to solve this problem: Vote with your wallet.

And I respect that there are a finite number of conflicts in storytelling. We overcome the monster; we go from rags to riches; we embark on a quest; we embark on a quest and return with knowledge; we laugh our way through our troubles to a light and happy comic conclusion; we observe a villain crashing and burning; and, we observe a villain change and grow into a worthy person. And that's it. Everything is derivative of those plots. And that's fine, provided they are altered enough to be creative. Art is mostly innovation, not invention. You don't have to reinvent the wheel; you just have to change the tires. And I'm not the only one who thinks so. As British comedian Rob Brydon said in the artsy film *The Trip*, "It's 2010! Everything has been done before. All you can do is do something someone's done before, but do it better, or differently." And he's absolutely right. So, for 2015, let's aim for doing it better.

References

CHAPTER ONE: MOVE OVER, MERYL

"Academy Awards Summaries." *Filmsite.org.* American Movie Classics Company, n.d. Web. 03 Nov. 2014. <www.filmsite.org/oscars3.html>.

All Movie Guide. "Meryl Streep - Biography." *All Media Guide/NYTimes.org.* NY Times, Co., 2010. Web. 03 Nov. 2014. <www.nytimes.com/movies/person/68676/Meryl-Streep/biography>.

"Amy Adams." *Rotten Tomatoes.* Flixster, n.d. Web. 03 Nov. 2014. <http://www.rottentomatoes.com/celebrity/amy_adams/>.

"Angelina Jolie." *Rotten Tomatoes.* Flixster, n.d. Web. 03 Nov. 2014. <http://www.rottentomatoes.com/celebrity/angelina_jolie/>.

Barber, Lynn. "Helena Bonham Carter: Couldn't she just wear a babygro?" *The Guardian.* Guardian News and Media, 20 Apr. 1997. Web. 03 Nov. 2014. <www.theguardian.com/film/1997/apr/20/lynnbarber>.

"Cate Blanchett." *Rotten Tomatoes.* Flixster, n.d. Web. 03 Nov. 2014. <http://www.rottentomatoes.com/celebrity/cate_blanchett/>.

Costa, Maddy. "It's all gone widescreen." *The Guardian.* Guardian News and Media, 03 Nov. 2006. Web. 03 Nov. 2014. <www.theguardian.com/film/2006/nov/03/1>.

"The Dolby Theatre." *Dolby.com.* Dolby Laboratories, 2014. Web. 04 Nov. 2014. <www.dolby.com/us/en/about/dolby-theatre.html>.

"Emma Thompson." *Rotten Tomatoes*. Flixster, n.d. Web. 03 Nov. 2014.
<http://www.rottentomatoes.com/celebrity/emma_thompson/>
.

"Helena Bonham Carter." *IMDb.com*. n.d. Web. 03 Nov. 2014. <http://www.imdb.com/name/nm0000307/>.

---. *Rotten Tomatoes*. Flixster, n.d. Web. 03 Nov. 2014. <http://www.rottentomatoes.com/celebrity/helena-bonham-carter/>.

"Jennifer Lawrence." *Rotten Tomatoes*. Flixster, n.d. Web. 03 Nov. 2014.
<http://www.rottentomatoes.com/celebrity/jennifer_lawrence/>.

"Jennifer Shrader Lawrence." *Bio*. A&E Television Networks, 2014. Web. 04 Nov. 2014
<www.biography.com/people/jennifer-lawrence-20939797>.

"Jodie Foster." *Rotten Tomatoes*. Flixster, n.d. Web. 03 Nov. 2014.
<http://www.rottentomatoes.com/celebrity/jodie_foster/>.

"Judi Dench." *Bio*. A&E Television Networks, 2014. Web. 04 Nov. 2014. <www.biography.com/people/judi-dench-9271553>.

---. *Rotten Tomatoes*. Flixster, n.d. Web. 03 Nov. 2014. <http://www.rottentomatoes.com/celebrity/judi_dench/>.

Kaufman, Amy. "Oscar voters: Meet the academy's youngest members." *LATimes.com*. L.A. Times Entertainment, 23 Feb. 2012. Web. 04 Nov. 2014.
<http://latimesblogs.latimes.com/movies/2012/02/oscar-voters-meet-the-academys-youngest-members.html>.

"Maggie Smith." *Rotten Tomatoes*. Flixster, n.d. Web. 03 Nov. 2014.
<http://www.rottentomatoes.com/celebrity/maggie_smith/>.

Manuel, John. "Majoring In Moneyball." *Baseball America.* The Enthusiast Network, 23 Dec. 2003. Web. 03 Nov. 2014. <http://www.baseballamerica.com/today/features/031223colle gemoneyball.html>.

"Margaret Natalie Smith." *Bio.* A&E Television Networks, 2014. Web. 04 Nov. 2014. <www.biography.com/people/maggie-smith-9487030>.

"Meryl Streep." *IMDb.com.* n.d. Web. 03 Nov. 2014. <http://www.imdb.com/name/nm0000658/>.

---. *Rotten Tomatoes.* Flixster, n.d. Web. 03 Nov. 2014. <http://www.rottentomatoes.com/celebrity/meryl_streep/>.

Morris, Wesley. "Abba-cadabra." *Boston Globe.* NY Times, Co., 18 Jul. 2008. Web. 03 Nov. 2014. <www.boston.com/ae/movies/articles/2008/07/18/abba_cadab ra/>.

"Natalie Portman." *Rotten Tomatoes.* Flixster, n.d. Web. 03 Nov. 2014. <http://www.rottentomatoes.com/celebrity/natalie_portman/>.

"1987 Oscars." *Oscars.org.* Academy of Motion Picture Arts and Sciences, 1987. Web. 05 Nov. 2014. <www.oscars.org/oscars/ceremonies/1987>.

"1998 Oscars." *Oscars.org.* Academy of Motion Picture Arts and Sciences, 1998. Web. 05 Nov. 2014. <www.oscars.org/oscars/ceremonies/1998>.

"1994 Oscars." *Oscars.org.* Academy of Motion Picture Arts and Sciences, 1994. Web. 05 Nov. 2014. <www.oscars.org/oscars/ceremonies/1994>.

"1999 Oscars." *Oscars.org.* Academy of Motion Picture Arts and Sciences, 1999. Web. 05 Nov. 2014. <www.oscars.org/oscars/ceremonies/1999>.

"1996 Oscars." *Oscars.org.* Academy of Motion Picture Arts and Sciences, 1996. Web. 05 Nov. 2014. <www.oscars.org/oscars/ceremonies/1996>.

194

"1993 Oscars." *Oscars.org.* Academy of Motion Picture Arts and Sciences, 1993. Web. 05 Nov. 2014. <www.oscars.org/oscars/ceremonies/1993>.

"1970 Oscars." *Oscars.org.* Academy of Motion Picture Arts and Sciences, 1970. Web. 05 Nov. 2014. <www.oscars.org/oscars/ceremonies/1970>.

"1979 Oscars." *Oscars.org.* Academy of Motion Picture Arts and Sciences, 1979. 05 Nov. 2014. <www.oscars.org/oscars/ceremonies/1979>.

"1973 Oscars." *Oscars.org.* Academy of Motion Picture Arts and Sciences, 1973. Web. 05 Nov. 2014. <www.oscars.org/oscars/ceremonies/1973>.

"1966 Oscars." *Oscars.org.* Academy of Motion Picture Arts and Sciences, 1966. Web. 05 Nov. 2014. <www.oscars.org/oscars/ceremonies/1966>.

Onorati, Claudia. "Jennifer Lawrence breaks record with Oscar nomination." *LATimes.com.* L.A. Times Entertainment, n.d. Web. 04 Nov. 2014. <www.latimes.com/entertainment/gossip/lat-hh17-oscar-nominations-wre0014173356-20131114-photo.html>.

Pfefferman, Naomi. "Helena Bonham Carter–Jewish mother?" *Jewish Journal.* Tribe Media Corp., 30 Jul. 2008. Web. 03 Nov. 2014. <www.jewishjournal.com/hollywood_jew/article/helena_bonham_carter_jewish_mother_20080730/>.

Pond, Steve. "'Silver Linings Playbook' Oscar Nominee Jennifer Lawrence Shares Her Acting Secret: Never Sweat." *Yahoo Movies.* Yahoo!, 15 Feb. 2013. Web. 04 Nov. 2014. <movies.yahoo.com/news/silver-linings-playbook-oscar-nominee-jennifer-lawrence-shares-220811334.html>.

Puchko, Kristy. "Carey Mulligan and Helena Bonham Carter Revolt in Suffragette First Look." *Cinema Blend.* 04 Jun. 2014. Web. 03 Nov. 2014.

<www.cinemablend.com/new/Carey-Mulligan-Helena-
Bonham-Carter-Revolt-Suffragette-First-Look-43307.html>.

"Rotten Tomatoes: About." *Rotten Tomatoes*. Flixster, n.d.
Web. 03 Nov. 2014. <http://www.rottentomatoes.com/about/>.

"Sigourney Weaver." *Rotten Tomatoes*. Flixster, n.d. Web. 03
Nov. 2014.
<http://www.rottentomatoes.com/celebrity/sigourney_weaver/
>.

Skillman, Cari. "Jennifer Lawrence compared to Laurence
Olivier by 'Hunger Games' Donald Sutherland." *On the Red
Carpet/ABC7.com*. KABC-TV Los Angeles, 22 Mar. 2012.
Web. 04 Nov. 2014. <www.ontheredcarpet.com/Jennifer-
Lawrence-compared-to-Laurence-Olivier-by-Hunger-Games-
Donald-Sutherland-Video/8591138>.

Speers, W. "Queen Honors Naipaul, Maggie Smith."
Philly.com. 30 Dec. 1989. Web. 03 Nov. 2014.
<http://articles.philly.com/1989-12-
30/news/26159758_1_british-empire-telephone-pole-police-
chase>.

Thornton, Michael. "A magnificent year for grandes dames
like Judi Dench and Maggie Smith." *The Telegraph*.
Telegraph Media Group, 29 Aug. 2014. Web. 04 Nov. 2014.
<www.telegraph.co.uk/culture/film/11061703/A-magnificent-
year-for-grandes-dames-like-Judi-Dench-and-Maggie-
Smith.html>.

"2008 Oscars." *Oscars.org*. Academy of Motion Picture Arts
and Sciences, 2008. Web. 05 Nov. 2014.
<www.oscars.org/oscars/ceremonies/2008>.

"2011 Oscars." *Oscars.org*. Academy of Motion Picture Arts
and Sciences, 2011. Web. 05 Nov. 2014.
<www.oscars.org/oscars/ceremonies/2011>.

"2005 Oscars." *Oscars.org*. Academy of Motion Picture Arts
and Sciences, 2005. Web. 05 Nov. 2014.
<www.oscars.org/oscars/ceremonies/2005>.

"2014 Oscars." *Oscars.org*. Academy of Motion Picture Arts and Sciences, 2014. Web. 05 Nov. 2014. <www.oscars.org/oscars/ceremonies/2014>.

"2001 Oscars." *Oscars.org*. Academy of Motion Picture Arts and Sciences, 2001. Web. 05 Nov. 2014. <www.oscars.org/oscars/ceremonies/2001>.

"2007 Oscars." *Oscars.org*. Academy of Motion Picture Arts and Sciences, 2007. Web. 05 Nov. 2014. <www.oscars.org/oscars/ceremonies/2007>.

"2006 Oscars." *Oscars.org*. Academy of Motion Picture Arts and Sciences, 2006. Web. 05 Nov. 2014. <www.oscars.org/oscars/ceremonies/2006>.

"2013 Oscars." *Oscars.org*. Academy of Motion Picture Arts and Sciences, 2013. Web. 05 Nov. 2014. <www.oscars.org/oscars/ceremonies/2013>.

"2002 Oscars." *Oscars.org*. Academy of Motion Picture Arts and Sciences, 2002. Web. 05 Nov. 2014. <www.oscars.org/oscars/ceremonies/2002>.

"Uma Thurman." *Rotten Tomatoes*. Flixster, n.d. Web. 03 Nov. 2014. <http://www.rottentomatoes.com/celebrity/uma_thurman/>.

Wilmoth, Peter. "Can-do Cate." *The Age*. Fairfax Media, 02 Mar. 2008. Web. 04 Nov. 2014. <www.theage.com.au/news/in-depth/strongpeoplestrong-cando-cate-the-woman-whos-everywhere/2008/03/01/1204227051340.html>.

CHAPTER TWO: TO DO OR NOT TO DO

Boonstra, Heather D. "Advocates Call for a New Approach After the Era of 'Abstinence-Only' Sex Education." *Guttmacher.org*. Guttmacher Institute, 2009. Web. 15 Nov. 2014. <https://www.guttmacher.org/pubs/gpr/12/1/gpr120106.html>.

---. "Teen Pregnancy: Trends And Lessons Learned." *Guttmacher Report on Public Policy* 5.1 (2002). Web. 27 Nov. 2014. <www.guttmacher.org/pubs/tgr/05/1/gr050107.html>.

The Breakfast Club. Dir. John Hughes. Perf. Emilio Estevez, Paul Gleason, and Anthony Michael Hall. 1985. DVD. Universal, 2008.

Castle, Jennifer. "'Nobody's really trying to get laid': How John Hughes reinvented the teen comedy." *Salon.com.* Salon Media Group, Inc., 07 May 2014. Web. 15 Nov. 2014. <http://www.salon.com/2014/05/07/nobodys_really_trying_to _get_laid_how_john_hughes_reinvented_the_teen_comedy_p artner/>.

Ebert, Roger. "John Hughes: When You're 16, You're More Serious Than You'll Ever Be Again." *Roger Ebert's Journal.* Ebert Digital, 29 Apr. 1984. Web. 15 Nov. 2014. <http://www.rogerebert.com/rogers-journal/john-hughes-when-youre-16-youre-more-serious-than-youll-ever-be-again>.

Ferris Bueller's Day Off. Dir. John Hughes. Perf. Matthew Broderick, Mia Sara, and Alan Ruck. 1986. DVD. Paramount, 2006.

Home Alone. Dir. Chris Columbus. Perf. Macaulay Culkin, Joe Pesci, and Daniel Stern. 1990. DVD. Twentieth Century Fox, 1999.

Home Alone 2: Lost in New York. Dir. Chris Columbus. Perf. Macaulay Culkin, Joe Pesci, and Daniel Stern. 1992. DVD. Twentieth Century Fox, 1999.

Howell, Marcela, and Marilyn Keefe. "The History of Federal Abstinence-Only Funding." *Advocates for Youth.* Advocates for Youth, Jul. 2007. Web. 15 Nov. 2014. <http://www.advocatesforyouth.org/publications/publications-a-z/429-the-history-of-federal-abstinence-only-funding>.

National Lampoon's Christmas Vacation. Dir. Jeremiah S. Chechik. Perf. Chevy Chase, Beverly D'Angelo, and Randy Quaid. 1989. DVD. Warner Bros., 2009.

National Lampoon's Vacation. Dir. Harold Ramis. Perf. Chevy Chase, Beverly D'Angelo, and Imogene Coca. 1983. DVD. Warner Bros., 2009.

Pretty in Pink. Dir. Howard Deutch. Perf. Molly Ringwald, Harry Dean Stanton, and Jon Cryer. 1986. DVD. Paramount, 2006.

Ross, Julianne. "17 Lies We Need to Stop Teaching Boys About Sex." *Mic.com.* Mix Network Inc., 15 May 2014. Web. 21 Dec. 2014. <mic.com/articles/89301/17-lies-we-need-to-stop-teaching-boys-about-sex>.

"Sexually Active Teens." *Child Trends Data Bank.* Child Trends, Jul. 2014. Web. 27 Nov. 2014. <www.childtrends.org/?indicators=sexually-active-teens>.

Sixteen Candles. Dir. John Hughes. Perf. Molly Ringwald, Paul Dooley, and Justin Henry. 1984. DVD. Universal, 2004.

Some Kind of Wonderful. Dir. Howard Deutch. Perf. Eric Stoltz, Mary Stuart Masterson, and Craig Sheffer. 1987. DVD. Paramount, 2002.

"Statistics." *PAVE: Shattering the Silence of Sexual Violence.* PAVE, n.d. Web. 31 Dec. 2014. <pavingtheway.net/statistics-2/>.

Sternbergh, Adam. "The Post-Hughes Teenager." *NYMag.com.* New York Media, 16 Aug. 2009. Web. 15 Nov. 2014. <http://nymag.com/news/intelligencer/58338/>.

Uncle Buck. Dir. John Hughes. Perf. John Candy, Amy Madigan, and Jean Louisa Kelly. 1989. DVD. Universal, 2007.

Weird Science. Dir. John Hughes. Perf. Anthony Michael Hall, Ilan Mitchell-Smith, and Kelly LeBrock. 1985. DVD. Universal, 2008.

CHAPTER THREE: JACK OF ALL TRADES, MASTER OF NONE

"Addicts." *Undeclared: The Complete Series*. Writ. Jennifer Konner and Alexandra Rushfield. Dir. Greg Mottola. Series prod. Judd Apatow. DVD. Shout! Factory, 2007.

Anchorman: The Legend of Ron Burgundy. Dir. Adam McKay. Perf. Will Ferrell, Christina Applegate, and Paul Rudd. 2004. DVD. DreamWorks, 2006.

Austin Powers: International Man of Mystery. Dir. Jay Roach. Perf. Mike Myers, Elizabeth Hurley, and Michael York. 1997. DVD. New Line, 2002.

Austin Powers: The Spy Who Shagged Me. Dir. Jay Roach. Perf. Mike Myers, Heather Graham, and Michael York. 1999. DVD. New Line, 2002.

Bewitched. Dir. Nora Ephron. Perf. Nicole Kidman, Will Ferrell, and Shirley MacLaine. 2005. DVD. Sony Pictures Home Entertainment, 2006.

Blades of Glory. Dir. Will Speck and Josh Gordon. Perf. Will Ferrell, Jon Heder, and Will Arnett. 2007. DVD. DreamWorks, 2007.

The Campaign. Dir. Jay Roach. Perf. Will Ferrell, Zach Galifianakis, and Jason Sudeikis. 2012. DVD. Warner Bros., 2012.

Casa de mi Padre. Dir. Matt Piedmont. Perf. Will Ferrell, Gael García Bernal, and Diego Luna. 2012. DVD. New Line, 2012.

Dick. Dir. Andrew Fleming. Perf. Kirsten Dunst, Michelle Williams, and Dan Hedaya. 1999. DVD. Sony Picture Home Entertainment, 2005.

Elf. Dir. Jon Favreau. Perf. Will Ferrell, James Caan, and Zooey Deschanel. 2003. DVD. New Line, 2010.

"Goodbye, Michael." *The Office: Season Seven*. Writ. Greg Daniels. Dir. Paul Feig. Prod. Randy Cordray. Series prod. Greg Daniels. DVD. Universal, 2011.

Heylighen, F. "The generalized 'Peter Principle'." *Principia Cybernetica Web*. Principia Cybernetica, 30 Nov. 1993. Web. 11 Nov. 2014. <pespmc1.vub.ac.be/PETERPR.html>.

"The Inner Circle." *The Office: Season Seven*. Writ. Charlie Grandy. Dir. Matt Sohn. Prod. Randy Cordray. Series prod. Greg Daniels. DVD. Universal, 2011.

Jay and Silent Bob Strike Back. Dir. Kevin Smith. Perf. Jason Mewes, Kevin Smith, and Ben Affleck. 2001. DVD. Buena Vista, 2011.

Kicking & Screaming. Dir. Jesse Dylan. Perf. Will Ferrell, Robert Duvall, and Mike Ditka. 2005. DVD. Universal, 2005.

Land of the Lost. Dir. Brad Silberling. Perf. Will Ferrell, Danny McBride, and Anna Friel. 2009. DVD. Universal, 2009.

"Lee Marvin vs. Derek Jeter." *30 Rock: Season 4*. Writ. Kay Cannon and Tina Fey. Dir. Don Scardino. Prod. Jerry Kupfer. Series prod. Tina Fey. DVD. Universal, 2010.

Megamind. Dir. Tom McGrath. Perf. Will Ferrell, Tina Fey, and Jonah Hill. 2010. DVD. DreamWorks, 2011.

"Michael's Last Dundies." *The Office: Season Seven*. Writ. Mindy Kaling. Dir. Mindy Kaling. Prod. Randy Cordray. Series prod. Greg Daniels. DVD. Universal, 2011.

"The Moms." *30 Rock: Season 4*. Writ. Kay Cannon and Robert Carlock. Dir. John Riggi. Prod. Jerry Kupfer. Series prod. Tina Fey. DVD. Universal, 2010.

"Mr. Saturday Knight." *Family Guy: Volume Two*. Writ. Steve Callaghan. Dir. Michael Dante DiMartino. Prod. Kara Vallow. Series prod. Seth MacFarlane. DVD. Twentieth Century Fox, 2010.

"My Name Is Robbie." *The Oblongs: The Complete Twisted Series*. Writ. Jill Soloway. Dir. Vincent Waller. Prod. J.

Michael Mendel and Richard Quan. Series prod. Angus
Oblong and Jace Richdale. DVD. Warner Bros., 2005.

"My Whole Life Is Thunder." *30 Rock: Season 7.* Writ. Jack
Burditt and Colleen McGuinness. Dir. Linda Mendoza. Prod.
Jerry Kupfer. Series prod. Tina Fey. DVD. Universal, 2013.

The Other Guys. Dir. Adam McKay. Perf. Will Ferrell, Mark
Wahlberg, and Eva Mendes. 2010. DVD. Sony Pictures Home
Entertainment, 2010.

The Producers. Dir. Susan Stroman. Perf. Nathan Lane,
Matthew Broderick, and Uma Thurman. 2005. DVD.
Universal, 2006.

Semi-Pro. Dir. Kent Alterman. Perf. Will Ferrell, Woody
Harrelson, and André Benjamin. 2008. DVD. New Line, 2008.

Talladega Nights: The Ballad of Ricky Bobby. Dir. Adam
McKay. Perf. Will Ferrell, John C. Reilly, and Sacha Baron
Cohen. 2006. DVD. Sony Pictures Home Entertainment, 2006.

Taylor, M. Susan, Kay B. Tracy, Monika K. Renard, J. Kline
Harrison, and Stephen J. Carroll. "Due Process in Performance
Appraisal: A Quasi-experiment in Procedural Justice."
Administrative Science Quarterly 40 (1995): 495-523. Web.
11 Nov. 2014.

"Training Day." *The Office: Season Seven.* Writ. Daniel Chun.
Dir. Paul Lieberstein. Prod. Randy Cordray. Series prod. Greg
Daniels. DVD. Universal, 2011.

"2014 Performance Management Survey."
PerformanceReviews.net. That Network LLC, n.d. Web. 15
Nov. 2014. <http://performancereviews.net/survey/>.

Zoolander. Dir. Ben Stiller. Perf. Ben Stiller, Owen Wilson,
and Will Ferrell. 2001. DVD. Paramount, 2002.

CHAPTER FOUR: WHAT DOESN'T KILL YOU MAKES YOU DEPRESSED

Andreasen, Nancy C. "A journey into chaos: Creativity and the unconscious." *Mens Sana Monographs* 9.1 (2011). Web. 26 Dec. 2014. doi:10.4103/0973-1229.77424.

America's Sweethearts. Dir. Joe Roth. Perf. Julia Roberts, Billy Crystal, and Catherine Zeta-Jones. 2001. DVD. Sony Pictures Home Entertainment, 2002.

August: Osage County. Dir. John Wells. Perf. Meryl Streep, Julia Roberts, and Ewan McGregor. 2013. DVD. The Weinstein Company, 2014.

Ballantyne, Coco. "Hypothermia: How long can someone survive in frigid water?" *Scientific American.* Nature America, Inc., 16 Jan. 2009. Web. 19 Nov. 2014. <www.scientificamerican.com/article/airplane-1549-hudson-hypothermia/>.

Cano, Annmarie, and K. Daniel O'Leary. "Infidelity and separations precipitate major depressive episodes and symptoms of nonspecific depression and anxiety." *Journal of Consulting and Clinical Psychology* 68.5 (2000). Web. 25 Dec. 2014. doi:http://dx.doi.org/10.1037/0022-006X.68.5.774.

Charlie Wilson's War. Dir. Mike Nichols. Perf. Tom Hanks, Julia Roberts, and Philip Seymour Hoffman. 2007. DVD. Universal, 2007.

Clark, C. Brendan, Christopher B. Thorne, Sonya Hardy, and Karen L. Cropsey. "Cooperation and depressive symptoms." *Journal of Affective Disorders* 150.3 (2013): 1184-7. Web. 08 Dec. 2014. doi:10.1016/j.jad.2013.05.011.

"Climate of Cape Cod." Coast Guard Beach, n.d. Web. 19 Nov. 2014. <www.coastguard-americabeach.com/about_us/Climate_of_Cape_Cod.html>.

Closer. Dir. Mike Nichols. Perf. Julia Roberts, Jude Law, and Natalie Portman. 2004. DVD. Sony Pictures Home Entertainment, 2005.

Confessions of a Dangerous Mind. Dir. George Clooney. Perf. Sam Rockwell, Drew Barrymore, and George Clooney. 2002. DVD. Alliance Films, 2005.

Conspiracy Theory. Dir. Richard Donner. Perf. Mel Gibson, Julia Roberts, and Patrick Stewart. 1997. DVD. Warner Bros., 2009.

Delgado, Pedro L. and Jason Schillerstrom. "Cognitive Difficulties Associated With Depression: What Are the Implications for Treatment?" *Psychiatric Times* 26.3 (2009). Web. 23 Nov. 2014. <www.psychiatrictimes.com/articles/cognitive-difficulties-associated-depression-what-are-implications-treatment>.

"Depression." *The Ernest E. Kennedy Center.* 2014. Web. 23 Nov. 2014. <www.ekcenter.org/services/eap-services/depression/>.

Drudi, Dino. "Fishing for a Living is Dangerous Work." *Compensation and Working Conditions.* U.S. Bureau of Labor Statistics, 1998. Web. 18 Nov. 2014. <www.bls.gov/opub/mlr/cwc/fishing-for-a-living-is-dangerous-work.pdf>.

Eat Pray Love. Dir. Ryan Murphy. Perf. Julia Roberts, Javier Bardem, and Richard Jenkins. 2010. DVD. Sony Pictures Home Entertainment, 2010.

Elliott, Timothy R., and Robert G. Frank. "Depression Following Spinal Cord Injury." *Archives of Physical Medicine and Rehabilitation* 77 (1996). Web. 25 Dec. 2014. doi:http://dx.doi.org/10.1016/S0003-9993(96)90263-4.

Erin Brockovich. Dir. Steven Soderbergh. Perf. Julia Roberts, Albert Finney, and Aaron Eckhart. 2000. DVD. Universal, 2006.

"Facts on Sexually Transmitted Infections in the United States." *Guttmacher.org.* Guttmacher Institute, n.d. Web. 11 Nov. 2014. <www.guttmacher.org/pubs/FIB_STI_US.html>.

Flatliners. Dir. Joel Schumacher. Perf. Kiefer Sutherland, Julia Roberts, and Kevin Bacon. 1990. DVD. Sony Pictures Home Entertainment, 1998.

Fallon, Jr., L. Fleming. "Rhinoplasty." *Encyclopedia of Surgery*. Advameg, Inc., n.d. Web. 23 Nov. 2014. <www.surgeryencyclopedia.com/Pa-St/Rhinoplasty.html>.

Frey, Rebecca. "Mentoplasty." *Encyclopedia of Surgery*. Advameg, Inc., n.d. Web. 23 Nov. 2014. <www.surgeryencyclopedia.com/La-Pa/Mentoplasty.html>.

"Gender and women's mental health." *WHO International Mental Health*. World Health Organization, n.d. Web. 23 Nov. 2014. <www.who.int/mental_health/prevention/genderwomen/en/>.

Gradin, V. B., A. Pérez. J. A. MacFarlane, I. Cavin, G. Waiter, J. Engelmann, B. Dritschel, A. Pomi, K. Matthews, and J.D. Steele. "Abnormal brain responses to social fairness in depression: an fMRI study using the Ultimatum Game." *Psychological Medicine* (2014). Web. 08 Dec. 2014. doi:10.1017/S0033291714002347.

Grant, BF. "Comorbidity between DSM-IV drug use disorders and major depression: Results of a national survey of adults." *Journal of Substance Abuse* 7.4 (1995): 481-7. Web. 23 Nov. 2014. doi:10.1016/0899-3289(95)90017-9.

Grunebaum, Michael. "Ask the Experts." *Columbia Psychiatry*. Columbia University Medical Center, 2010. Web. 31 Dec. 2014. <asp.cumc.columbia.edu/psych/asktheexperts/ask_the_experts_inquiry.asp?SI=668>.

"Health Effects of Cigarette Smoking." *CDC.gov*. Centers of Disease Control, 06 Feb. 2014. Web. 15 Nov. 2014. <http://www.cdc.gov/tobacco/data_statistics/fact_sheets/health_effects/effects_cig_smoking/>.

"Hepatitis B Vaccine." *HepB.org*. Hepatitis B Foundation, 26 Feb. 2013. Web. 15 Nov. 2014. <http://www.hepb.org/hepb/vaccine_information.htm>.

"Homicide Rate Breaks Record In Dade County." *Ocala Star-Banner* 29 Dec. 1980: 2B. Web. 19 Nov. 2014.

"Human Papillomavirus." *The Pink Book/CDC.gov*. Centers of Disease Control, 07 May 2012. Web. 15 Nov. 2014. <http://www.cdc.gov/vaccines/pubs/pinkbook/hpv.html>.

"In-depth study on all forms of violence against women." United Nations, 06 Jul. 2006: 54. Web. 19 Nov. 2014. <www.un.org/ga/search/view_doc.asp?symbol=A/61/122/Add.1>.

Kennedy, S.H., B.R. Welsh, K. Fulton, J.K. Soczynska, R.S. McIntyre, et al. "Frequency and correlates of gambling problems in outpatients with major depressive disorder and bipolar disorder." *The Canadian Journal of Psychiatry* 55 (2010): 568-75. Web. 23 Nov. 2014. <www.gamblingresearch.org/content/frequency-and-correlates-gambling-problems-outpatients-major-depressive-disorder-and-bipolar>.

Larry Crowne. Dir. Tom Hanks. Perf. Tom Hanks, Julia Roberts, and Bryan Cranston. 2011. DVD. Alliance Films, 2011.

Law, Samuel. "Major Mood Disorders." *Problem Gambling Institute of Ontario*. Centre for Addiction and Mental Health, n.d. Web. 18 Nov. 2014. <www.problemgambling.ca/en/resourcesforprofessionals/pages/majormooddisorders.aspx>.

Levinson, Douglas F. "Major Depression and Genetics." *Genetics of Brain Function*. Stanford University School of Medicine, 2009. Web. 15 Dec. 2014. <depressiongenetics.stanford.edu/mddandgenes.html>.

Loftus, Mary. "The Other Side of Fame." *PsychologyToday.com*. Sussex Publishers, 01 May 1995. Web. 15 Nov. 2014. <http://www.psychologytoday.com/articles/199505/the-other-side-fame>.

Luyten, P., B. Sabbe, SJ Blatt, S Meganck, B Jansen, C De Grave, F Maes, and J Corveleyn. "Dependency and self-criticism: relationship with major depressive disorder, severity of depression, and clinical presentation." *Depression and Anxiety* 24.8 (2007): 586-96. Web. 18 Nov. 2014.

Martinez Jr., Ramiro, Matthew T. Lee, and Amie L. Nielsen. "Segmented Assimilation, Local Context and Determinants of Drug Violence in Miami and San Diego: Does Ethnicity and Immigration Matter?" *International Migration Review* 38.1 (2004): 131-57. Web. 19 Nov. 2014. <http://www.jstor.org/stable/27645360>.

Mary Reilly. Dir. Stephen Frears. Perf. Julia Roberts, John Malkovich, and Glenn Close. 1996. DVD. Sony Pictures Home Entertainment, 2001.

Massara, Marisa. "Sex work." *The California Aggie*. Creative Media, 07 Mar. 2013. Web. 18 Nov. 2014. <www.theaggie.org/2013/03/07/column-sex-work/>.

"Measuring Intimate Partner (Domestic) Violence." *NIJ: Intimate Partner Violence*. National Institute of Justice, 12 May 2010. Web. 19 Nov. 2014. <www.nij.gov/topics/crime/intimate-partner-violence/pages/measuring.aspx>.

The Mexican. Dir. Gore Verbinski. Perf. Brad Pitt, Julia Roberts, and James Gandolfini. 2001. DVD. Warner Bros., 2013.

"Mirror Image." *Miami Vice: Season Four*. Writ. Robert Palm and Daniel Sackheim. Dir. Richard Compton. Prod. Richard Brams. Series prod. Dick Wolf. DVD. Universal, 2007.

Mirror Mirror. Dir. Tarsem Singh Dhandwar. Perf. Julia Roberts, Lily Collins, and Armie Hammer. 2012. DVD. Twentieth Century Fox, 2012.

Mona Lisa Smile. Dir. Mike Newell. Perf. Julia Roberts, Kirsten Dunst, and Julia Stiles. 2003. DVD. Sony Pictures Home Entertainment, 2004.

My Best Friend's Wedding. Dir. P.J. Hogan. Perf. Julia Roberts, Dermot Mulroney, and Cameron Diaz. 1997. DVD. Sony Pictures Home Entertainment, 2007.

Mystic Pizza. Dir. Donald Petrie. Perf. Annabeth Gish, Julia Roberts, and Lili Taylor. 1988. DVD. MGM, 2004.

National Institute of Mental Health. "Depression." U.S. Department of Health & Human Services, 2008. Web. 23 Nov. 2014. <http://www.nimh.nih.gov/health/publications/depression/nim hdepression.pdf>.

The Normal Heart. Dir. Ryan Murphy. Perf. Mark Ruffalo, Matt Bomer, and Julia Roberts. 2014. DVD. HBO, 2014.

Notting Hill. Dir. Roger Michell. Perf. Julia Roberts, Hugh Grant, and Hugh Bonneville. 1999. DVD. Universal, 2004.

Ocean's Eleven. Dir. Steven Soderbergh. Perf. George Clooney, Brad Pitt, and Andy Garcia. 2001. DVD. Warner Bros., 2002.

Ocean's Twelve. Dir. Steven Soderbergh. Perf. George Clooney, Brad Pitt, and Matt Damon. 2004. DVD. Warner Bros., 2005.

"The One After the Super Bowl." *Friends: The Complete Second Season*. Writ. Jeffrey Astrof, Mike Sikowitz, and Michael Borkow. Dir. Michael Lembeck. Prod. Todd Stevens. Series prod. Kevin S. Bright, Marta Kauffman, and David Crane. DVD. Warner Bros., 2002.

The Pelican Brief. Dir. Alan J. Pakula. Perf. Julia Roberts, Denzel Washington, and Sam Shepard. 1993. DVD. Warner Bros., 2009.

Picardi, A, P Morosini, P Gaetano, M Pasquini, and M Biondi. "Higher levels of anger and aggressiveness in major depressive disorder than in anxiety and somatoform disorders." *Journal of Clinical Psychiatry* 65.3 (Mar. 2004): 442-3. Web. 23 Nov. 2014.

The Player. Dir. Robert Altman. Perf. Tim Robbins, Greta Scacchi, and Fred Ward. 1992. DVD. New Line, 1997.

Pöldinger, W. "The relation between depression and art." *Psychopathology* 19 (1986). Web. 26 Dec. 2014. doi:10.1159/000285163.

Potterat, John J., Devon D. Brewer, Stephen Q. Muth, Richard B. Rothenberg, Donald E. Woodhouse, John B. Muth, Heather K. Stites, and Stuart Brody. "Mortality in a Long-term Open Cohort of Prostitute Women." *American Journal of Epidemiology* 159.8 (2004): 778-85. Web. 18 Nov. 2014. doi:10.1093/aje/kwh110.

Pretty Woman. Dir. Garry Marshall. Perf. Richard Gere, Julia Roberts, and Ralph Bellamy. 1990. DVD. Buena Vista, 2013.

Price, Michael. "Revenge and the people who seek it." *APA.org*. American Psychological Association, 2009. Web. 15 Nov. 2014. <http://www.apa.org/monitor/2009/06/revenge.aspx>.

"Prostitution in The United States - The Statistics." *Sex Workers' Education Network*. Bayswan, n.d. Web. 18 Nov. 2014. <www.bayswan.org/stats.html>.

Runaway Bride. Dir. Garry Marshall. Perf. Julia Roberts, Richard Gere, and Joan Cusack. 1999. DVD. Paramount, 2000.

Schwartz, Allan. "Of Troubled Marriages, Sexual Compulsions and Depression." *MentalHelp.net*. CenterSite, 13 Dec. 2009. Web. 25 Dec. 2014. <www.mentalhelp.net/poc/view_doc.php?type=doc&id=3403 6>.

"Sexually Transmitted Disease Surveillance 2012." *CDC.gov*. Centers for Disease Control, 07 Jan. 2014. Web. 12 Nov. 2014. <http://www.cdc.gov/std/stats12/surv2012.pdf>.

"Sexually transmitted infections (STIs)." *WHO International Media Centre*. World Health Organization, Nov. 2013. Web.

11 Nov. 2014.
<www.who.int/mediacentre/factsheets/fs110/en/>.

Silbert, Mimi, and Ayala Pines. "Occupational Hazards of
Street Prostitutes." *Criminal Justice and Behavior* 8.4 (1981):
395-9. Web. 11 Nov. 2014.
doi:10.1177/009385488100800401.

Silver, J. R. "Spinal injuries resulting from horse riding
accidents." *Spinal Cord* 40.6 (Jun. 2002): 264-71. Web. 18
Nov. 2014. doi:10.1038/sj.sc.3101280.

Simonton, Dean Keith. "Are Genius and Madness Related?
Contemporary Answers to an Ancient Question." *Psychiatric
Times*. UBM Medica, 31 May 2005. Web. 26 Dec. 2014.
<www.psychiatrictimes.com/articles/are-genius-and-madness-
related-contemporary-answers-ancient-question>.

Sleeping With the Enemy. Dir. Joseph Ruben. Perf. Julia
Roberts, Patrick Bergin, and Kevin Anderson. 1991. DVD.
Twentieth Century Fox, 2009.

Something to Talk About. Dir. Lasse Hallström. Perf. Julia
Roberts, Dennis Quaid, and Robert Duvall. 1995. DVD.
Warner Bros., 2010.

Stauffer, Éric. "Homicides in Miami Dade County, Florida:
An Extensive Study for the Year 1999 Using the Data of the
Medical Examiner's Office." Florida International University,
2001. Web. 19 Nov. 2014.
<www.swissforensic.org/publications/documents/assets/rpmia
mi.pdf>.

Steel Magnolias. Dir. Herbert Ross. Perf. Sally Field, Dolly
Parton, and Shirley MacLaine. 1989. DVD. Sony Pictures
Home Entertainment, 2000.

"A Study of Homicide in Eight U.S. Cities: An NIJ Intramural
Research Project." *NIJ Research in Brief*. U.S. Department of
Justice, Nov. 1997. Web. 19 Nov. 2014.
<https://www.ncjrs.gov/pdffiles/167263.pdf>.

210

"Tobacco-Related Mortality." *CDC.gov*. Centers of Disease Control, 06 Feb. 2014. Web. 15 Nov. 2014. <http://www.cdc.gov/tobacco/data_statistics/fact_sheets/health _effects/tobacco_related_mortality/>.

"Traffic Safety Facts, 2007 Data: Motorcycles." *NHTSA's National Center for Statistics and Analysis*. National Highway Traffic Safety Administration, 2007. Web. 18 Nov. 2014. <www-nrd.nhtsa.dot.gov/Pubs/810990.PDF>.

"2001 Oscars." *Oscars.org*. Academy of Motion Picture Arts and Sciences, 2001. Web. 05 Nov. 2014. <www.oscars.org/oscars/ceremonies/2001>.

Valentine's Day. Dir. Garry Marshall. Perf. Ashton Kutcher, Jennifer Garner, and Anne Hathaway. 2010. DVD. Warner Bros., 2011.

Vorvick, Linda J., and Timothy Rogge. "Major depression with psychotic features." *MedlinePlus*. U.S. National Library of Medicine, 07 Nov. 2014. Web. 23 Nov. 2014. <www.nlm.nih.gov/medlineplus/ency/article/000933.htm>.

White, Ian R., Dan R. Altmann, and Kiran Nanchahal. "Alcohol consumption and mortality: modelling risks for men and women at different ages." *BMJ* 325:191 (27 Jul. 2002). Web. 15 Nov. 2014. <www.bmj.com/content/325/7357/191>.

Willingham, Val. "Study: Rates of many mental disorders much higher in soldiers than in civilians." *CNN*. Turner Broadcasting System, Inc., 04 Mar. 2014. Web. 23 Nov. 2014. <www.cnn.com/2014/03/03/health/jama-military-mental-health/>.

CHAPTER FIVE: BACHELOR NUMBER TWO

Askin, Pauline. "Romantic comedies affecting off-screen love lives." *Reuters*. Thomson Reuters, 21 Jul. 2010. Web. 31 Dec. 2014. <www.reuters.com/article/2010/07/21/us-love-odd-idUSTRE66K4JK20100721>.

"Contact Us." *Cornell School of Hotel Administration*. Cornell University, 2014. Web. 23 Dec. 2014. <https://www.hotelschool.cornell.edu/about/contactus.html>.

DeParle, Jason. "Two Classes, Divided by 'I Do'." *NYTimes.com*. NY Times, Co., 14 Jul. 2012. Web. 23 Dec. 2014. <www.nytimes.com/2012/07/15/us/two-classes-in-america-divided-by-i-do.html>.

Dirty Dancing. Dir. Emile Ardolino. Perf. Patrick Swayze, Jennifer Grey, and Jerry Orbach. 1987. DVD. Lions Gate, 2007.

Fisher, Helen E. "Brains Do It: Lust, Attraction, and Attachment." *Dana.org*. The Dana Foundation, 01 Jan. 2000. Web. 28 Nov. 2014. <http://www.dana.org/Cerebrum/Default.aspx?id=39351>.

Fox, Kate. "The Smell Report - Sexual Attraction." *SIRC.org*. Social Issues Research Centre, n.d. Web. 23 Dec. 2014. <www.sirc.org/publik/smell_attract.html>.

Gwin, Peter. "The Mystery of Risk." *National Geographic Magazine*. National Geographic Society, Jun. 2013. Web. 28 Nov. 2014. <http://ngm.nationalgeographic.com/2013/06/125-risk-takers/gwin-text>.

Harry Potter and the Deathly Hallows, Part 2. Dir. David Yates. Perf. Daniel Radcliffe, Rupert Grint, and Emma Watson. 2011. DVD. Warner Bros., 2011.

Harry Potter and the Order of the Phoenix. Dir. David Yates. Perf. Daniel Radcliffe, Rupert Grint, and Emma Watson. 2007. DVD. Warner Bros., 2007.

"Inflation Calculator." *US Inflation Calculator*. Coin News Media Group, 17 Dec. 2014. Web. 23 Dec. 2014. <http://www.usinflationcalculator.com/>.

Iyengar, Sheena S., and Mark R. Lepper. "When Choice is Demotivating: Can One Desire Too Much of a Good Thing?" *Journal of Personality and Social Psychology* 79.6 (2000):

995-1006. Web. 05 Dec. 2014. doi: 10.1037//0022-3514.79.6.995.

Lee, Thomas R. "Factors That Make a Difference in Marital Success." *StrongerMarriage.org*. Utah Marriage Commission, 2001. Web. 10 Dec. 2014. <http://strongermarriage.org/htm/married/factors-that-make-a-difference-in-marital-success>.

Lehman, Jerry D. *Understanding Marriage, Family, and Intimate Relationships*. Springfield, IL: Charles C Thomas Publisher, 2005. Print.

Lenton, Alison P., and Marco Francesconi. "Too much of a good thing? Variety is confusing in mate choice." *Biology Letters* (2011). Web. 05 Dec. 2014. doi: 10.1098/rsbl.2011.0098.

Moulin Rouge. Dir. Baz Luhrmann. Perf. Nicole Kidman, Ewan McGregor, and John Leguizamo. 2001. DVD. Twentieth Century Fox, 2002.

"Mount Holyoke College." *Mount Holyoke College*. Trustees of Mount Holyoke College, 2014. Web. 23 Dec. 2014. <https://www.mtholyoke.edu>.

The Notebook. Dir. Nick Cassavetes. Perf. Ryan Gosling, Rachel McAdams, and James Garner. 2004. DVD. New Line, 2004.

Pretty in Pink. Dir. Howard Deutch. Perf. Molly Ringwald, Harry Dean Stanton, and Jon Cryer. 1986. DVD. Paramount, 2006.

Toelle, Stephanie C., and Victor W. Harris. "Are You Marrying Someone from a Different Culture or Religion?" *EDIS - UF/IFAS Extension*. University of Florida, Sep. 2012. Web. 23 Dec. 2014. <http://edis.ifas.ufl.edu/fy1337>.

"Tuberculosis in Europe and North America, 1800-1922." *Harvard University Library Open Collections Program*. The Presidents and Fellows of Harvard College, n.d. Web. 31 Dec. 2014. <ocp.hul.harvard.edu/contagion/tuberculosis.html>.

The Twilight Saga: New Moon. Dir. Chris Weitz. Perf. Kristen Stewart, Robert Pattinson, and Taylor Lautner. 2009. DVD. Summit Entertainment, 2010.

The Twilight Saga: Eclipse. Dir. David Slade. Perf. Kristen Stewart, Robert Pattinson, and Taylor Lautner. 2010. DVD. Summit Entertainment, 2010.

Wright, Cindy. "Thinking of Marrying Someone From Another Culture?" *Marriage Missions.* Marriage Missions International, 5 Aug. 2007. Web. 23 Dec. 2014. <marriagemissions.com/thinking-of-marrying-someone-from-another-culture/>.

X-Men: Days of Future Past. Dir. Bryan Singer. Perf. Hugh Jackman, James McAvoy, and Michael Fassbender. 2014. DVD. Twentieth Century Fox, 2014.

X-Men: First Class. Dir. Matthew Vaughn. Perf. James McAvoy, Michael Fassbender, and Rose Byrne. 2011. DVD. Twentieth Century Fox, 2011.

X-Men: The Last Stand. Dir. Brett Ratner. Perf. Hugh Jackman, Halle Berry, and Ian McKellen. 2006. DVD. Twentieth Century Fox, 2008.

CHAPTER SIX: THE RAZZIE DAZZLE

"The Adventures of Ford Fairlane." *Rotten Tomatoes.* Flixster, n.d. Web. 08 Dec. 2014. <http://www.rottentomatoes.com/m/adventures_of_ford_fairlane/>.

"The Adventures of Pluto Nash." *Rotten Tomatoes.* Flixster, n.d. Web. 08 Dec. 2014. <http://www.rottentomatoes.com/m/adventures_of_pluto_nash/>.

"After Earth." *Rotten Tomatoes.* Flixster, n.d. Web. 08 Dec. 2014. <http://www.rottentomatoes.com/m/after_earth/>.

"An Alan Smithee Film: Burn, Hollywood, Burn." *Rotten Tomatoes*. Flixster, n.d. Web. 08 Dec. 2014. <http://www.rottentomatoes.com/m/an_alan_smithee_film_bu rn_hollywood_burn/>.

"An Alan Smithee Film: Burn Hollywood Burn (1997) - Company Credits." *IMDb.com*. n.d. Web. 06 Dec. 2014. <http://www.imdb.com/title/tt0118577/companycredits?ref_=t t_ql_dt_5>.

"Alexander." *Rotten Tomatoes*. Flixster, n.d. Web. 08 Dec. 2014. <http://www.rottentomatoes.com/m/alexander/>.

"All About Steve." *Rotten Tomatoes*. Flixster, n.d. Web. 08 Dec. 2014. <http://www.rottentomatoes.com/m/all_about_steve/>.

"Anaconda." *Rotten Tomatoes*. Flixster, n.d. Web. 08 Dec. 2014. <http://www.rottentomatoes.com/m/anaconda/>.

"Annie." *Rotten Tomatoes*. Flixster, n.d. Web. 08 Dec. 2014. <http://www.rottentomatoes.com/m/annie_1981/>.

"Armageddon." *Rotten Tomatoes*. Flixster, n.d. Web. 08 Dec. 2014. <http://www.rottentomatoes.com/m/armageddon/>.

"The Avengers." *Rotten Tomatoes*. Flixster, n.d. Web. 08 Dec. 2014. <http://www.rottentomatoes.com/m/1083461-avengers/>.

"Barb Wire." *Rotten Tomatoes*. Flixster, n.d. Web. 08 Dec. 2014. <http://www.rottentomatoes.com/m/barb_wire/>.

"Basic Instinct 2." *Rotten Tomatoes*. Flixster, n.d. Web. 08 Dec. 2014. <http://www.rottentomatoes.com/m/basic_instinct_2/>.

"Batman & Robin." *Rotten Tomatoes*. Flixster, n.d. Web. 08 Dec. 2014. <http://www.rottentomatoes.com/m/1077027-batman_and_robin/>.

"Battlefield Earth." *Rotten Tomatoes.* Flixster, n.d. Web. 08 Dec. 2014. <http://www.rottentomatoes.com/m/battlefield_earth/>.

"Battleship." *Rotten Tomatoes.* Flixster, n.d. Web. 08 Dec. 2014. <http://www.rottentomatoes.com/m/battleship/>.

"Big Daddy." *Rotten Tomatoes.* Flixster, n.d. Web. 08 Dec. 2014. <http://www.rottentomatoes.com/m/big_daddy/>.

"The Blair Witch Project." *Rotten Tomatoes.* Flixster, n.d. Web. 08 Dec. 2014. <http://www.rottentomatoes.com/m/blair_witch_project/>.

Blended. Dir. Frank Coraci. Perf. Adam Sandler, Drew Barrymore, and Kevin Nealon. 2014. DVD. Warner Bros., 2014.

"Blended." *Rotten Tomatoes.* Flixster, n.d. Web. 08 Dec. 2014. <http://www.rottentomatoes.com/m/blended/>.

"Bloodrayne." *Rotten Tomatoes.* Flixster, n.d. Web. 08 Dec. 2014. <http://www.rottentomatoes.com/m/bloodrayne/>.

"Blue City." *Rotten Tomatoes.* Flixster, n.d. Web. 08 Dec. 2014. <http://www.rottentomatoes.com/m/blue_city/>.

"The Bodyguard." *Rotten Tomatoes.* Flixster, n.d. Web. 08 Dec. 2014. <http://www.rottentomatoes.com/m/1042108-bodyguard/>.

"Body of Evidence." *Rotten Tomatoes.* Flixster, n.d. Web. 08 Dec. 2014. <http://www.rottentomatoes.com/m/body_of_evidence/>.

"Bolero (1984)." *Rotten Tomatoes.* Flixster, n.d. Web. 08 Dec. 2014. <http://www.rottentomatoes.com/m/1002858-bolero/>.

"The Bonfire of the Vanities." *Rotten Tomatoes.* Flixster, n.d. Web. 08 Dec. 2014. <http://www.rottentomatoes.com/m/bonfire_of_the_vanities/>.

"Book of Shadows - Blair Witch 2." *Rotten Tomatoes.* Flixster, n.d. Web. 08 Dec. 2014. <http://www.rottentomatoes.com/m/book_of_shadows_blair_witch_2/>.

"The Bounty Hunter." *Rotten Tomatoes.* Flixster, n.d. Web. 08 Dec. 2014. <http://www.rottentomatoes.com/m/1220551-bounty_hunter/>.

"Box office/business for The Adventures of Ford Fairlane (1990)." *IMDb.com.* n.d. Web. 06 Dec. 2014. <http://www.imdb.com/title/tt0098987/business>.

"Box office/business for Bolero (1984)." *IMDb.com.* n.d. Web. 06 Dec. 2014. <http://www.imdb.com/title/tt0086987/business?ref_=tt_dt_bus>.

"Box office/business for Cocktail (1988)." *IMDb.com.* n.d. Web. 06 Dec. 2014. <http://www.imdb.com/title/tt0094889/business>.

"Box office/business for Color of Night (1994)." *IMDb.com.* n.d. Web. 06 Dec. 2014. <http://www.imdb.com/title/tt0109456/business>.

"Box office/business for Dirty Love (2005)." *IMDb.com.* n.d. Web. 06 Dec. 2014. <http://www.imdb.com/title/tt0327643/business?ref_=tt_ql_dt_4>.

"Box office/business for Ghosts Can't Do It (1989)." *IMDb.com.* n.d. Web. 06 Dec. 2014. <http://www.imdb.com/title/tt0099656/business>.

"Box office/business for I Know Who Killed Me (2007)." *IMDb.com.* n.d. Web. 06 Dec. 2014. <http://www.imdb.com/title/tt0897361/business?ref_=tt_ql_dt_4>.

"Box office/business for Indecent Proposal (1993)." *IMDb.com.* n.d. Web. 06 Dec. 2014. <http://www.imdb.com/title/tt0107211/business>.

"Box office/business for Leonard Part 6 (1987)." *IMDb.com*. n.d. Web. 06 Dec. 2014. <http://www.imdb.com/title/tt0093405/business>.

"Box office/business for Shining Through (1992)." *IMDb.com*. n.d. Web. 06 Dec. 2014. <http://www.imdb.com/title/tt0105391/business>.

"Box office/business for The Lonely Lady (1983)." *IMDb.com*. n.d. Web. 06 Dec. 2014. <http://www.imdb.com/title/tt0085863/business>.

"Box office/business for Under the Cherry Moon (1986)." *IMDb.com*. n.d. Web. 06 Dec. 2014. <http://www.imdb.com/title/tt0092133/business>.

"Bratz: The Movie." *Rotten Tomatoes*. Flixster, n.d. Web. 08 Dec. 2014. <http://www.rottentomatoes.com/m/bratz_the_movie/>.

"Bucky Larson: Born to Be a Star." *Rotten Tomatoes*. Flixster, n.d. Web. 08 Dec. 2014. <http://www.rottentomatoes.com/m/bucky_larson_born_to_be_a_star/>.

"Butterfly." *Rotten Tomatoes*. Flixster, n.d. Web. 08 Dec. 2014. <http://www.rottentomatoes.com/m/butterfly_1982/>.

"Caddyshack II." *Rotten Tomatoes*. Flixster, n.d. Web. 08 Dec. 2014. <http://www.rottentomatoes.com/m/caddyshack_2/>.

"Cannonball Run II." *Rotten Tomatoes*. Flixster, n.d. Web. 08 Dec. 2014. <http://www.rottentomatoes.com/m/cannonball_run_2/>.

"Can't Stop the Music (1980) - Company Credits." *IMDb.com*. n.d. Web. 06 Dec. 2014. <http://www.imdb.com/title/tt0080492/companycredits>.

"Catwoman." *Rotten Tomatoes*. Flixster, n.d. Web. 08 Dec. 2014. <http://www.rottentomatoes.com/m/catwoman/>.

"Charlie's Angels - Full Throttle." *Rotten Tomatoes*. Flixster, n.d. Web. 08 Dec. 2014. <http://www.rottentomatoes.com/m/charlies_angels_full_throt tle/>.

"Christopher Columbus: The Discovery." *Rotten Tomatoes*. Flixster, n.d. Web. 08 Dec. 2014. <http://www.rottentomatoes.com/m/christopher_columbus_the _discovery/>.

"Cliffhanger." *Rotten Tomatoes*. Flixster, n.d. Web. 08 Dec. 2014. <http://www.rottentomatoes.com/m/1044214- cliffhanger/>.

"Cobra." *Rotten Tomatoes*. Flixster, n.d. Web. 08 Dec. 2014. <http://www.rottentomatoes.com/m/1004407-cobra/>.

"Cocktail." *Rotten Tomatoes*. Flixster, n.d. Web. 08 Dec. 2014. <http://www.rottentomatoes.com/m/1004420-cocktail/>.

"Color of Night." *Rotten Tomatoes*. Flixster, n.d. Web. 08 Dec. 2014. <http://www.rottentomatoes.com/m/color_of_night/>.

"Color of Night (1994) - Company Credits." *IMDb.com*. n.d. Web. 06 Dec. 2014. <http://www.imdb.com/title/tt0109456/companycredits?ref_=t t_ql_dt_5>.

"Congo." *Rotten Tomatoes*. Flixster, n.d. Web. 08 Dec. 2014. <http://www.rottentomatoes.com/m/congo/>.

"Cool as Ice." *Rotten Tomatoes*. Flixster, n.d. Web. 08 Dec. 2014. <http://www.rottentomatoes.com/m/cool_as_ice/>.

"Crossroads." *Rotten Tomatoes*. Flixster, n.d. Web. 08 Dec. 2014. <http://www.rottentomatoes.com/m/1112549- crossroads/>.

"Cruising." *Rotten Tomatoes*. Flixster, n.d. Web. 08 Dec. 2014. <http://www.rottentomatoes.com/m/cruising/>.

"Daddy Day Camp." *Rotten Tomatoes.* Flixster, n.d. Web. 08 Dec. 2014.
<http://www.rottentomatoes.com/m/daddy_day_camp/>.

"Deuce Bigalow: European Gigolo." *Rotten Tomatoes.* Flixster, n.d. Web. 08 Dec. 2014.
<http://www.rottentomatoes.com/m/deuce_bigelow_european_gigolo/>.

"Dice Rules." *Rotten Tomatoes.* Flixster, n.d. Web. 08 Dec. 2014. <http://www.rottentomatoes.com/m/andrew-dice-clay-dice-rules/>.

"Dirty Love." *Rotten Tomatoes.* Flixster, n.d. Web. 08 Dec. 2014. <http://www.rottentomatoes.com/m/dirty_love/>.

"Disaster Movie." *Rotten Tomatoes.* Flixster, n.d. Web. 08 Dec. 2014.
<http://www.rottentomatoes.com/m/disaster_movie/>.

"Driven." *Rotten Tomatoes.* Flixster, n.d. Web. 08 Dec. 2014.
<http://www.rottentomatoes.com/m/1107198-driven/>.

"Dr. Seuss - The Cat in the Hat." *Rotten Tomatoes.* Flixster, n.d. Web. 08 Dec. 2014.
<http://www.rottentomatoes.com/m/cat_in_the_hat/>.

"The Dukes of Hazzard." *Rotten Tomatoes.* Flixster, n.d. Web. 08 Dec. 2014.
<http://www.rottentomatoes.com/m/dukes_of_hazzard/>.

"Ed." *Rotten Tomatoes.* Flixster, n.d. Web. 08 Dec. 2014.
<http://www.rottentomatoes.com/m/ed/>.

"Endless Love." *Rotten Tomatoes.* Flixster, n.d. Web. 08 Dec. 2014. <http://www.rottentomatoes.com/m/endless_love/>.

"Fever Pitch." *Rotten Tomatoes.* Flixster, n.d. Web. 08 Dec. 2014. <http://www.rottentomatoes.com/m/1007230-fever_pitch/>.

"Final Analysis." *Rotten Tomatoes.* Flixster, n.d. Web. 08 Dec. 2014. <http://www.rottentomatoes.com/m/final_analysis/>.

"Fire Down Below." *Rotten Tomatoes.* Flixster, n.d. Web. 08 Dec. 2014. <http://www.rottentomatoes.com/m/1078038-fire_down_below/>.

"The Flintstones in Viva Rock Vegas." *Rotten Tomatoes.* Flixster, n.d. Web. 08 Dec. 2014. <http://www.rottentomatoes.com/m/flintstones_in_viva_rock_vegas/>.

"The Formula." *Rotten Tomatoes.* Flixster, n.d. Web. 08 Dec. 2014. <http://www.rottentomatoes.com/m/formula/>.

"Freddy Got Fingered." *Rotten Tomatoes.* Flixster, n.d. Web. 08 Dec. 2014. <http://www.rottentomatoes.com/m/freddy_got_fingered/>.

"Friday the 13th." *Rotten Tomatoes.* Flixster, n.d. Web. 08 Dec. 2014. <http://www.rottentomatoes.com/m/friday_the_13th_part_1/>.

"From Justin to Kelly." *Rotten Tomatoes.* Flixster, n.d. Web. 08 Dec. 2014. <http://www.rottentomatoes.com/m/from_justin_to_kelly/>.

"Ghosts Can't Do It." *Rotten Tomatoes.* Flixster, n.d. Web. 08 Dec. 2014. <http://www.rottentomatoes.com/m/ghosts_cant_do_it/>.

"Gigli." *Rotten Tomatoes.* Flixster, n.d. Web. 08 Dec. 2014. <http://www.rottentomatoes.com/m/gigli/>.

"G.I. Joe: The Rise of Cobra." *Rotten Tomatoes.* Flixster, n.d. Web. 08 Dec. 2014. <http://www.rottentomatoes.com/m/gi_joe_the_rise_of_cobra/>.

"Glitter." *Rotten Tomatoes.* Flixster, n.d. Web. 08 Dec. 2014. <http://www.rottentomatoes.com/m/glitter/>.

"Godzilla." *Rotten Tomatoes.* Flixster, n.d. Web. 08 Dec. 2014. <http://www.rottentomatoes.com/m/godzilla/>.

"Google Trends - Web Search." *Google Trends.* Google, 28 Dec. 2014. Web. 28 Dec. 2014. <http://www.google.ca/trends/>.

"Graffiti Bridge." *Rotten Tomatoes.* Flixster, n.d. Web. 08 Dec. 2014. <http://www.rottentomatoes.com/m/graffiti_bridge/>.

"Grown Ups 2." *Rotten Tomatoes.* Flixster, n.d. Web. 08 Dec. 2014. <http://www.rottentomatoes.com/m/grown_ups_2/>.

"The Happening." *Rotten Tomatoes.* Flixster, n.d. Web. 08 Dec. 2014. <http://www.rottentomatoes.com/m/10007985-happening/>.

"The Haunting." *Rotten Tomatoes.* Flixster, n.d. Web. 08 Dec. 2014. <http://www.rottentomatoes.com/m/1090789-haunting/>.

"Heaven's Gate." *Rotten Tomatoes.* Flixster, n.d. Web. 08 Dec. 2014. <http://www.rottentomatoes.com/m/heavens_gate/>.

"Hercules." *Rotten Tomatoes.* Flixster, n.d. Web. 08 Dec. 2014. <http://www.rottentomatoes.com/m/1009518-hercules/>.

"The Hottie and the Nottie." *Rotten Tomatoes.* Flixster, n.d. Web. 08 Dec. 2014. <http://www.rottentomatoes.com/m/hottie_and_the_nottie/>.

"Hot to Trot." *Rotten Tomatoes.* Flixster, n.d. Web. 08 Dec. 2014. <http://www.rottentomatoes.com/m/hot_to_trot/>.

"House of Wax." *Rotten Tomatoes.* Flixster, n.d. Web. 08 Dec. 2014. <http://www.rottentomatoes.com/m/house_of_wax_2005/>.

"Howard the Duck." *Rotten Tomatoes.* Flixster, n.d. Web. 08 Dec. 2014. <http://www.rottentomatoes.com/m/howard_the_duck/>.

"Hudson Hawk." *Rotten Tomatoes.* Flixster, n.d. Web. 08 Dec. 2014. <http://www.rottentomatoes.com/m/hudson_hawk/>.

"I Know Who Killed Me." *Rotten Tomatoes.* Flixster, n.d. Web. 08 Dec. 2014. <http://www.rottentomatoes.com/m/i_know_who_killed_me/>.

"Inchon." *Rotten Tomatoes.* Flixster, n.d. Web. 08 Dec. 2014. <http://www.rottentomatoes.com/m/inchon/>.

"Inchon (1981) - Company Credits." *IMDb.com.* n.d. Web. 06 Dec. 2014. <http://www.imdb.com/title/tt0084132/companycredits>.

"Indecent Proposal." *Rotten Tomatoes.* Flixster, n.d. Web. 08 Dec. 2014. <http://www.rottentomatoes.com/m/indecent_proposal/>.

"I Now Pronounce You Chuck and Larry." *Rotten Tomatoes.* Flixster, n.d. Web. 08 Dec. 2014. <http://www.rottentomatoes.com/m/i_now_pronounce_you_chuck_and_larry/>.

"In the Name of the King: A Dungeon Siege Tale." *Rotten Tomatoes.* Flixster, n.d. Web. 08 Dec. 2014. <http://www.rottentomatoes.com/m/in-the-name-of-the-king-a-dungeon-siege-tale/>.

"Ishtar." *Rotten Tomatoes.* Flixster, n.d. Web. 08 Dec. 2014. <http://www.rottentomatoes.com/m/ishtar/>.

"The Island of Dr. Moreau." *Rotten Tomatoes.* Flixster, n.d. Web. 08 Dec. 2014. <http://www.rottentomatoes.com/m/1072156-island_of_dr_moreau/>.

"It's Pat." *Rotten Tomatoes.* Flixster, n.d. Web. 08 Dec. 2014. <http://www.rottentomatoes.com/m/its-pat/>.

"Jack and Jill." *Rotten Tomatoes.* Flixster, n.d. Web. 08 Dec. 2014. <http://www.rottentomatoes.com/m/jack_and_jill_2011/>.

"Jaws 4 - The Revenge." *Rotten Tomatoes.* Flixster, n.d. Web. 08 Dec. 2014. <http://www.rottentomatoes.com/m/jaws-the-revenge/>.

"Jaws 3." *Rotten Tomatoes.* Flixster, n.d. Web. 08 Dec. 2014. <http://www.rottentomatoes.com/m/jaws_3/>.

"The Jazz Singer." *Rotten Tomatoes.* Flixster, n.d. Web. 08 Dec. 2014. <http://www.rottentomatoes.com/m/1010979-jazz_singer/>.

"The Karate Kid, Part III." *Rotten Tomatoes.* Flixster, n.d. Web. 08 Dec. 2014. <http://www.rottentomatoes.com/m/the_karate_kid_part_iii/>.

"Lady in the Water." *Rotten Tomatoes.* Flixster, n.d. Web. 08 Dec. 2014. <http://www.rottentomatoes.com/m/lady_in_the_water/>.

"Land of the Lost." *Rotten Tomatoes.* Flixster, n.d. Web. 08 Dec. 2014. <http://www.rottentomatoes.com/m/10009083-land_of_the_lost/>.

"Last Action Hero." *Rotten Tomatoes.* Flixster, n.d. Web. 08 Dec. 2014. <http://www.rottentomatoes.com/m/last_action_hero/>.

"The Last Airbender." *Rotten Tomatoes.* Flixster, n.d. Web. 08 Dec. 2014. <http://www.rottentomatoes.com/m/last_airbender/>.

"The Legend of the Lone Ranger." *Rotten Tomatoes.* Flixster, n.d. Web. 08 Dec. 2014. <http://www.rottentomatoes.com/m/1012184-legend_of_the_lone_ranger/>.

"Leonard Part 6." *Rotten Tomatoes.* Flixster, n.d. Web. 08 Dec. 2014. <http://www.rottentomatoes.com/m/leonard-part-6/>.

"Little Man." *Rotten Tomatoes.* Flixster, n.d. Web. 08 Dec. 2014. <http://www.rottentomatoes.com/m/little_man/>.

"Little Nicky." *Rotten Tomatoes.* Flixster, n.d. Web. 08 Dec. 2014. <http://www.rottentomatoes.com/m/little_nicky/>.

"Lock Up." *Rotten Tomatoes.* Flixster, n.d. Web. 08 Dec. 2014. <http://www.rottentomatoes.com/m/1012605-lock_up/>.

"The Lonely Lady." *Rotten Tomatoes.* Flixster, n.d. Web. 08 Dec. 2014. <http://www.rottentomatoes.com/m/lonely_lady/>.

"The Lonely Lady (1983) - Company Credits." *IMDb.com.* n.d. Web. 06 Dec. 2014. <http://www.imdb.com/title/tt0085863/companycredits>.

"The Lone Ranger." *Rotten Tomatoes.* Flixster, n.d. Web. 08 Dec. 2014. <http://www.rottentomatoes.com/m/the_lone_ranger/>.

"The Love Guru." *Rotten Tomatoes.* Flixster, n.d. Web. 08 Dec. 2014. <http://www.rottentomatoes.com/m/love_guru/>.

"Mac and Me." *Rotten Tomatoes.* Flixster, n.d. Web. 08 Dec. 2014. <http://www.rottentomatoes.com/m/mac_and_me/>.

"Megaforce." *Rotten Tomatoes.* Flixster, n.d. Web. 08 Dec. 2014. <http://www.rottentomatoes.com/m/megaforce/>.

"Men, Women & Children." *Rotten Tomatoes.* Flixster, n.d. Web. 08 Dec. 2014. <http://www.rottentomatoes.com/m/men_women_and_children/>.

"Mommie Dearest." *Rotten Tomatoes.* Flixster, n.d. Web. 08 Dec. 2014. <http://www.rottentomatoes.com/m/mommie_dearest/>.

"Movie Budgets." *The Numbers: Where Data and the Movie Business Meet.* Nash Information Services, 2014. Web. 05 Dec. 2014. <www.the-numbers.com/movie/budgets/all>.

"Movie 43." *Rotten Tomatoes.* Flixster, n.d. Web. 08 Dec. 2014. <http://www.rottentomatoes.com/m/movie_43/>.

"Newsies." *Rotten Tomatoes.* Flixster, n.d. Web. 08 Dec. 2014. <http://www.rottentomatoes.com/m/newsies/>.

"New Year's Eve." *Rotten Tomatoes.* Flixster, n.d. Web. 08 Dec. 2014. <http://www.rottentomatoes.com/m/new_years_eve_2011/>.

"The Next Best Thing." *Rotten Tomatoes.* Flixster, n.d. Web. 08 Dec. 2014. <http://www.rottentomatoes.com/m/next_best_thing/>.

"1977 Oscars." *Oscars.org.* Academy of Motion Picture Arts and Sciences, 1987. Web. 08 Dec. 2014. <www.oscars.org/oscars/ceremonies/1977>.

"Norbit." *Rotten Tomatoes.* Flixster, n.d. Web. 08 Dec. 2014. <http://www.rottentomatoes.com/m/norbit/>.

"North." *Rotten Tomatoes.* Flixster, n.d. Web. 08 Dec. 2014. <http://www.rottentomatoes.com/m/north/>.

"Nothing But Trouble." *Rotten Tomatoes.* Flixster, n.d. Web. 08 Dec. 2014. <http://www.rottentomatoes.com/m/nothing_but_trouble_1998/>.

"The Nude Bomb (The Return of Maxwell Smart)." *Rotten Tomatoes.* Flixster, n.d. Web. 08 Dec. 2014. <http://www.rottentomatoes.com/m/nude_bomb/>.

"Old Dogs." *Rotten Tomatoes.* Flixster, n.d. Web. 08 Dec. 2014. <http://www.rottentomatoes.com/m/10009596-old_dogs/>.

226

"On Deadly Ground." *Rotten Tomatoes.* Flixster, n.d. Web. 08 Dec. 2014. <http://www.rottentomatoes.com/m/on_deadly_ground/>.

"The Oogieloves in the Big Balloon Adventure." *Rotten Tomatoes.* Flixster, n.d. Web. 08 Dec. 2014. <http://www.rottentomatoes.com/m/the_oogieloves_in_the_big_balloon_adventure/>.

"Pearl Harbor." *Rotten Tomatoes.* Flixster, n.d. Web. 08 Dec. 2014. <http://www.rottentomatoes.com/m/1108389-pearl_harbor/>.

"Pinocchio." *Rotten Tomatoes.* Flixster, n.d. Web. 08 Dec. 2014. <http://www.rottentomatoes.com/m/1119026-pinocchio/>.

"The Pirate Movie." *Rotten Tomatoes.* Flixster, n.d. Web. 08 Dec. 2014. <http://www.rottentomatoes.com/m/pirate_movie/>.

"The Postman." *Rotten Tomatoes.* Flixster, n.d. Web. 08 Dec. 2014. <http://www.rottentomatoes.com/m/postman/>.

"Rambo: First Blood Part II." *Rotten Tomatoes.* Flixster, n.d. Web. 08 Dec. 2014. <http://www.rottentomatoes.com/m/rambo-first-blood-part-ii/>.

"Rambo III." *Rotten Tomatoes.* Flixster, n.d. Web. 08 Dec. 2014. <http://www.rottentomatoes.com/m/rambo_iii/>.

"Raise the Titanic." *Rotten Tomatoes.* Flixster, n.d. Web. 08 Dec. 2014. <http://www.rottentomatoes.com/m/raise_the_titanic/>.

"The Real Cancun." *Rotten Tomatoes.* Flixster, n.d. Web. 08 Dec. 2014. <http://www.rottentomatoes.com/m/real_cancun/>.

"Return to the Blue Lagoon." *Rotten Tomatoes.* Flixster, n.d. Web. 08 Dec. 2014. <http://www.rottentomatoes.com/m/return_to_the_blue_lagoon/>.

"Revolution." *Rotten Tomatoes*. Flixster, n.d. Web. 08 Dec. 2014. <http://www.rottentomatoes.com/m/1028715-revolution/>.

"Rhinestone." *Rotten Tomatoes*. Flixster, n.d. Web. 08 Dec. 2014. <http://www.rottentomatoes.com/m/rhinestone/>.

"Road House." *Rotten Tomatoes*. Flixster, n.d. Web. 08 Dec. 2014. <http://www.rottentomatoes.com/m/1017666-road_house/>.

"Rocky IV." *Rotten Tomatoes*. Flixster, n.d. Web. 08 Dec. 2014. <http://www.rottentomatoes.com/m/rocky_iv/>.

"Rocky V." *Rotten Tomatoes*. Flixster, n.d. Web. 08 Dec. 2014. <http://www.rottentomatoes.com/m/rocky_v/>.

"Saturn 3." *Rotten Tomatoes*. Flixster, n.d. Web. 08 Dec. 2014. <http://www.rottentomatoes.com/m/saturn_3/>.

"The Scarlet Letter." *Rotten Tomatoes*. Flixster, n.d. Web. 08 Dec. 2014. <http://www.rottentomatoes.com/m/1066120-scarlet_letter/>.

"Sex and the City 2." *Rotten Tomatoes*. Flixster, n.d. Web. 08 Dec. 2014. <http://www.rottentomatoes.com/m/sex_and_the_city_2/>.

Sex Tape. Dir. Jake Kasdan. Perf. Cameron Diaz, Jason Segel, and Rob Corddry. 2014. DVD. Sony Pictures Home Entertainment, 2014.

"Shanghai Surprise." *Rotten Tomatoes*. Flixster, n.d. Web. 08 Dec. 2014. <http://www.rottentomatoes.com/m/shanghai_surprise/>.

"Sheena." *Rotten Tomatoes*. Flixster, n.d. Web. 08 Dec. 2014. <http://www.rottentomatoes.com/m/sheena/>.

"Shining Through." *Rotten Tomatoes*. Flixster, n.d. Web. 08 Dec. 2014. <http://www.rottentomatoes.com/m/shining_through/>.

"Showgirls." *Rotten Tomatoes.* Flixster, n.d. Web. 08 Dec. 2014. <http://www.rottentomatoes.com/m/showgirls/>.

"The Specialist." *Rotten Tomatoes.* Flixster, n.d. Web. 08 Dec. 2014. <http://www.rottentomatoes.com/m/1056079-specialist/>.

"Speed 2 - Cruise Control." *Rotten Tomatoes.* Flixster, n.d. Web. 08 Dec. 2014. <http://www.rottentomatoes.com/m/speed_2_cruise_control/>.

"Speed Zone." *Rotten Tomatoes.* Flixster, n.d. Web. 08 Dec. 2014. <http://www.rottentomatoes.com/m/speed_zone/>.

"Spice World." *Rotten Tomatoes.* Flixster, n.d. Web. 08 Dec. 2014. <http://www.rottentomatoes.com/m/spice_world/>.

"Star Trek V - The Final Frontier." *Rotten Tomatoes.* Flixster, n.d. Web. 08 Dec. 2014. <http://www.rottentomatoes.com/m/star_trek_v_the_final_frontier/>.

"Star Wars: Episode I - The Phantom Menace." *Rotten Tomatoes.* Flixster, n.d. Web. 08 Dec. 2014. <http://www.rottentomatoes.com/m/star_wars_episode_i_the_phantom_menace/>.

"Star Wars: Episode II - Attack of the Clones 3D." *Rotten Tomatoes.* Flixster, n.d. Web. 08 Dec. 2014. <http://www.rottentomatoes.com/m/star_wars_episode_ii_attack_of_the_clones_3d/>.

"Striptease." *Rotten Tomatoes.* Flixster, n.d. Web. 08 Dec. 2014. <http://www.rottentomatoes.com/m/striptease/>.

"Stroker Ace." *Rotten Tomatoes.* Flixster, n.d. Web. 08 Dec. 2014. <http://www.rottentomatoes.com/m/stroker_ace/>.

"The Stupids." *Rotten Tomatoes.* Flixster, n.d. Web. 08 Dec. 2014. <http://www.rottentomatoes.com/m/stupids/>.

"Superbabies: Baby Geniuses 2." *Rotten Tomatoes.* Flixster, n.d. Web. 08 Dec. 2014. <http://www.rottentomatoes.com/m/super_babies_baby_geniuses_2/>.

"Surviving Christmas." *Rotten Tomatoes.* Flixster, n.d. Web. 08 Dec. 2014. <http://www.rottentomatoes.com/m/surviving_christmas/>.

"Swept Away." *Rotten Tomatoes.* Flixster, n.d. Web. 08 Dec. 2014. <http://www.rottentomatoes.com/m/1116774-swept_away/>.

Tammy. Dir. Ben Falcone. Perf. Melissa McCarthy, Susan Sarandon, and Allison Janney. DVD. Warner Bros., 2014.

"Tarzan, the Ape Man." *Rotten Tomatoes.* Flixster, n.d. Web. 08 Dec. 2014. <http://www.rottentomatoes.com/m/1020897-tarzan_the_ape_man/>.

"That's My Boy." *Rotten Tomatoes.* Flixster, n.d. Web. 08 Dec. 2014. <http://www.rottentomatoes.com/m/thats_my_boy/>.

"A Thousand Words." *Rotten Tomatoes.* Flixster, n.d. Web. 08 Dec. 2014. <http://www.rottentomatoes.com/m/a-thousand-words/>.

"3000 Miles to Graceland." *Rotten Tomatoes.* Flixster, n.d. Web. 08 Dec. 2014. <http://www.rottentomatoes.com/m/3000_miles_to_graceland/>.

"Tough Guys Don't Dance." *Rotten Tomatoes.* Flixster, n.d. Web. 08 Dec. 2014. <http://www.rottentomatoes.com/m/tough_guys_dont_dance/>.

"Transformers: Age of Extinction." *Rotten Tomatoes.* Flixster, n.d. Web. 08 Dec. 2014. <http://www.rottentomatoes.com/m/transformers_age_of_extinction/>.

"Transformers: Dark of the Moon." *Rotten Tomatoes*. Flixster, n.d. Web. 08 Dec. 2014. <http://www.rottentomatoes.com/m/transformers_dark_of_the _moon/>.

"Transformers: Revenge of the Fallen." *Rotten Tomatoes*. Flixster, n.d. Web. 08 Dec. 2014. <http://www.rottentomatoes.com/m/transformers_revenge_of_ the_fallen/>.

"Twilight Saga: Breaking Dawn Part 1." *Rotten Tomatoes*. Flixster, n.d. Web. 08 Dec. 2014. <http://www.rottentomatoes.com/m/twilight_saga_breaking_d awn/>.

"The Twilight Saga: Breaking Dawn Part 2." *Rotten Tomatoes*. Flixster, n.d. Web. 08 Dec. 2014. <http://www.rottentomatoes.com/m/the_twilight_saga_breakin g_dawn_part_2/>.

"The Twilight Saga: Eclipse." *Rotten Tomatoes*. Flixster, n.d. Web. 08 Dec. 2014. < http://www.rottentomatoes.com/m/1210749-eclipse/>.

"Two of a Kind." *Rotten Tomatoes*. Flixster, n.d. Web. 08 Dec. 2014. < http://www.rottentomatoes.com/m/1022225- two_of_a_kind/>.

"Tyler Perry's A Madea Christmas." *Rotten Tomatoes*. Flixster, n.d. Web. 08 Dec. 2014. <http://www.rottentomatoes.com/m/tyler_perrys_a_madea_ch ristmas_2013/>.

"Under the Cherry Moon." *Rotten Tomatoes*. Flixster, n.d. Web. 08 Dec. 2014. <http://www.rottentomatoes.com/m/under_the_cherry_moon/ >.

"Vampires Suck." *Rotten Tomatoes*. Flixster, n.d. Web. 08 Dec. 2014. <http://www.rottentomatoes.com/m/vampires_suck/>.

"Village People - Can't Stop the Music." *Rotten Tomatoes.* Flixster, n.d. Web. 08 Dec. 2014. <http://www.rottentomatoes.com/m/cant_stop_the_music/>.

"Waterworld." *Rotten Tomatoes.* Flixster, n.d. Web. 08 Dec. 2014. < http://www.rottentomatoes.com/m/waterworld/>.

"Where The Boys Are '84." *Rotten Tomatoes.* Flixster, n.d. Web. 08 Dec. 2014. <http://www.rottentomatoes.com/m/where_the_boys_are_84/> .

"White Chicks." *Rotten Tomatoes.* Flixster, n.d. Web. 08 Dec. 2014. <http://www.rottentomatoes.com/m/white_chicks/>.

"The Wicker Man." *Rotten Tomatoes.* Flixster, n.d. Web. 08 Dec. 2014. <http://www.rottentomatoes.com/m/the_wicker_man_2006/>.

"Who's That Girl?" *Rotten Tomatoes.* Flixster, n.d. Web. 08 Dec. 2014. <http://www.rottentomatoes.com/m/whos-that-girl/>.

"Wild Wild West." *Rotten Tomatoes.* Flixster, n.d. Web. 08 Dec. 2014. <http://www.rottentomatoes.com/m/wild_wild_west/>.

Wilson, John. "Bio." *The Official Razzie Forum.* Golden Raspberry Award Foundation, 23 Jan. 2011. Web. 16 Dec. 2014. <www.razzies.com/forum/bio_topic4783.html>.

---. "A Brief History of The Razzie Awards." *The Official Razzie Forum.* Golden Raspberry Award Foundation, 04 Dec. 2005. Web. 16 Dec. 2014. <www.razzies.com/forum/topic326_page1&TPN=1.html>.

"Windows." *Rotten Tomatoes.* Flixster, n.d. Web. 08 Dec. 2014. <http://www.rottentomatoes.com/m/windows/>.

"Wyatt Earp." *Rotten Tomatoes.* Flixster, n.d. Web. 08 Dec. 2014. <http://www.rottentomatoes.com/m/1052698-wyatt_earp/>.

"Xanadu." *Rotten Tomatoes.* Flixster, n.d. Web. 08 Dec. 2014.
<http://www.rottentomatoes.com/m/xanadu/>.

"Year of the Dragon." *Rotten Tomatoes.* Flixster, n.d. Web. 08
Dec. 2014. <http://www.rottentomatoes.com/m/1024232-
year_of_the_dragon/>.

CHAPTER SEVEN: IT'S THE END OF THE WORLD AS WE KNOW IT AND IT'S RATED G

Belkin, Lisa. "Are Fairytales Too Scary for Children?"
NYTimes.com. NY Times, Co., 12 Jan. 2009. Web. 11 Nov.
2014. <parenting.blogs.nytimes.com/2009/01/12/are-
fairytales-to-scary-for-children/>.

Brave. Dir. Mark Andrews and Brenda Chapman. Perf. Kelly
Macdonald, Billy Connolly, and Emma Thompson. 2012.
DVD. Buena Vista, 2012.

A Bug's Life. Dir. John Lasseter. Perf. Dave Foley, Kevin
Spacey, and Julia Louis-Dreyfus. 1998. DVD. Buena Vista,
2009.

Callahan, Yesha. "Are You Raising a Homophobic Child?"
The Root. The Graham Holdings Company, 07 Jul. 2014.
Web. 21 Dec. 2014.
<http://www.theroot.com/articles/culture/2014/07/are_you_rai
sing_a_homophobic_child.html>.

Cars. Dir. John Lasseter and Joe Ranft. Perf. Owen Wilson,
Bonnie Hunt, and Paul Newman. 2006. DVD. Buena Vista,
2006.

Cars 2. Dir. John Lasseter and Brad Lewis. Perf. Owen
Wilson, Larry the Cable Guy, and Michael Caine. 2011. DVD.
Buena Vista, 2011.

"Disney Pixar Movies We Love." *Common Sense Media.*
Common Sense Media, n.d. Web. 08 Dec. 2014.
<https://www.commonsensemedia.org/lists/disney-pixar-
movies-we-love>.

Eller, Claudia. "Disney, Pixar Try To Patch Things Up."
Orlando Sentinel. Orlando Sentinel, 07 May 2003. Web. 08
Dec. 2014. <articles.orlandosentinel.com/2003-05-
07/news/0305070180_1_pixar-finding-nemo-walt-disney>.

Finding Nemo. Dir. Andrew Stanton. Perf. Albert Brooks,
Ellen DeGeneres, and Alexander Gould. 2003. DVD. Buena
Vista, 2003.

Fleming, Michael. "Jessica Rabbit revealed." *Variety*. Penske
Business Media, 13 Mar. 1994. Web. 08 Dec. 2014.
<variety.com/1994/voices/columns/jessica-rabbit-revealed-
119154/>.

The Incredibles. Dir. Brad Bird. Perf. Craig T. Nelson, Holly
Hunter, and Samuel L. Jackson. 2004. DVD. Buena Vista,
2005.

Knapp, Don. "Jonestown massacre + 20: Questions linger."
CNN. Turner Broadcasting System, Inc., 18 Nov. 1998. Web.
21 Nov. 2014.
<http://www.cnn.com/US/9811/18/jonestown.anniv.01>.

Lieberman, David. "Pixar split from Disney could be on the
horizon." *USA Today*. Gannett Co. Inc., 09 Feb. 2003. Web.
08 Dec. 2014.
<usatoday30.usatoday.com/money/media/columnist/lieberman
/2003-02-09-pixar_x.htm>.

The Little Mermaid. Dir. Ron Clements and John Musker.
Perf. Jodi Benson, Christopher Daniel Barnes, and Pat Carroll.
1989. DVD. Walt Disney Studios Home Entertainment, 2013.

Mandel, Susannah. "Mask and Closet, Or, 'Under the Hood':
Metaphors and Representations of Homosexuality in
American Superhero Comics After 1985." Diss. Massachusetts
Institute of Technology, 22 Aug. 2003. Web.

McPake, Joanna, and Lydia Plowman. "Seven Myths About
Young Children And Technology." *Childhood Education* 89.1
(2013). Web. 08 Dec. 2014.
doi:10.1080/00094056.2013.757490.

Monsters, Inc. Dir. Pete Docter. Perf. John Goodman, Billy Crystal, and Mary Gibbs. 2001. DVD. Buena Vista, 2002.

Monsters University. Dir. Dan Scanlon. Perf. Billy Crystal, John Goodman, and Helen Mirren. 2013. DVD. Buena Vista, 2013.

Noe, Denise. "Christianity, Promiscuity and Pedophilia Inside 'The Family' Cult." *Crime Library.* Turner Entertainment Networks, Inc., 12 Jan. 2014. Web. 21 Dec. 2014. <www.crimelibrary.com/blog/article/christianity-promiscuity-and-pedophilia-inside-the-family-cult/index.html>.

Osherow, Neal. "Making Sense of the Nonsensical: An Analysis of Jonestown." *Guyana.org.* Guyana News and Information, 24 Jun. 2000. Web. 21 Dec. 2014. <www.guyana.org/features/jonestown.html>.

Ratatouille. Dir. Brad Bird. Perf. Patton Oswalt, Ian Holm, and Lou Romano. 2007. DVD. Buena Vista, 2007.

Reilly, Nicholas. "Powerful anti-hate ad teaches: 'What we learn as children can last a lifetime'." *Metro.co.uk.* Associated Newspapers Limited, 10 Nov. 2014. Web. 21 Dec. 2014. <metro.co.uk/2014/11/10/powerful-anti-hate-ad-teaches-what-we-learn-as-children-can-last-a-lifetime-4942867>.

Reiterman, Tim. "For Those Who Were There, Jonestown's A Part Of Each Day." *The Seattle Times.* Seattle Times Company, 18 Nov. 1998. Web. 21 Dec. 2014. <community.seattletimes.nwsource.com/archive/?date=19981118&slug=2784066>.

Salemi, Michelle. "Experts say parents infect their children with racial ignorance." *Medill Reports.* Northwestern University, 03 May 2012. Web. 21 Dec. 2014. <news.medill.northwestern.edu/chicago/news.aspx?id=205068>.

Schussler, Arielle. "The Case Against Fairytales." Caliber Mag. Associated Students of the University of California, 13

Mar. 2013. Web. 11 Nov. 2014. <calibermag.org/articles/the-case-against-fairytales/>.

Smith, Leef. "Disney's Loin King? Group Sees Dirt in the Dust." *Washington Post*. Washington Post Company, 01 Sep. 1995. Web. 08 Dec. 2014. <www.washingtonpost.com/wp-srv/style/longterm/review96/flionking.htm>.

Talmadge, Eric. "The North Korean indoctrination festival where children trained like the 'Hitler Youth' celebrate regime." *National Post*. Postmedia Network Inc., 12 Apr. 2013. Web. 21 Nov. 2014. <news.nationalpost.com/2013/04/12/the-north-korean-indoctrination-festival-where-schoolchildren-trained-like-the-hitler-youth-celebrate-the-regime>.

Toy Story. Dir. John Lasseter. Perf. Tom Hanks, Tim Allen, and Laurie Metcalf. 1995. DVD. Buena Vista, 2010.

Toy Story 2. Dir. John Lasseter. Perf. Tom Hanks, Tim Allen, and Joan Cusack. 1999. DVD. Buena Vista, 2005.

Toy Story 3. Dir. Lee Unkrich. Perf. Tom Hanks, Tim Allen, and Joan Cusack. 2010. DVD. Buena Vista, 2010.

"Treatment For Abandonment & Attachment." *The Refuge*. n.d. Web. 31 Dec. 2014. <www.therefuge-ahealingplace.com/ptsd-treatment/abandonment>.

Up. Dir. Pete Docter. Perf. Ed Asner, Christopher Plummer, and Jordan Nagai. 2009. DVD. Buena Vista, 2009.

WALL-E. Dir. Andrew Stanton. Perf. Ben Burtt, Elissa Knight, and Jeff Garlin. 2008. DVD. Buena Vista, 2008.

"What's Wrong With Being A Princess?" *ABC News*. ABC News Internet Ventures, 22 Apr. 2007. Web. 08 Dec. 2014. <abcnews.go.com/GMA/Health/story?id=3065469&page=1>.

Wilkinson, Will. "Natural-Born Homophobes?" *Forbes*. Forbes.com LLC, 17 Mar. 2011. Web. 21 Dec. 2014. <www.forbes.com/sites/willwilkinson/2011/03/17/natural-born-homophobes>.

236

Wolfe, Ireland. "Fear of Abandonment in Childhood Development." *Global Post*. International News, n.d. Web. 31 Dec. 2014. <everydaylife.globalpost.com/fear-abandonment-childhood-development-5299.html>.

Wright, Lawrence. "The Apostate: Paul Haggis vs. the Church of Scientology." *The New Yorker*. Condé Nast, 14 Feb. 2011. Web. 21 Dec. 2014. <www.newyorker.com/magazine/2011/02/14/the-apostate-3>.

CHAPTER EIGHT: STIRRING THE POT

"The Ballad of Magellan." *Animaniacs*: *Volume 4*. Writ. John P. McCann and Paul Rugg. Dir. Audu Paden and Barry Caldwell. Prod. Peter Hastings and Rusty Mills. Series prod. Steven Spielberg. DVD. Warner Bros., 2013.

"Bart the Fink." *The Simpsons: The Complete Seventh Season*. Writ. John Swartzwelder. Dir. Jim Reardon. Prod. J. Michael Mendel, Richard Raynis, David Silverman, and Richard Sakai. Series prod. Matt Groening. DVD. Twentieth Century Fox, 2005.

"Exploring the Alpabet." *SesameStreet.org*. Sesame Workshop, n.d. Web. 29 Oct. 2014. <http://www.sesamestreet.org/parents/topicsandactivities/topics/abc>.

Legally Blonde. Dir. Robert Luketic. Perf. Reese Witherspoon, Luke Wilson, and Selma Blair. 2001. DVD. MGM, 2004.

"Lemon of Troy." *The Simpsons: The Complete Sixth Season*. Writ. Brent Forrester. Dir. Jim Reardon. Prod. J. Michael Mendel, Richard Raynis, David Silverman, and Richard Sakai. Series prod. Matt Groening. DVD. Twentieth Century Fox, 2005.

Leung, Marianne. "Sponge Like Brain." *Serendip Studio*. Bryn Mawr College, 29 Apr. 2010. Web. 29 Oct. 2014. <serendip.brynmawr.edu/exchange/node/7240>.

"MacBeth." *Animaniacs*: *Volume 3*. Writ. Deanna Oliver. Dir. Michael Gerard and Jon McClenahan. Prod. Rich Arons. Series prod. Steven Spielberg. DVD. Warner Bros., 2007.

Misery. Dir. Rob Reiner. Perf. James Caan, Kathy Bates, and Frances Sternhagen. 1990. DVD. Twentieth Century Fox, 2014.

"Multiplication." *Animaniacs*: *Volume 4*. Writ. Randy Rogel. Dir. Liz Holzman and Al Zegler. Prod. Peter Hastings and Rusty Mills. Series prod. Steven Spielberg. DVD. Warner Bros., 2013.

National Research Council. *The Growth of Incarceration in the United States: Exploring Causes and Consequences*. Washington, DC: The National Academies Press, 2014. Web. 31 Oct 2014. < http://www.nap.edu/catalog.php?record_id=18613>.

Orange Is The New Black. Series prod. Jenji Kohan. Perf. Taylor Schilling, Laura Prepon, and Uzo Aduba. 2013. DVD. Lions Gate, 2014.

Pasnik, Shelley. "TV and Kids under Age 3." *PBS Parents*. Public Broadcasting Service, n.d. Web. 29 Oct. 2014. < http://www.pbs.org/parents/childrenandmedia/article-faq.html>.

"The Perfect Present." *Sex and the City: Season Six: Part One*. Writ. Jenny Bicks. Dir. David Frankel. Series prod. Darren Star. DVD. HBO, 2004.

"The President's Song." *Animaniacs*: *Volume 3*. Writ. Randy Rogel. Dir. Al Zegler. Prod. Peter Hastings and Rusty Mills. Series prod. Steven Spielberg. DVD. Warner Bros., 2007.

"Secret Sex." *Sex and the City: The Complete First Season*. Writ. Darren Star. Dir. Michael Fields. Series prod. Darren Star. DVD. HBO, 2000.

"$pringfield (Or, How I Learned to Stop Worrying and Love Legalized Gambling)." *The Simpsons: The Complete Fifth Season*. Writ. Bill Oakley and Josh Weinstein. Dir. Wes

Archer. Prod. Richard Raynis, David Silverman, and Richard Sakai. Series prod. Matt Groening. DVD. Twentieth Century Fox, 2004.

"Wakko's America." *Animaniacs*: *Volume 1*. Writ. Randy Rogel and Tom Ruegger. Dir. Rusty Mills and Ron Fleischer. Prod. Rich Arons and Sherri Stone. Series prod. Steven Spielberg. DVD. Warner Bros., 2006.

CHAPTER NINE: THE LUCRATIVE LORE OF LORRE

"The American-Western European Values Gap." *PewGlobal.org*. Pew Research Center, 29 Feb. 2012. Web. 11 Nov. 2014. <www.pewglobal.org/2011/11/17/the-american-western-european-values-gap/>.

Andre, Claire, and Manuel Velasquez. "Creating the Good Society." *Issues in Ethics* 5.1 (1992). Web. 11 Nov. 2014. <www.scu.edu/ethics/publications/iie/v5n1/>.

"Back Off, Mary Poppins." *Two and a Half Men: The Complete Second Season*. Writ. Lee Aronsohn and Susan Beavers. Dir. Pamela Fryman. Series prod. Chuck Lorre and Lee Aronsohn. DVD. Warner Bros., 2008.

"The Benefactor Factor." *The Big Bang Theory: The Complete Fourth Season*. Writ. Chuck Lorre, Eric Kaplan, and Steve Holland. Dir. Mark Cendrowski. Prod. Faye Oshima Belyeu. Series prod. Chuck Lorre and Bill Prady. DVD. Warner Bros., 2011.

Bibler, Frank. "Complete TV Ratings 1995-1996." *Top Rated Programs*. 26 Jul. 2002. Web. 31 Dec. 2014. < http://fbibler.chez.com/tvstats/recent_data/1995-96.html>.

---. "Complete TV Ratings 1994-1995." *Top Rated Programs*. 26 Jul. 2002. Web. 31 Dec. 2014. <http://fbibler.chez.com/tvstats/recent_data/1994-95.html>.

---. "Complete TV Ratings 1997-1998." *Top Rated Programs*. 26 Jul. 2002. Web. 31 Dec. 2014. < http://fbibler.chez.com/tvstats/recent_data/1997-98.html>.

---. "Complete TV Ratings 1996-1997." *Top Rated Programs.* 26 Jul. 2002. Web. 31 Dec. 2014. < http://fbibler.chez.com/tvstats/recent_data/1996-97.html>.

"A Big Bag of Dog." *Two and a Half Men: The Complete Tenth Season.* Writ. Jim Patterson and Eddie Gorodetsky. Dir. James Widdoes. Series prod. Chuck Lorre and Lee Aronsohn. DVD. Warner Bros., 2013.

"The Big Bran Hypothesis." *The Big Bang Theory: The Complete First Season.* Writ. Robert Cohen and Dave Goetsch. Dir. Mark Cendrowski. Prod. Faye Oshima Belyeu. Series prod. Chuck Lorre and Bill Prady. DVD. Warner Bros., 2008.

"Big Girls Don't Throw Food." *Two and a Half Men: The Complete Ninth Season.* Writ. Eddie Gorodetsky and Jim Patterson. Dir. James Widdoes. Series prod. Chuck Lorre and Lee Aronsohn. DVD. Warner Bros., 2012.

"The Cooper-Nowitzki Theorem." *The Big Bang Theory: The Complete Second Season.* Writ. Tim Doyle and Richard Rosenstock. Dir. Mark Cendrowski. Prod. Faye Oshima Belyeu. Series prod. Chuck Lorre and Bill Prady. DVD. Warner Bros., 2009.

"The Crazy Bitch Gazette." *Two and a Half Men: The Complete Eighth Season.* Writ. Don Foster, Eddie Gorodetsky, and Jim Patterson. Dir. James Widdoes. Series prod. Chuck Lorre and Lee Aronsohn. DVD. Warner Bros., 2011.

"David Copperfield Slipped Me a Roofie." *Two and a Half Men: The Complete Sixth Season.* Writ. Don Foster and Jim Patterson. Dir. Jeff Melman. Series prod. Chuck Lorre and Lee Aronsohn. DVD. Warner Bros., 2009.

"The Duchess of Dull-in-Sack." *Two and a Half Men: The Complete Ninth Season.* Writ. Eddie Gorodetsky, Jim Patterson, and Don Reo. Dir. James Widdoes. Series prod. Chuck Lorre and Lee Aronsohn. DVD. Warner Bros., 2012.

"The Electric Can Opener Fluctuation." *The Big Bang Theory: The Complete Third Season*. Writ. Steven Molaro. Dir. Mark Cendrowski. Prod. Faye Oshima Belyeu. Series prod. Chuck Lorre and Bill Prady. DVD. Warner Bros., 2010.

"Four Balls, Two Bats and One Mitt." *Two and a Half Men: The Complete Tenth Season*. Writ. Chuck Lorre and Eddie Gorodetsky. Dir. James Widdoes. Series prod. Chuck Lorre and Lee Aronsohn. DVD. Warner Bros., 2013.

"Frodo's Headshots." *Two and a Half Men: The Complete Ninth Season*. Writ. Susan Beavers, Don Reo, and David Richardson. Dir. James Widdoes. Series prod. Chuck Lorre and Lee Aronsohn. DVD. Warner Bros., 2012.

"A Giant Cat Holding a Churro." *Two and a Half Men: The Complete Ninth Season*. Writ. Susan Beavers, Don Reo, and David Richardson. Dir. James Widdoes. Series prod. Chuck Lorre and Lee Aronsohn. DVD. Warner Bros., 2012.

"The Hamburger Postulate." *The Big Bang Theory: The Complete First Season*. Writ. Dave Goetsch and Steven Molaro. Dir. Mark Cendrowski. Prod. Faye Oshima Belyeu. Series prod. Chuck Lorre and Bill Prady. DVD. Warner Bros., 2008.

"I Changed My Mind About The Milk." *Two and a Half Men: The Complete Tenth Season*. Writ. Don Reo and Jim Patterson. Dir. James Widdoes. Series prod. Chuck Lorre and Lee Aronsohn. DVD. Warner Bros., 2013.

"The Irish Pub Formulation." *The Big Bang Theory: The Complete Fourth Season*. Writ. Bill Prady, Eric Kaplan, and Maria Ferrari. Dir. Mark Cendrowski. Prod. Faye Oshima Belyeu. Series prod. Chuck Lorre and Bill Prady. DVD. Warner Bros., 2011.

"Just Like Buffalo." *Two and a Half Men: The Complete First Season*. Writ. Lee Aronsohn and Don Foster. Dir. Rob Schiller. Series prod. Chuck Lorre and Lee Aronsohn. DVD. Warner Bros., 2007.

"The Lizard-Spock Expansion." *The Big Bang Theory: The Complete Second Season*. Writ. Dave Goetsch and Jennifer Glickman. Dir. Mark Cendrowski. Prod. Faye Oshima Belyeu. Series prod. Chuck Lorre and Bill Prady. DVD. Warner Bros., 2009.

"The Luminous Fish Effect." *The Big Bang Theory: The Complete First Season*. Writ. David Litt and Lee Aronsohn. Dir. Mark Cendrowski. Prod. Faye Oshima Belyeu. Series prod. Chuck Lorre and Bill Prady. DVD. Warner Bros., 2008.

"The Maternal Capacitance." *The Big Bang Theory: The Complete Second Season*. Writ. Richard Rosenstock and Steven Molaro. Dir. Mark Cendrowski. Prod. Faye Oshima Belyeu. Series prod. Chuck Lorre and Bill Prady. DVD. Warner Bros., 2009.

"Merry Thanksgiving." *Two and a Half Men: The Complete First Season*. Writ. Chuck Lorre and Lee Aronsohn. Dir. Jay Sandrich. Series prod. Chuck Lorre and Lee Aronsohn. DVD. Warner Bros., 2007.

"Most Chicks Won't Eat Veal." *Two and a Half Men: The Complete First Season*. Writ. Chuck Lorre and Lee Aronsohn. Dir. James Burrows. Series prod. Chuck Lorre and Lee Aronsohn. DVD. Warner Bros., 2007.

"No Sniffing, No Wowing." *Two and a Half Men: The Complete First Season*. Writ. Chuck Lorre and Don Foster. Dir. Rob Schiller. Series prod. Chuck Lorre and Lee Aronsohn. DVD. Warner Bros., 2007.

"Not in My Mouth!" *Two and a Half Men: The Complete Ninth Season*. Writ. Chuck Lorre and Lee Aronsohn. Dir. James Widdoes. Series prod. Chuck Lorre and Lee Aronsohn. DVD. Warner Bros., 2012.

The Odd Couple. Dir. Gene Saks. Perf. Jack Lemmon, Walter Matthau, and John Fiedler. 1968. DVD. Paramount, 2006.

"An Old Flame with a New Wick." *Two and a Half Men: The Complete First Season*. Writ. Lee Aronsohn and Mark

Roberts. Dir. Andrew D. Weyman. Series prod. Chuck Lorre and Lee Aronsohn. DVD. Warner Bros., 2007.

"One False Move, Zimbabwe!" *Two and a Half Men: The Complete Ninth Season.* Writ. Eddie Gorodetsky, Jim Patterson, and Don Reo. Dir. James Widdoes. Series prod. Chuck Lorre and Lee Aronsohn. DVD. Warner Bros., 2012.

"Palmdale, Ech." *Two and a Half Men: The Complete Ninth Season.* Writ. Eddie Gorodetsky, Jim Patterson, and Don Reo. Dir. James Widdoes. Series prod. Chuck Lorre and Lee Aronsohn. DVD. Warner Bros., 2012.

"The Peanut Reaction." *The Big Bang Theory: The Complete First Season.* Writ. Dave Goetsch and Steven Molaro. Dir. Mark Cendrowski. Prod. Faye Oshima Belyeu. Series prod. Chuck Lorre and Bill Prady. DVD. Warner Bros., 2008.

"People Who Love Peepholes." *Two and a Half Men: The Complete Ninth Season.* Writ. Chuck Lorre, Lee Aronsohn, Eddie Gorodetsky, and Jim Patterson. Dir. James Widdoes. Series prod. Chuck Lorre and Lee Aronsohn. DVD. Warner Bros., 2012.

"The Plimpton Stimulation." *The Big Bang Theory: The Complete Third Season.* Writ. Steven Molaro, Jim Reynolds, and Maria Ferrari. Dir. Mark Cendrowski. Prod. Faye Oshima Belyeu. Series prod. Chuck Lorre and Bill Prady. DVD. Warner Bros., 2010.

"The Proton Displacement." *The Big Bang Theory: The Complete Seventh Season.* Writ. Steven Molaro, Eric Kaplan, and Jim Reynolds. Dir. Mark Cendrowski. Prod. Kristy Cecil. Series prod. Chuck Lorre and Bill Prady. DVD. Warner Bros., 2014.

"The Raiders Minimization." *The Big Bang Theory: The Complete Seventh Season.* Writ. Steven Molaro, Steve Holland, and Maria Ferrari. Dir. Mark Cendrowski. Prod. Kristy Cecil. Series prod. Chuck Lorre and Bill Prady. DVD. Warner Bros., 2014.

"The Rhinitis Revelation." *The Big Bang Theory: The Complete Fifth Season*. Writ. Bill Prady, Steven Molaro, and Jim Reynolds. Dir. Howard Murray. Prod. Faye Oshima Belyeu. Series prod. Chuck Lorre and Bill Prady. DVD. Warner Bros., 2012.

"The Scavenger Vortex." *The Big Bang Theory: The Complete Seventh Season*. Writ. Steven Molaro, Jim Reynolds, and Maria Ferrari. Dir. Mark Cendrowski. Prod. Kristy Cecil. Series prod. Chuck Lorre and Bill Prady. DVD. Warner Bros., 2014.

"Springtime on a Stick." *Two and a Half Men: The Complete Eighth Season*. Writ. Eddie Gorodetsky and Jim Patterson. Dir. James Widdoes. Series prod. Chuck Lorre and Lee Aronsohn. DVD. Warner Bros., 2011.

"The Staircase Implementation." *The Big Bang Theory: The Complete Third Season*. Writ. Chuck Lorre, Dave Goetsch, and Maria Ferrari. Dir. Mark Cendrowski. Prod. Faye Oshima Belyeu. Series prod. Chuck Lorre and Bill Prady. DVD. Warner Bros., 2010.

"The Status Quo Combustion." *The Big Bang Theory: The Complete Seventh Season*. Writ. Steven Molaro, Steve Holland, and Tara Hernandez. Dir. Mark Cendrowski. Prod. Kristy Cecil. Series prod. Chuck Lorre and Bill Prady. DVD. Warner Bros., 2014.

"The Straw In My Donut Hole." *Two and a Half Men: The Complete Ninth Season*. Writ. Chuck Lorre, Lee Aronsohn, and Susan Beavers. Dir. James Widdoes. Series prod. Chuck Lorre and Lee Aronsohn. DVD. Warner Bros., 2012.

"The Thanksgiving Decoupling." *The Big Bang Theory: The Complete Seventh Season*. Writ. Steven Molaro, Jim Reynolds, and Jeremy Howe. Dir. Mark Cendrowski. Prod. Kristy Cecil. Series prod. Chuck Lorre and Bill Prady. DVD. Warner Bros., 2014.

"That Voodoo That I Do Do." *Two and a Half Men: The Complete Third Season*. Writ. Eddie Gorodetsky and Mark

Roberts. Dir. Gary Halvorson. Series prod. Chuck Lorre and Lee Aronsohn. DVD. Warner Bros., 2008.

"Those Fancy Japanese Toilets." *Two and a Half Men: The Complete Ninth Season.* Writ. Eddie Gorodetsky and Jim Patterson. Dir. James Widdoes. Series prod. Chuck Lorre and Lee Aronsohn. DVD. Warner Bros., 2012.

"Two Adults, One Kid, No Grown Ups" (supplementary material). *Two and a Half Men: The Complete First Season.* DVD. Warner Bros., 2007.

"Virgin, Mother, Crone." *Cybill: The Complete First Series.* Writ. Chuck Lorre. Dir. Robert Berlinger. Prod. Lee Aronsohn, Elaine Aronson, and Dottie Dartland. Series prod. Jay Daniel and Chuck Lorre. DVD. Anchor Bay Home Entertainment, 2006.

"Waiting for the Right Snapper." *Two and a Half Men: The Complete Fifth Season.* Writ. Mark Roberts, Lee Aronsohn, and Chuck Lorre. Dir. Jeff Melman. Series prod. Chuck Lorre and Lee Aronsohn. DVD. Warner Bros., 2009.

"The War Against Gingivitis." *Two and a Half Men: The Complete Ninth Season.* Writ. Eddie Gorodetsky, Jim Patterson, and Don Reo. Dir. James Widdoes. Series prod. Chuck Lorre and Lee Aronsohn. DVD. Warner Bros., 2012.

"Weekend in Bangkok with Two Olympic Gymnasts." *Two and a Half Men: The Complete Third Season.* Writ. Chuck Lorre and Lee Aronsohn. Dir. Gary Halvorson. Series prod. Chuck Lorre and Lee Aronsohn. DVD. Warner Bros., 2008.

"What a Lovely Landing Strip." *Two and a Half Men: The Complete Ninth Season.* Writ. Eddie Gorodetsky, Jim Patterson, and Don Reo. Dir. James Widdoes. Series prod. Chuck Lorre and Lee Aronsohn. DVD. Warner Bros., 2012.

"Whipped Unto The Third Generation." *Two and a Half Men: The Complete Second Season.* Writ. Mark Roberts. Dir. James Widdoes. Series prod. Chuck Lorre and Lee Aronsohn. DVD. Warner Bros., 2008.

"The White Asparagus Triangulation." *The Big Bang Theory: The Complete Second Season.* Writ. Stephen Engel and Richard Rosenstock. Dir. Mark Cendrowski. Prod. Faye Oshima Belyeu. Series prod. Chuck Lorre and Bill Prady. DVD. Warner Bros., 2009.

"Why We Gave Up Women." *Two and a Half Men: The Complete Ninth Season.* Writ. Eddie Gorodetsky, Jim Patterson, and Don Reo. Dir. James Widdoes. Series prod. Chuck Lorre and Lee Aronsohn. DVD. Warner Bros., 2012.

"The Zazzy Substitution." *The Big Bang Theory: The Complete Fourth Season.* Writ. Lee Aronsohn, Steven Molaro, and Maria Ferrari. Dir. Mark Cendrowski. Prod. Faye Oshima Belyeu. Series prod. Chuck Lorre and Bill Prady. DVD. Warner Bros., 2011.

CHAPTER TEN: A BLUE-COLLAR BLUE RIBBON

Adams, John S. *Housing America in the 1980s.* New York: Russell Sage Foundation, 1988. Web. 05 Dec. 2014.

"Ally's F." *Everybody Loves Raymond: The Complete Ninth Season.* Writ. Steve Skrovan. Dir. Kenneth Shapiro. Prod. Holli Gailen and Ken Ornstein. Series prod. Philip Rosenthal. DVD. HBO, 2007.

'The Angry Family." *Everybody Loves Raymond: The Complete Sixth Season.* Writ. Philip Rosenthal. Dir. Gary Halvorson. Prod. Ken Ornstein. Series prod. Philip Rosenthal. DVD. HBO, 2006.

Apple, Alyssa Ziegler, and Marnie Perez. "ABC News and People Magazine Present: 'Best in TV: The Greatest TV Shows of Our Time With By Barbara Walters,' A Special Edition of '20/20'." *ABC Medianet.* American Broadcasting Companies, Inc., 06 Sep. 2012. Web. 17 Dec. 2014. <psc.video.go.com/web/dnr/dispDNR.aspx?id=090612_01>.

"Beaver Gets 'Spelled'." *Leave It To Beaver: Season One.* Writ. Joe Connelly and Bob Mosher. Dir. Norman Tokar.

246

Prod. Joe Connelly and Bob Mosher. Series prod. Joe
Connelly and Bob Mosher. DVD. Universal, 2013.

"Becoming, Part Two." *Buffy the Vampire Slayer: The
Complete Second Season*. Writ. Joss Whedon. Dir. Joss
Whedon. Prod. Gareth Davies. Series prod. Joss Whedon.
DVD. Twentieth Century Fox, 2009.

"Best in TV: Best TV Mom." *ABC News*. ABC News Internet
Ventures, n.d. Web. 21 Dec. 2014.
<abcnews.go.com/2020/video/Best-tv-family-lucy-variety-
shows-brady-bunch-Henderson-Florence-winfrey-letterman-
dwts-American-idol-survivor-cheers-Seinfeld-comedy-tv-
17266917>.

"A Bitter Pill to Swallow." *Roseanne: The Complete Fourth
Season*. Writ. Amy Sherman and Jennifer Heath. Dir. Andrew
D. Weyman. Prod. Al Lowenstein. Series prod. Tom Werner
and Marcy Carsey. DVD. Anchor Bay Entertainment, 2006.

"Boys' Therapy." *Everybody Loves Raymond: The Complete
Ninth Season*. Writ. Philip Rosenthal. Dir. Kenneth Shapiro.
Prod. Holli Gailen and Ken Ornstein. Series prod. Philip
Rosenthal. DVD. HBO, 2007.

"Cashing in on Climate Change." *PR Newswire*. PR Newswire
Association, 29 May 2008. Web. 21 Dec. 2014.
<www.prnewswire.com/news-releases/cashing-in-on-climate-
change-57320232.html>.

Clark, Airial. "What is Sex-Positive Parenting?" *The Sex-
Positive Parent*. n.d. Web. 21 Dec. 2014.
<thesexpositiveparent.com/about/what-is-sex-positive-
parenting/>.

"The Dark Ages." *Roseanne: The Complete Fifth Season*.
Writ. Eric Gilliland and Mike Gandolfi. Dir. Andrew D.
Weyman. Prod. Al Lowenstein. Series prod. Tom Werner and
Marcy Carsey. DVD. Anchor Bay Entertainment, 2006.

"Darlene Fades to Black." *Roseanne: The Complete Fourth
Season*. Writ. Jeff Abugov. Dir. Andrew D. Weyman. Prod. Al

Lowenstein. Series prod. Tom Werner and Marcy Carsey. DVD. Anchor Bay Entertainment, 2006.

"The Disciplinarian." *Everybody Loves Raymond: The Complete Seventh Season.* Writ. Mike Royce. Dir. Jerry Zaks. Prod. Ken Ornstein. Series prod. Philip Rosenthal. DVD. HBO, 2006.

"D-I-V-O-R-C-E." *Roseanne: The Complete First Season.* Writ. Lauren Eve Anderson. Dir. Ellen Falcon. Series prod. Tom Werner and Marcy Carsey. DVD. Mill Creek Entertainment, 2011.

"A Fistful Of Reasons." *The Brady Bunch: The Complete Second Season.* Writ. Tam Spiva. Dir. Oscar Rudolph. Prod. Howard Leeds. Series prod. Sherwood Schwartz. DVD. Paramount, 2005.

Gaddis, Jayson. "What Happens When We Don't Teach Boys About Sex?" *The Good Men Project.* 22 May 2012. Web. 21 Dec. 2014. <goodmenproject.com/featured-content/what-happens-when-we-dont-teach-our-boys-about-sex/>.

"Going, Going... Steady." *The Brady Bunch: The Complete Second Season.* Writ. David P. Harmon. Dir. Oscar Rudolph. Prod. Howard Leeds. Series prod. Sherwood Schwartz. DVD. Paramount, 2005.

"Good Cop, Bad Dog." *Modern Family: The Complete Second Season.* Writ. Abraham Higginbotham and Jeffrey Richman. Dir. Fred Savage. Series prod. Christopher Lloyd and Steven Levitan. DVD. Twentieth Century Fox, 2011.

"The Haircut." *Leave It To Beaver: Season One.* Writ. Bill Manhoff. Dir. Norman Tokar. Prod. Joe Connelly and Bob Mosher. Series prod. Joe Connelly and Bob Mosher. DVD. Universal, 2013.

Hilton, G. "Sex Education - the issues when working with boys." *Sex Education* 1.1 (2001). Web. 21 Dec. 2014.

"Homer the Heretic." *The Simpsons: The Complete Fourth Season.* Writ. George Meyer. Dir. Jim Reardon. Prod. Richard

Raynis, David Silverman, and Richard Sakai. Series prod.
Matt Groening. DVD. Twentieth Century Fox, 2011.

"Homeward Bound." *Roseanne: The Complete Sixth Season*.
Writ. Michael Borkow. Dir. Philip Charles MacKenzie. Prod.
Al Lowenstein. Series prod. Tom Werner and Marcy Carsey.
DVD. Anchor Bay Entertainment, 2006.

"How Ugly Is He?" *The Cosby Show: Seasons 1 & 2*. Writ.
John Markus. Dir. Jay Sandrich. Prod. Caryn Sneider. Series
prod. Tom Werner and Marcy Carsey. DVD. Mill Creek
Entertainment, 2014.

Humphrey, Nicholas. "What Shall We Tell The Children?"
Edge.org. Edge Foundation, Inc., 21 Feb. 1997. Web. 17 Dec.
2014. <edge.org/conversation/what-shall-we-tell-the-
children>.

"Jealousy!" *The Dick Van Dyke Show: Season 1*. Writ. Carl
Reiner. Dir. Sheldon Leonard. Series prod. Carl Reiner. DVD.
Image Entertainment, 2003.

"Life and Stuff." *Roseanne: The Complete First Season*. Writ.
Matt Williams. Dir. Ellen Falcon. Series prod. Tom Werner
and Marcy Carsey. DVD. Mill Creek Entertainment, 2011.

"Looking For Loans In All The Wrong Places." *Roseanne:
The Complete Fifth Season*. Writ. Eileen Heisler and DeAnn
Heline. Dir. Andrew D. Weyman. Prod. Al Lowenstein. Series
prod. Tom Werner and Marcy Carsey. DVD. Anchor Bay
Entertainment, 2006.

"Manny Get Your Gun." *Modern Family: The Complete
Second Season*. Writ. Danny Zuker. Dir. Michael Spiller.
Series prod. Christopher Lloyd and Steven Levitan. DVD.
Twentieth Century Fox, 2011.

"My Sister, My Sitter." *The Simpsons: The Complete Eighth
Season*. Writ. Dan Greaney. Dir. Jim Reardon. Prod. J.
Michael Mendel, Richard Raynis, David Silverman, Richard
Sakai, and Denise Sirkot. Series prod. Matt Groening. DVD.
Twentieth Century Fox, 2011.

"National Average Wage Index." *SSA.gov*. U.S. Social Security Administration, 2013. Web. 05 Dec. 2014. <http://www.ssa.gov/oact/cola/AWI.html>.

Novak, Matt. "Recapping 'The Jetsons': Episode 01- Rosey the Robot." *Smithsonian.com*. Smithsonian Institution, 24 Sep. 2012. Web. 10 Nov. 2014. <http://www.smithsonianmag.com/history/recapping-the-jetsons-episode-01-rosey-the-robot-48001715/?no-ist>.

Pappas, Stephanie. "10 Scientific Tips For Raising Happy Kids." *LiveScience*. Purch, 12 Jan. 2012. Web. 05 Dec. 2014. <www.livescience.com/17894-10-scientific-parenting-tips.html>.

"Pilot." *Modern Family: The Complete First Season*. Writ. Christopher Lloyd and Steven Levitan. Dir. Jason Winer. Prod. Jeff Morton. Series prod. Christopher Lloyd and Steven Levitan. DVD. Twentieth Century Fox, 2010.

"Pilot." *The Wonder Years: Season One*. Writ. Neal Marlens and Carol Black. Dir. Steve Miner. Prod. Jeffrey Silver. Series prod. Neal Marlens and Carol Black. DVD. Twentieth Century Fox/StarVista, 2014.

"Religion's Negative Effects on Brain Development and Functions." *Letters to my Christian Mother*. 6 Oct. 2011. Web. 17 Dec. 2014. <mychristianmother.blogspot.ca/2011/10/week-1-religions-negative-effects-on.html>.

Ross, Julianne. "17 Lies We Need to Stop Teaching Boys About Sex." Mic.com. Mix Network Inc., 15 May 2014. Web. 21 Dec. 2014. <mic.com/articles/89301/17-lies-we-need-to-stop-teaching-boys-about-sex>.

"Rudy's Sick." *The Cosby Show: Seasons 1 & 2*. Writ. Matt Williams. Dir. Jay Sandrich. Prod. Caryn Sneider. Series prod. Tom Werner and Marcy Carsey. DVD. Mill Creek Entertainment, 2014.

"Sally is a Girl." *The Dick Van Dyke Show: Season 1*. Writ. David Adler. Dir. John Rich. Series prod. Carl Reiner. DVD. Image Entertainment, 2003.

"The Sick Boy and the Sitter." *The Dick Van Dyke Show: Season 1*. Writ. Carl Reiner. Dir. Sheldon Leonard. Series prod. Carl Reiner. DVD. Image Entertainment, 2003.

Silverman, Stephen M. "Marge Simpson Named Most-Admired Mom." *People.com*. Time Inc., 17 Mar. 2004. Web. 17 Dec. 2014.
<www.people.com/people/article/0,,627865,00.html>.

Stevenson, Betsey. "Aspirations, Not Current Income." *NYTimes.com*. NY Times, Co., 17 Aug. 2012. Web. 10 Nov. 2014.
<http://www.nytimes.com/roomfordebate/2010/12/22/what-does-middle-class-mean-today/aspirations-not-current-income>.

"Swingers." *The Wonder Years: Season One*. Writ. Neal Marlens and Carol Black. Dir. Neal Marlens and Carol Black. Prod. Jeffrey Silver. Series prod. Neal Marlens and Carol Black. DVD. Twentieth Century Fox/StarVista, 2014.

"Talk to Your Daughter." *Everybody Loves Raymond: The Complete Sixth Season*. Writ. Tucker Cawley and Ray Romano. Dir. Jerry Zaks. Prod. Ken Ornstein. Series prod. Philip Rosenthal. DVD. HBO, 2006.

Taylor, Paul. "Who Should Be the Judge of Middle Class?" *NYTimes.com*. NY Times, Co., 23 Dec. 2010. Web. 10 Nov. 2014. <www.nytimes.com/roomfordebate/2010/12/22/what-does-middle-class-mean-today/who-should-be-the-judge-of-middle-class>.

"Terms of Estrangement (Part 1)." *Roseanne: The Complete Fifth Season*. Writ. Sy Dukane and Denise Moss. Dir. Andrew D. Weyman. Prod. Al Lowenstein. Series prod. Tom Werner and Marcy Carsey. DVD. Anchor Bay Entertainment, 2006.

"To Tell or Not to Tell." *The Dick Van Dyke Show: Season 1*. Writ. David Adler. Dir. John Rich. Series prod. Carl Reiner. DVD. Image Entertainment, 2003.

"Trends in New York City Housing Price Appreciation." *FurmanCenter.org*. The Furman Center for Real Estate & Urban Policy, 2008. Web. 05 Dec. 2014. <http://furmancenter.org/files/Trends_in_NYC_Housing_Pric e_Appreciation.pdf>.

"Two Down, One to Go." *Roseanne: The Complete Sixth Season*. Writ. Amy Sherman. Dir. Philip Charles MacKenzie. Prod. Al Lowenstein. Series prod. Tom Werner and Marcy Carsey. DVD. Anchor Bay Entertainment, 2006.

Valenti, Jessica. *The Purity Myth*. Berkeley, CA: Seal Press, 2010. Print.

"We're in the Money." *Roseanne: The Complete First Season*. Writ. David McFadzean. Dir. Ellen Falcon. Series prod. Tom Werner and Marcy Carsey. DVD. Mill Creek Entertainment, 2011.

"Where There's Smoke." *The Brady Bunch: The Complete Second Season*. Writ. David P. Harmon. Dir. Oscar Rudolph. Prod. Howard Leeds. Series prod. Sherwood Schwartz. DVD. Paramount, 2005.

"You're Not A Mother Night." *The Cosby Show: Seasons 1 & 2*. Writ. Karyl Geld Miller and Korby Siamis. Dir. Jay Sandrich. Prod. Caryn Sneider. Series prod. Tom Werner and Marcy Carsey. DVD. Mill Creek Entertainment, 2014.

CHAPTER ELEVEN: T-REX INFESTED WATERS

Booker, Christopher. *The Seven Basic Plots: Why We Tell Stories*. London: Bloomsbury, 2006. Print.

Cieply, Michael. "Sequels Ruled Hollywood in 2011: Familiarity Breeds Hollywood Sequels." *NYTimes.com*. NY Times, Co., 28 Dec. 2011. Web. 23 Dec. 2014. <www.nytimes.com/2011/12/29/movies/sequels-ruled-hollywood-in-2011.html>.

Cunningham, Todd. "Steven Spielberg's 'Jurassic World' to Hit Theaters in June 2015." *The Wrap*. The Wrap News Inc.,

10 Sep. 2013. Web. 20 Dec. 2014.
<www.thewrap.com/steven-spielbergs-jurassic-world-to-hit-theaters-in-june-2015/>.

Jaws. Dir. Steven Spielberg. Perf. Roy Scheider, Robert Shaw, and Richard Dreyfuss. 1975. DVD. Universal, 2012.

"Jaws." *Rotten Tomatoes*. Flixster, n.d. Web. 20 Dec. 2014. <http://www.rottentomatoes.com/m/jaws/>.

Jurassic Park. Dir. Steven Spielberg. Perf. Sam Neill, Laura Dern, and Jeff Goldblum. 1993. DVD. Universal, 2004.

"Jurassic Park." *Rotten Tomatoes*. Flixster, n.d. Web. 20 Dec. 2014. <http://www.rottentomatoes.com/m/jurassic_park/>.

Moore, Ben. "'Jurassic Park 4' Titled 'Jurassic World'; Gets Summer 2015 Release Date." *Screen Rant*. 2013. Web. 20 Dec. 2014. <screenrant.com/jurassic-park-4-world-summer-2015/>.

Scheib, Richard. "Jaws: The Revenge (1987)." *Moria: The Science Fiction, Horror and Fantasy Film Review*. 2011. Web. 12 Jul. 2014. <http://moria.co.nz/horror/jaws4-therevenge.htm>.

"Top 100 Movies of 2014." *Rotten Tomatoes*. Flixster, 2014. Web. 20 Dec. 2014. <http://www.rottentomatoes.com/top/bestofrt/?year=2014>.

The Trip. Dir. Michael Winterbottom. Perf. Steve Coogan and Rob Brydon. 2010. DVD. MPI Home Video, 2011.

"2014 Yearly Box Office Results." *Box Office Mojo*. IMDb.com, 2014. Web. 20 Dec. 2014. <http://www.boxofficemojo.com/yearly/chart/?yr=2014>.

www.ingramcontent.com/pod-product-compliance
Lightning Source LLC
Chambersburg PA
CBHW071335280526
45787CB00001B/103